Two Years of Wonder

By

Ted Neill

Praise for Two Years of Wonder:

"As the author, even Neill asks if the world needs another book about a white man 'losing and finding himself' in Africa. In the case of *Two Years of Wonder*, the answer is an emphatic 'Yes.' With unflinching honesty, Ted shows us the inner workings of a mind in the grips of severe depression. It is a harrowing read and a *must*-read if you know someone grappling with mental illness much less the complexities and contradictions of aid work."

- Rasheed Newson, author of *The Singletons of Ashmount* and *Bring a Shovel and a Gun.*

"There are two urgent reasons to read Ted Neill's book, *Two Years of Wonder*. First, it informs us of the grave plight of children infected and affected by HIV/AIDS in Africa. It would take so little for us to help, and it starts with awareness. Read Ted's book if you believe that all life is sacred and to be respected and protected. Second, this book is especially important for change agents who sometimes feel frustration with how difficult it is to do lasting good in the world. Ted has been there. His successes, and also his failures, are instructive, and ultimately inspiring."

- Jack Hoban, USMC and author of *The Ethical Warrior.*

"Blending incisive self-reflection and autobiography, Ted Neill's *Two Years of Wonder* deconstructs our comfortable preconceptions about Africa, AIDS orphans, volunteerism, and the world of international aid. Told through a shifting kaleidoscope of stories, Neill's book constantly tumbles truth to provide his readers with a new view of the world as a complex, ambiguous, and interconnected whole."

- Tara Sullivan, author of *Golden Boy and The Bitter Side of Sweet.*

"What is most evident in *Two Years of Wonder*, is the transforming power of caring human presence. No great fixes are offered in the stories of vulnerable Kenyan children, no conclusive plan for solving enormous social problems. But this book offers hope. Through story-telling about the lives he encounters, Ted Neill provides an honest view of what it means to respectfully bear witness to the suffering of others and our own. The writing is candid, clear and provides encouragement that coming along side another person to live daily life together, even for a short season, can make a profound difference."

- Ruby Takushi, Director of Programs, *Recovery Cafe Seattle.*

"In *Two Years of Wonder,* Ted Neill takes his readers halfway around the world to laugh with, cry for, and be deeply moved by children in a Kenyan school and orphanage. Through engaging prose, Neill tells compelling stories that come full circle. For most of us, *Two Years of Wonder* is an inspiring read. It is a must read for anyone post-college or post-retirement considering volunteer work in an African orphanage or school."

- Dean Owen, author of *November 22, 1963: Reflections on the Life, Assassination, and Legacy of John F. Kennedy.*

Dedicated to Binyavanga Wainaina, my big brother of the word who opened my eyes. I hope I have not let you down.

Without your wound where would your power be? . . . The very angels themselves cannot persuade the wretched and blundering children on earth as can one human being broken in the wheels of living. In Love's service, only the wounded soldiers can serve.

—Thornton Wilder, *The Angel That Troubled the Waters*

Foreword
by
Dr. Helene D. Gayle

When I began my career at the CDC in 1984, few appreciated that AIDS was going to become a major public health threat. In 1981 when AIDS was first described by the Centers for Disease Control (CDC) in its Morbidity and Mortality Weekly Report (MMWR), I had just finished medical school and was just about to start my residency training in pediatrics. Two years later, in 1983, AIDS was recognized as a disease affecting children. So, although I probably treated children with HIV, I was never aware of it during my 3-year pediatric training.

For my first three years at CDC, I sat on the sidelines of the epidemic focused on other seemingly more important public health issues affecting children both domestically and globally. I watched with interest and concern as the HIV/AIDS epidemic continued to evolve. By 1987, it was clear that HIV/AIDS was deeply interwoven with issues of social justice and equity, the same issues that had led me to the field of public health in the first place. It was inescapable that HIV/AIDS was likely to be one of the defining public health issues of my lifetime. That is when I began my own journey tackling HIV/AIDS and the effort has lasted throughout the multiple decades of my career.

In the 1980s, and even through to the present day, HIV/AIDS is a disease that carries an unjust social and even moral stigma. HIV has disproportionally impacted populations that were historically marginalized in society, including gay men, IV drug users, sex workers, people of color, and poor women. Moral blame and stigma were attached to the disease to a degree not seen in most other epidemics. Even into the 1990s the unfortunate appellation "innocent victim" was applied to children born with HIV through mother-to-child transmission or hemophiliacs who were infected through blood transfusions. The clear implication being that others with HIV infection had done something to deserve it or intentionally bring it upon themselves. This moral blame not only released many parts of society from an evidence-based, public health approach to solutions, but also unduly burdened people at risk of HIV/AIDS or living with the infection with a sense of shame and denial—this often kept them from the very services that could make a crucial difference between life or death.

We have come a long way. To see the progress we have made brings me a mix of relief, accomplishment, and inspiration. We know more about the infection and how to prevent its spread and how to treat it. Effective treatment has allowed many people to live long, meaningful lives with HIV/AIDS as a chronic disease. And HIV/AIDS has advanced our understanding of the root causes or the social determinants of health—things such education, access to nutritious foods, safe neighborhoods and environments, economic stability. This understanding has led to broader solutions for decreasing health inequity. There is also less stigma attached to the diagnosis HIV/AIDS, although that still varies based on societal and cultural factors.

I give this bit of context because HIV/AIDS is an important backdrop for this story. But what Ted's work with his own story and the children's stories makes plain, is that this narrative is not just about HIV/AIDS, but about the larger story of the inequity and marginalization we see in the world and how one individual tried to come to terms with that.

The stories of Oliver, Miriam, Ivy, Harmony, Tabitha, Sofie, Nea and others, are still happening today. In some cases, HIV/AIDS is the culprit. In others it is Ebola, or it is the vulnerabilities that come from poverty, migration or dislocation due to climate change, war, or ethnic-based conflicts. Common to all of these is the contributing factor of the vast inequalities of wealth that currently characterize our globe. Inequality manifests as unequal freedom *to* resources, information, education, expression, and safety. It appears as unequal freedom *from* discrimination and oppression. We, as a global community, have made great progress in the fight against HIV/AIDS, but the challenges posed by an increasingly unequal and inequitable society remain. As long as they do, people, children, families will still be vulnerable.

Even in the face of this, I see hope. Hope is apparent to me in the children portrayed in these pages. In those who were able to survive due to their own grit and resilience—not to mention the generosity and love from those who answered the call to compassion when they heard it. I see reason to hope in the fierce determination of young women like Miriam, Sophie, and Alexis whose stories unfold in the chapters to follow. I see hope in the network of social workers, caregivers, medical workers, community health advocates, and educators, striving on both local and global levels, contributing not just to the ideal of health for all, but also for justice.

And I see it in Ted Neill—even as he wrestles with his own sense of vulnerability, brought on by his own struggles and his own "white-savior-complex," and his journey to reconcile his privilege with the lives he encountered. He details this journey here with refreshing honesty and humor.

I've known Ted since 2006. I was the President and CEO of the international development organization, CARE. I started in my role at CARE, the same month he began working as a graduate school intern. I had just transitioned from the Bill and Melinda Gates Foundation where I had directed the HIV, TB, and Reproductive Health Programs. Before then I had led the HIV/AID programs at the CDC and the US Agency for Development (USAID).

Over time, I got to know Ted as someone with a penchant for bad puns, cheesy jokes, a keen intellect and a huge heart. I've been able to witness Ted's career evolution as well as the peaks and valleys of his personal struggle with clinical depression and anxiety. I know his transparency regarding his mental health issues in this memoir emerges from an effort to expose himself to the same level of vulnerability and personal scrutiny that the children, through their stories, have opened themselves to. Ted's candor is also a valuable exercise in dispelling the stigma that still attaches to mental illness. As with HIV/AIDS, stigma itself becomes a barrier to support and treatment. It results in needless suffering, shame, discrimination, and isolation. In this way, Ted's experiences as a result of depression and anxiety has given him a shared solidarity with many of the children and young adults of Rainbow Children's home. Many of them suffer from depression and anxiety as a result of the trauma of personal loss, social isolation/discrimination, and the stress of chronic disease. This is something that has brought them closer together with Ted.

Ted's approach to telling their stories is warm and intimate. This is especially true considering the difficulties in asking children to relive their trauma without the help of professional counsellors. Although many differences in language, ethnicity, and privilege, exist among us, *Two Years of Wonder* shows us that humans can connect through this sharing of stories with their joys and their pains. These are messages we need today more than ever.

Although most of the stories are of children thousands of miles away on another continent, we don't need to hop on a plane and fly across oceans, or half of a dozen time zones, to find people who are different from ourselves. We don't need to be a frequent flyer to see others who have less privilege and access to opportunity than we do. Sometimes it only requires a car or bus ride. Sometimes all we have to do is get off at a different subway stop. Sometimes it just means opening our eyes.

We don't all have the opportunity to make a transcontinental journey. But we all can benefit from experiencing difference and seeing beyond our own circumstances. Ted did both, in his trip to Kenya, but also through his experience with those living with addiction and/or mental health issues in his home city. Ted's retelling of this journey is valuable for the deep, enduring

connections among us all that it reveals. These are the connections that make siblings in the human family. I know the children who will benefit from the telling of this story and the friends Ted made in the recovery community are glad he made the journey.
I am too.

Helene D. Gayle
October 2018

Dr. Helene Gayle is currently CEO of The Chicago Community Trust. She was president and CEO of McKinsey Social Initiative (now McKinsey.org) and the humanitarian organization CARE from 2006 to 2015. She was director of the HIV, TB, and Reproductive Health Program at the Bill & Melinda Gates Foundation. She also served at the Centers for Disease Control and Prevention (CDC) for over 20 years. Dr. Gayle has been named a "Top 100 Global Thinkers," by Foreign Policy, "Top 10 Women in Leadership," by Newsweek, and "50 Women to Watch," by the Wall Street Journal. Forbes has recognized her among its "100 Most Powerful Women." Dr. Gayle has published numerous scientific articles and has been featured by media outlets like The New York Times, The Washington Post, Forbes Woman, Harvard Business Review, Glamour, O magazine, National Public Radio, CNN, and more. She serves on the board of Coca Cola, Colgate Palmolive, the ONE Campaign, the Rockefeller Foundation, the Brookings Institution, the New America Foundation, and others. She has received over three dozen honorary degrees, awards, and distinctions.

Author's Note

In my recovery from depression and my near suicide, I read *The Things They Carried*, by Tim O'Brien. His collection of interconnected short stories, based on his experiences and the experience of men he served with during the Vietnam War, became my model for crafting a narrative—however fractured—of my story and the children's. I identified with the torn nature of the soldier in O'Brien's work: hating the front line and yet craving it as an opportunity to feel awake, alive, relevant, and significant. I know that feeling. I feel it every day when I look up at trees that are just trees and not acacia; birds that are not the brightly colored jewels that flitter about East Africa; gray sky that is not the spectacular blue shade of the tropics; stars that are dimmer; cars that do not move you to pray for your own safety; a society where suffering is not around every corner. For a long time after returning from Kenya, I yearned for the same level of stimulation, the same challenge to push against. Yet I know I am not *of* there, Kenya is not my home. I was a visitor, a storyteller. As I sorted through my longing and loss, somehow the process of writing soothed me.

So I kept trying to write about it. This memoir, a mix of fact and fiction, is the result.

My story here in first person is the best as I remember it with a few caveats: I have changed the sequence of some events and borrowed from the experience of other volunteers in a few instances, for the purpose of story pacing and flow. I wrote much of this in the years after Kenya, drawing mostly on tape recorded conversations with the children and old journals. Sofie and Judith's story as well as Maina and Hezekiah's were based on interviews with Judith and Maina that I conducted for the Rainbow Children's newsletter. The sections written in third person, from the point of view of Miriam, Oliver, Harmony, Ivy, and Tabitha, are inventions. They are my best attempts at recounting the stories I heard from the children, from their point of view, in a cohesive narrative. The sections are reconstructions of what these children I knew experienced, although some characters are composites and some scenes are reimagined, built around the few details I could garner. I have approached the children's narrative as a storyteller, not as a journalist, which is why I consider these sections a type of fiction or metafiction.

The stories are crafted around the major turning points of the children's lives they shared with me—the details, the internal monologues, the dialogues, and some of the characters, are mine. I have tried to stay true to their recollections and their personalities (as I knew them) and I feel these imaginings add something to the narrative, but I have taken literary license and owe the reader that admission. Strict constructions might object, yet I felt this was a more effective and compelling way to convey their experiences and surroundings than straight exposition. It was also an opportunity to take the spotlight off myself and put it onto them.

Finally, any and all royalties I earn from this story will go to these children and children like them. That is no fiction.

For some of the most traumatic scenes, such as those involving sexual abuse of children or violence, I did not feel qualified or justified in interviewing the children for details of their personal traumas. I know even the recollection of trauma can be additionally painful and damaging. My guiding principle was always to do no harm. I used secondary sources, published accounts, articles, and informal conversations to illuminate those scenes and create characters. Harmony's story is a composite built from the experience of many. The tragedy being that such stories of repeated violence and sexual abuse at the hands of men who betrayed their roles as protectors are all too common and easy to find. Their victims are many and the stories of those survivors are out there, if we are willing to listen—willing to witness. It is the least we can do to acknowledge and honor their suffering and begin the process of healing and taking account.

This book itself is an effort to bear witness to the suffering, but also resilience, of these children and young adults. And, as *they* see it, this is an attempt to illuminate a corner of the world often misunderstood and caricatured. As I reached out to them over the years to seek their permission to use their stories as inspiration for this project, they would often tell me how necessary such a book was. They would reiterate that we westerners, ensconced with a paperback or e-reader in our coffee shops, airport lounges, or living room reading chairs, those of us living in "developed" countries, *we* were the ones in need of help. *We* needed to remove our blinders and come to see a truth of the world too often hidden from us. We were the ones who needed to be educated, as we were far too ignorant, and that is a loss to us all.

Chapter 1

What would Sebastian Junger Do?

September 25, 2012, I picked up a knife to kill myself.

I have to rewind to show how I got here.

While in undergrad at Georgetown University, I had to withdraw from Intensive Italian. Even with four years of high school Latin it was, well, too intensive for me. In order to still graduate on time I had the option of making up the credits by doing community service work that was somehow connected to one of my classes—service work for school credit was not unheard of at a Jesuit University. I was taking an English course in literature related to the HIV crisis. We read works like *Borrowed Time* and *The Way We Write Now.* Long story short, I ended up volunteering at a downtown shelter for children with HIV.

Vulnerable, sick, abandoned children quickly became a passion for me. I volunteered at the shelter for six years. Like many English majors, I had dreams of becoming a journalist. I thought I had found my cause. I wrote about the children and I expanded my range to other marginalized groups at risk for HIV such as IV drug users and sex workers. I volunteered with outreach volunteers who did needle exchange, passed out condoms, and provided HIV testing to these groups late at night. I befriended addicts sex workers, and the social workers and even police who tried, in their own ways, to help them. For a sensitive, idealistic young man who had been the target of the word "fag," punched, kicked, and generally intimidated and marginalized by others in the jungle that is high school, it felt as if I had found my niche.

With years to reflect and look back, I can also see the extent to which my upbringing, my generation, even my race and socioeconomic status all played into who I was and who (I thought) I

1

wanted to become. I grew up in Fairfax, Virginia, a county of suburbs that surrounded Washington D.C. Fairfax was an enclave of highly educated, driven, middle and upper middleclass people, who during my childhood in the eighties and nineties, were predominantly white. I felt pressure for performance and upward mobility at a young age and with so many resources and advantages, kids like me were set up for success. The channels of high schools, colleges, and universities further separated us out according to ability, advantages, and expectations. We all strived to be the best, of course.

I was lucky enough to be accepted into Georgetown, which, although not an Ivy League school, was considered the Catholic or Jesuit Harvard, Yale, or Princeton. Once there, it was hard to escape the sense that I was with a rarified elite. The notion was cultivated. The selection process alone guaranteed that I was surrounded by dozens upon dozens of valedictorians, who were now just in the middle of the pack, so to speak. We were reminded of our talents often with stats such as Georgetown's ninety-nine percent rejection rate. This was disguised as school spirit. I can't speak for others, but for me, it had a more insidious effect of inculcating me with a sense of grandiosity. I thinkd all of us were infected with a sort of assumption that we were great and great things were expected of us. I remember, in what I thought was a show of modesty, I hung the Bible verse from Luke 28:48, "To whom much is given, much is required," over my dorm room door.

This was the extra ingredient that was added to my mix of big dreams and youthful ambition: Georgetown is a Jesuit school, founded by the Society of Jesus, an order of priests who in theory had a deep commitment to social justice and more progressive causes. In practice, the Jesuits have often been known for this, but also for cozying up to society's elite through education—not to mention participating in the cultural genocide of indigenous people throughout the new world.

2

To me, a twenty-two-year-old graduate with a lingering sense of being undervalued, desperate to be relevant, and desperate to be significant as an adult, I became driven to achieve, but achieve through the heroic act of saving others. And for me, the English major with a concentration in writing was where I knew I had found my vocation, where my talents and the needs of the world would meet (another phrase scribbled into my pocket notebook of inspirational quotes I carried everywhere on campus).

I had precedents for the mark I wanted to leave on the world through my writing. The old adage was that journalism's work was to "afflict the comfortable and comfort the afflicted." And these were the late nineties, when the celebrity print journalist was having a bit of a resurgence, giving hope to all of us English majors. The most notable example came in the form of Sebastian Junger, author of *The Perfect Storm* and *Fire,* Sebastian putting himself in harrowing danger for the stories in the latter. He was the intrepid western journalist braving the world's hellholes to spread the story of man versus *danger.* One read half in awe of the fighters, smugglers, and smoke jumpers, and half in suspense of whether or not Sebastian himself would make it out without a terrible, life altering injury. And as the large photo on the back cover of *Fire* reminded us, who wouldn't want this beautiful square-jawed man, with angled cheekbones and blazing blue eyes, to escape unscathed (well perhaps a little scathed would be acceptable—after all, if someone could pull off a scar or even an eye patch, it would be Sebastian).

In the 2000s we had an even better prototype for the hero-activist-journalist in the person of Greg Mortenson, who with his selfless and courageous work in Afghanistan, and the book by himself and David Oliver Relin chronicling his exploits, *Three Cups of Tea: One Man's Mission to Fight Terrorism and Build Nations ... One School at a Time,* seemingly burst onto the scene in a *kufi* and a *perahan tunban* on a ray of light from the heavens, or rather, Penguin Press.

But Greg would come later. By 2002, my stories had not yet been accepted by any journals or papers. I was paying my bills as a waiter at a white-tablecloth seafood restaurant on K street near the White House, and I realized the scope of my story was too small. So I worked my networks and contacted a Jesuit priest from Georgetown, Father Devon McLeod, who was based in Nairobi, Kenya. He had founded a hospice in 1992 for orphans with HIV. I told him I wanted to come for two years, as if I were a Peace Corps volunteer (local expats referred to such volunteers as Two Year Wonders). He said he would be stateside soon and we could meet.

I visited him at the Jesuit residences on Georgetown campus. The male receptionist—a seminarian student—let me in with little question, just another non-descript bookish white guy in glasses assuming the privilege and non-threatening status of another. Father McLeod met me as I got off the elevator to his floor. He reminded me of Ian McKellen's portrayal of Gandalf, if Gandalf had moved to Miami and traded in his beard for a goatee and his hat for a pair of photochromic reading glasses. Tall and imposing, he still had a gentle air about him and eyes that conveyed heartbreak at the state of the world. If there ever was a holy man who would have rescued orphans, this was him right from central casting. I was surprised that he didn't talk much, allowing me to do most of the talking, however, I was left with no doubt that there were a great many thoughts crossing his mind. They played across his face with a bemused smile. After a discussion that was much briefer than I had anticipated, he asked me when I would be coming to Kenya.

I remember walking out to the brick quad in front of Dahlgren Chapel after he told me I could join the work at the orphanage, Rainbow Children's Home—visions of lions, elephants, ostriches, and other safari-themed adventures dancing through my mind. But it was shadowed briefly by a tiny thought: what if this trip, this adventure, was nothing like I thought it would be? What if it was heartbreaking? What if my own well-being was put at risk?

4

But it was grist for the mill, as far as I was concerned. I could be the impartial, objective writer. I could keep my attachment at bay and righteously channel my anger into the writing—to everyone's admiration. I would craft my own eye-opening work of staggering genius.

But I never truly pictured myself suffering. I saw myself as a modern-day George Orwell or Dorothy Day. I *would* bring comfort to the afflicted and afflict the comfortable. All while remaining objective. Fame awaited. Oprah's stage beckoned.

And if my face ended up on the back of a book cover next to Sebastian Junger, well then so be it.

Chapter 2

Fish and Chips

One of Miriam's earliest memories was of standing on her tip toes to see the rows of fish laid out at market. She had always been fascinated by fish, more so than anything else sold at market. Her father used to tell stories after dinner, often using Miriam's and her brother's names for the characters, and if there was ever a fish in the story, its name would inevitably be Miriam. The idea made her laugh as well as squirm, for she found the prospect horrid. Miriam was fascinated by fish, but the last thing Miriam wanted was to be turned into one, for they were smelly, ugly, and their eyes were yellow, green, or even red.

Despite this, her fascination continued, drawing her attention to the men that brought the fish to the market each morning, making her forget that she was tired or hungry. Here was a creature that had no arms, no legs, no wings even, yet it could move, somehow, in the water. Miriam knew its tail, which was different from any tail she had ever seen on a dog, a cat, or a rat, had something to do with it. Even a fish's color, silvery, shimmering, was different than anything she had ever seen except for perhaps a new shilling coin, which made her think for a time that coins were made from fish, until she saw the skin taken off one and she realized that it was not stiff or hard like a coin but flimsy and prone to dry and shrivel.

One morning her father told Miriam that she would be accompanying him on an errand. Her father was lean and tall, like Miriam and like her mother. She also remembered him as gentle, with a deep but soft voice. Usually he worked at the truck depot, lifting and carrying things, but this day he said he was to go to a hotel to deliver an envelope to his cousin Maurito.

He insisted that Miriam wear her best clothes. He did the same. Miriam understood why when she saw the hotel. Miriam knew that hotels were for eating meals. There were many along the way to the market. They all were made of the same mud, sticks, and corrugated metal, like her family's house. Each was around the same size as their house as well—with two rooms, one for cooking and one for eating *chipatis, mandazis, oogali,* or *skuma weeki.*

But this hotel was nothing like the hotels Miriam knew. This building was huge, like a warehouse, or a church, but even bigger. The outside was covered with glass windows and the windows were also clean, not brown and dark. And the walls—there was no writing on them or remnants of posters. The garden was full of square hedges, banana trees, and flowers Miriam had never seen before. Shiny cars—small cars, not *matatus*—were parked in the parking lot and *wazungu* walked around everywhere. On the other side of the hotel from the road was the ocean—Miriam and her family lived in Mombasa, so the ocean was always near. But she had never been to this part of the ocean where the sand was white and people played in the waves or laid down beneath palm trees in their underwear.

Maurito met them in the back of the hotel where *wafrika* were moving very quickly carrying crates of milk and bananas. The kitchen must have been nearby, so perhaps people ate in this type of hotel as well. Maurito was wearing an apron so Miriam concluded he must have been a cook. Her father gave him his envelope and they talked about adult matters. Miriam knew to remain quiet and wait.

She knew they were finished when Maurito turned, greeted her, and asked, "So, you would like to see the fishes?"

Miriam did not know what fish he meant. She looked to her father who said, "They have many fish here. Maurito will show you."

Miriam followed Maurito, but she did not want get close to any smelly dead fish. She and her father were in their best clothes. Still, when adults spoke, it was best to do what they said. So Miriam continued after Maurito. He led them through a kitchen. Miriam

7

knew it had to be a kitchen from the way the men in it were dressed, the smells of cooking food, and the flames burning on the stoves. However, it looked nothing like the kitchens she knew—this one was many times larger than her house and everything was shiny and metal. The men greeted Maurito as he walked by. Miriam could tell they were making *wazungu* food because she did not recognize any of the smells—except for tea and *mandazis* which two men sitting on crates were enjoying.

They passed through swinging doors, down a hallway, through another set of doors, then they entered a whole other room entirely. It was giant like a church, but it was not a church, it did not have benches, although it did have chairs, but they all faced different directions. There were all sorts of people walking about. Most of the *wafrika* were wearing white suits, although there were a few in very fancy dark suits and wearing dark sunglasses. Then there were the *wazungu* wearing short pants and short shirts. Their skin was by turns red, pale white, or covered in what looked like moles. Some had white cream streaked across their shoulders or on their noses. The women wore shirts that showed their shoulders or just their brassieres. Miriam had seen *wazungu* before and she already knew they were rich, crazy, and disgusting.

Maurito tapped her shoulder and directed her attention to something large and colorful in the center of the room. It was the size of a *matatu* and was colorful like one too. *Wazungu* children gazed up at it, walking around it. Maurito encouraged Miriam to approach it as well.

She did not understand exactly what it was. Its surface seemed to waver and shimmer and inside things were moving. She looked more closely, where the *wazungu* children were tapping at the surface.

Then she realized: on the inside were fish. The first thing Miriam noticed was that they did not move up and down like she had always thought—with one eye on bottom and one eye on top—but rather side to side. She let out an exclamation: *"Gai!"* but the *wazungu* boys did not know the Kikuyu word for God. They said something to her in *Kizungu*, but it was unintelligible to Miriam. She shook her head "no" in response. They turned their attention back to the fish. By mutual understanding, Miriam ignored them and they her.

The fish moved their mouths like they were talking. It made Miriam laugh. She tapped the glass like the *wazungu* boys but it seemed to make no difference to the fish. Some of the fish looked like the ones in the market, only smaller. But others were fat and colorful, with long trailing fins and tails that hovered alongside them in the water. There were even two creatures swimming about that had four legs each and flat round bodies. From over her shoulder, her father called them "turtles." On the bottom there were the most disgusting creatures Miriam had ever seen, they were sand-colored with eyes on stems. They also had claws and shells on their backs. There were also snot-bugs on the inside, but unlike the snot-bugs Miriam had seen before, these had shells as well. Her father called them snails, and the creatures with the claws and eyes on stems, crabs.

There was such an array of vibrant colors that Miriam had never seen before, except in church when all the ladies were dressed up, or once on a TV in a bus station when cartoons were on. For a moment Miriam wondered if it was a giant TV that they were watching. Her father assured her it was not.

She watched silver dots shooting up from the bottom—air bubbles. There were colorful plants waving in the water, and Miriam wondered why this water was not gray like water in gutters, or brown like streams, or even blue like the ocean. She did not know how long she stood there, but eventually her father called to her. Maurito was already gone, so were the two *wazungu* boys, having been replaced by two girls. It was time to go. She followed her father out through the same side door they had entered.

Something good had happened. Oliver's mother had gotten a job in Nairobi. Oliver knew this was good because his mother came home singing. Oliver's grandfather was also happy. He killed a goat and invited all of the neighbors as well as Oliver's mother's friends over for dinner.

Oliver liked it when his mother's friends were around—it was like having many mothers and although Oliver did not know his father, he did not miss one—he had his grandfather, Babu.

But with his mother's new job they moved out of Babu's house to an apartment that was between Babu's house and Nairobi. This made Oliver sad. They had never lived anywhere else and Oliver did not want to leave Babu's house which was large. He loved Babu and would miss him. He would also miss the spacious fields of potatoes and cabbage that grew around the house. Most of all he would miss his favorite bush. It had long branches covered by passion fruit vines. The branches arched up and away from the trunk of the bush and touched the ground a little further out, creating a space within where Oliver played. Babu called the bush "Oliver's house." When Babu wanted a passion fruit from the garden, he always asked Oliver if he could take a fruit from his "house."

Oliver's mother told him not to be sad about leaving Babu's house. She promised that they would return to visit and that Oliver would grow to like their new apartment. She also promised Oliver that he would be able to go to a very good school.

Oliver did not like the new apartment at first. There were no fields and no bushes and the hallway outside was dark and smelled strangely. But since Oliver's mother did not return from Nairobi until late at night, Babu would ride a *matatu* down from his house so he could meet Oliver after school and walk him home. His new school, St. James Primary, was nicer than the old one, Busara Academy. The children had their own desks and did not have to share them with others. The paint was fresh and not peeling and the school even had computers.

When they reached the apartment Babu would help Oliver with his homework. They always finished quickly so they could play a game of chess together afterwards. On other days when his grandfather had Quaker meetings, one of Oliver's mother's friends would come down to meet him. Sometimes it was even Pricilla, who would not walk but drove—her very own car—to pick up Oliver. After a while Oliver began to like the new apartment.

Nairobi was a good place. Oliver always believed this because it was the place that his mother went to make her living and many people were impressed with this. Babu was proud of her, as were the *cucus* that lived near him. It was after his mother got her job in Nairobi that Oliver was able to go to St. James Primary School, where he became number one in his class.

But when his mother took him for his first trip to Nairobi, the city scared him. Some of the buildings were so high that he was afraid that they might topple over on him. When his mother said that they would not and that they were perfectly stable, Oliver looked up at them more carefully. They were as tall as mountains and the sky seemed just above their roofs. He remembered that Jesus had gone up into the sky to live in heaven with his father, God. He wondered if God lived on the roof of one of these buildings and that was why so many people came together in the city. He remembered that one was not supposed to look into the face of God so he looked away from the tops of the buildings so he would not see God by accident.

In Nairobi people walked very quickly while cars moved very slowly. Oliver's mother said there were too many cars. There were certainly more than Oliver had ever seen in his entire life. Their fumes made the air stink and Oliver felt ill as he followed his mother, holding on to her hand.

Eventually they left the street and entered a Nando's. This Nando's was special because unlike the one near their apartment, this one had two floors. Oliver's mother bought him French fries and ice cream. After that they walked down the street to the cinema where they watched a movie, which was like watching TV but on a screen that was as big as a house. The theater was cold inside, so Oliver's mother bought him a red-knit cap to wear inside. He liked the cap, it was soft and indeed kept him warm in the dark and cold theater.

On another trip to Nairobi they waited at a *matatu* stage for what his mother said was a special *matatu*. As the line grew longer Oliver realized these *matatus* had to be special: there were many men in suits with briefcases waiting and then even a *mzungu* joined them.

Oliver had never seen a *mzungu* in person before. He had seen them on TV and in the cinema. There were even some on his mother's CDs. This one was a man. He was very tall and had long stringy hair and was wearing a backpack. He was terribly ugly. Oliver remembered that it was rude to stare so he tried not to.

When the *matatu* came, it was indeed special. It was large and blue. His mother called it a Kenya Shuttle. The inside had large seats and curtains on the windows. Oliver took his seat and pressed himself up against the window to make room for his mother and whoever else might sit down. His mother laughed and told him that on the Kenya Shuttle everyone had their own seat and they would not have to share like in a *matatu*. Sure enough, once everyone was seated the tout closed the door and would not allow anyone else on the bus. No one was even allowed to stand in the aisle even though there were still many people waiting in line.

Oliver looked around and saw that the *mzungu* was sitting a few rows ahead of them.

The shuttle moved out of the city where it was able to move more quickly. *Matatus* still passed them, but the shuttle was taller and Oliver could look down on their roofs. The tallest buildings disappeared but they still passed very large buildings. They went by the Ngong Uchumi which was ten times the size of the Uchumi by their apartment. Oliver's mother said she had once bought groceries there with Pricilla.

The *mzungu* got off, and as Oliver watched him walk away on the shoulder of the road, he noticed other *wazungu,* two girls with long light-colored hair. One had her hair braided like a *mfrika* woman but her scalp was bright white and looked funny between the braids. Both girls wore flip flops and Oliver could not understand why they would go outside wearing house shoes.

Soon the large buildings were replaced by market stalls that lined the side of the road. Then these were replaced by trees, forests, and walls that surrounded houses that looked so large that Oliver imagined many families must have lived inside.

They eventually alighted by a gas station. There was a busy market across the street with many cars and people, including *wazungu* and *wahindi.* Oliver's mother led him in the opposite direction. They crossed a road, passed a *matatu* stage then turned down a side road.

It smelled of sage and dry grass, the smell of sunlight to Oliver. Along this road they came to a yard that had no grass but dirt instead and was surrounded by a fence. Inside the fence were horses, which were huge and strange looking, but not as strange looking as the *wazungu* that were riding them. These were girls, older then Oliver, in small black helmets and long black boots. Once again Oliver tried hard not to stare.

An older *mzungu* lady named Shirley greeted them in *Kizungu.* Oliver's mother seemed to know her from her job. They spoke completely in *Kizungu,* which Oliver had some difficulty understanding, but he remembered to be polite and say "Fine, thank you," when Shirley asked him how he was doing.

Shirley helped Oliver and his mother onto a horse. Even though she was ugly and smelled badly, Shirley was very nice. She told Oliver not to be afraid, then she led them around the yard on the horse. When Oliver's mother said it was all right, Shirley let her take the reins of the horse herself. Shirley mounted her own horse and they went on a long ride through the forest.

Rarely had Oliver ever had so much fun in his life. When they returned to the stable Shirley made them tea—which Oliver did not like because it did not have any milk in it. Shirley realized this and brought him some, but it was cold—they only drank hot milk at their house. Oliver added the cold milk to his tea out of politeness but did not drink it.

He had been very excited about the horses and he asked Shirley questions about what they ate, how old they were, how big they grew, how smart they could be. Shirley gave him good responses and when Oliver had most of his questions answered, he started to think more about the things Shirley had said, just so he would not forget. Shirley laughed and said to Oliver's mother,

"A right intellectual he is."

Oliver made a point to remember what she said so he would not forget it either. When they were walking back to the Kenya Shuttle bus stop he asked his mother what Shirley had meant.

"She meant you are very smart for your age," she said.

This made Oliver happy since he knew mother wanted him to be smart.

As they waited for the Kenya Shuttle to return Oliver asked his mother if this was still Nairobi.

"No, this is Karen," she said.

Karen, he thought, was a very nice place. He hoped they could come back.

Chapter 3

Pre-School

There is no one to teach preschool. The orphanage, located in Karen, a leafy suburb outside of Nairobi, has an on-site school where about forty children under the age of nine attend. It's a one-story building with a red tile roof and a welcoming patio with two cut-out giraffe heads flanking the fading letters: RAINBOW CHILDREN'S HOME. The other fifty or so children that don't use the schoolhouse go to a private school down the road. They attend a private school because public schools would not accept them due to their HIV status. This private school that *did* accept them has watched half its student body leave for fear of our children and the virus they carry.

There are a number of three- to four-years-olds that are too young for kindergarten but too old to sit in the cottages with the house moms doing nothing. So they send these children to "pre-school," and give me the class. My classroom is about five feet by eleven feet with a chalkboard on one wall and shelves of donated books on the others. It reeks of draining ear fluid—half the children have such advanced ear infections that their ears regularly ooze a greenish yellow fluid. The smell is unlike anything I have encountered before. Composting grass mixed with burnt popcorn is the best way I can describe it. Their noses run copiously too, as much as their ears, so I keep rolls of toilet paper on the windowsill to clean them up when necessary.

I have thirteen pupils. I do not speak Kiswahili and they do not speak English—but they do speak loudly enough that each day by lunchtime my ears are ringing painfully. The Kenyan staff members are entertained on a daily basis as my voice echoes across

15

the schoolyard in my efforts to be heard over the din of the children. Chaos mostly reigns supreme.

I have a wide assortment of personalities and backgrounds in my class. There is Edison, who looks pugnacious like a boxer, but is quiet and sweet. His distended belly makes me think of him as a frat boy with a beer gut, even though it's actually from a hernia caused by malnutrition. He has scarring all over his abdomen; whether it is from a skin infection or a burn from when he was an infant, I don't know. Edison is the smartest boy in the class. Alice is the smartest girl. She is dark-skinned, curious, and has bad eyesight, so she can often be found around the orphanage leaning down closely to examine a flower, a snail, or even dog poop. I can barely keep her occupied and if she is not occupied she gets into mischief. Jennifer is her partner in crime who likes to put anything in her mouth—I have pried many a slimy rock, coin, or crayon out from between her molars. Diana has a bald head—shaved to treat the ringworm on her scalp—and big beautiful eyes that sparkle like dark jewels. Her eyelashes are so long and lustrous that she looks as if she is wearing mascara. She is by turns outgoing and then terrified of adults. Matthew has chubby cheeks and often wears a scowl—to me he bears a passing resemblance to Michael Jordan. He does not speak, only whispers. He was abandoned at another orphanage by his family and he will wet himself if you turn your back and begin walking away from him.

Then there are the children that cannot walk. There is Jacob who is four but unable to pull himself up to stand. He can't speak, although he seems to understand Kiswahili. The doctor who visits the orphanage suspects that Jacob has brain lesions that are inhibiting his development. There is Erick—whom the Kenyan staffers call "Little President" for his resemblance to the president of Kenya. He is knock-kneed and unsteady when standing. Finally there is Naila, a Sudanese girl who was locked in a room and tied to a bed for the first three years of her life—this was to protect her from the villagers that wanted to kill her because they suspected she had

HIV. Her parents had died of the disease and her grandmother who inherited Naila had to keep her hidden and leave her alone for long periods of time. Naila has yet to learn how to walk and she speaks a pidgin of Kiswahili and Arabic. I can't understand a word she says, although she is often eager to talk to—at—me. I try to make encouraging, excited sounds back to her.

When one child suddenly says he or she has to go to the bathroom, the other children immediately realize they need to go as well. Most can make it on their own but when one—or worse—two or all three of the children who cannot walk need to go, I have to scoop them up in my arms and run to the far end of the building where the toilets are, hoping that I make it before they relieve themselves on me. I usually don't and they usually do.

I am a horrible teacher. I know little about early childhood development. I know little about teaching. But to console myself I remind myself that if I were not trying to teach them how to count or say their ABCs no one would be, the stigma around HIV being what it is. Sadly, HIV-positive orphans have to settle for what they get and I'm what they got.

Each day by noon I am at my wits' end. Some days it only takes until midmorning. One day the teacher that handles the first through third grade classes in the larger room of the schoolhouse hears me screaming at the children to be quiet. My voice is ragged and cracking. My eardrums are fluttering painfully with even the smallest of giggles from the children. A tension headache is pulling a rope tighter and tighter around my temples. The teacher sends me help in the form of a thirteen-year-old girl.

She is old to be in third grade. I don't know why she is not off with the other students at the private school. Dressed in a donated, gray school uniform, she stands quietly in the doorway as if awaiting my instructions. She is very thin but has knowing eyes. I ask her if she is there to help. She nods, and I say, "Can you tell them to listen to me?"

She suddenly becomes a small fury. The voice that comes out of her is hoarse and strained, making her sound much older than she really is—as if she is channeling the spirit of an old shrew. She scolds the children in furious Kiswahili, wags her finger, picks Alice up off the floor and plops her into her seat. Jennifer, she wraps on the knuckles. When Jennifer begins to cry, a single look from the older girl silences her. Examining the children, she realizes Diana's nose is running. She takes a piece of toilet tissue from the roll on the windowsill and wipes Diana's face clean, tossing the tissues in a wastepaper basket and pulling Matthew down from a bookcase he was climbing in one fluid motion. She straightens Erick up in his seat and knocks crumbs off his sweatshirt. She returns to the doorway for a while, watching the now silent children, waiting for one of them to break order. No one does. She turns to me.

"They will be good now."

My helper's name is Miriam Mumbi. When the teacher can spare her she becomes my assistant—the children listen to her like an aunt. She assumes an air of confident authority around them, yet when I ask her a direct question she often will become shy and giggle nervously. But if I divert my attention from her, she will instantly answer—she, after all, is an orphan and craves attention.

The first time I actually remember noticing her was when I was painting one of the front buildings with two female volunteers, one from the UK, the other from the Netherlands. Miriam entered the room we were working on—she assumed she was allowed to even though there was a crowd of children standing at an obedient distance outside the door. The other volunteers did not raise a complaint, nor did the children, as if it was understood that Miriam was different and occupied a place between adult and child.

She sat down and began to read out loud from a faded and torn Winnie the Pooh book. The way she stumbled over phrases and mispronounced words irritated me. At her age she should have been able to read better, I thought with exasperation. I had a room to paint so I ignored her, letting the other volunteers help with words like cat, acre, and forest, their voices background noise to my headphones.

I never ignore Miriam now. She helps me keep my sanity.

Miriam teaches me key Kiswahili phrases to help me with the preschoolers: *kaa chini*, sit down; *yamazeni,* be quiet; *ushini shike,* don't touch; and her favorite: *ukinisambua nitakupiga,* if you disturb me, I will beat you.

Slowly the children begin to listen to me. I learn their rhythms. I know when they will be bored with an activity, when they need to be exercised, and when they need to go to the bathroom. I learn to use the entire orphanage as a classroom. The schoolhouse borders the quad that makes the heart of the orphanage. A hedge of trees bisects the space into a small playing field on one side and a playground with a sandpit, swings, and slides on the other. The cottages that the children live in with their house "Mums" or "Uncles" face the quad. Farther on the periphery are administrative medical buildings, a volunteer house where I live, a garden, a convent for the nuns who run the place, and sadly in the back corner a cemetery full of small graves.

It all takes up just a few acres but I learn to use every inch as a place for the children to explore. Getting them out of the small classroom spares my ears as well. The highlight of their school day is the walk we take before lunch to the gate of the home to watch the cars go by. Along the way, the kids pick flowers and clover, look at bugs, and throw fallen avocadoes at one another. For the children that can't walk, I grab a wagon or a wheelbarrow and wheel them along, which presents an opportunity to learn another Kiswahili word which they shout at me: *haraka,* faster.

It never fails—when we reach the gate, a good distance from the main buildings of the home, one of the children has to go to the bathroom. One day, tired of having to escort a child back or send Miriam to do so, I tell the child in question, in this case Edison, to go pee in the bushes.

Miriam scoffs.

"What?" I ask her.

"Me, I said nothing," she replies.

"You are lying," then I add, "Jesus says not to lie."

She turns on me, waving her finger. It turns out she is perfectly eager to correct me, given the chance.

"You should not tell the children to go *susu* in the bushes."

"Why not?" I enjoy baiting her. Sensing this, she crosses her arms and turns her head away.

The next day while at the gate, I turn to see Alice squatting and defecating in the bushes. I run over to tell her to stop but it is too late. My sudden approach startles her. As she stands up she steps in her own feces.

I stand stupefied, not knowing where to start. I don't need to. Miriam is immediately beside me, scolding Alice and sending her back to her cottage. Alice starts back, chastened. Miriam follows her.

"Miriam," I say. "Thank you. I'm sorry I did not listen to you."

She turns away in a show of haughtiness but I glimpse her face; she is smiling. She begins to skip down the drive as she follows Alice.

Class begins one morning and I notice that Jacob is not present. Usually one of the older children carries him over from his cottage. I can't leave the class alone to go get him, so I decide I will retrieve him when the class takes a bathroom break.

But Miriam appears first. She stands in the doorway, looking uncertain.

"Miriam, can you go get Jacob for me?"

"Jacob is sick," she says, then stares at me. The morning is cold and she is wearing a winter jacket with the hood pulled up around her head. She has pulled the strings taut so that the edges have closed in, close to her face. It is not just HIV-positive children, but rather many Kenyans I have seen piling on the layers on what would be considered only a mildly cold day outside the tropics. At a mile high, Nairobi can get cool, but there is something more to Miriam this morning. I've noticed she pulls the hood closed when she is upset, pensive, or wants to be alone. In an orphanage where all the children must share space, it is one of the only ways she can block out the encroaching world. I sense my reaction to the news is being carefully evaluated. My next words need to show care and reassurance at once.

"Is he in his cottage?"

"He is in the sickroom."

Now I know the seriousness of it.

"We will go see him on the break."

This seems to satisfy her and she returns to her own class.

At tea break I go to the nursing room. Miriam is waiting outside. I open the door and let her enter in front of me.

The nursing room, or sickroom as the children call it, is decorated with colorful curtains, cutouts of cartoon characters, and construction paper mobiles, as children's wards often are. I know such decorations are soothing to children, but I hate them, their promise of cheer rings false to me.

Jacob is in a crib. When nurse Ruth, a cheerful Kenyan woman with a melodious voice that seems to sing her words rather than speak them, gives her permission, Miriam walks over to him.

"*Habari,* Jacob," she says.

I have read a great deal about AIDS from a comfortable place in the developed world. That has hardly prepared me to see a child I have taught to walk, pinned to a mattress by a virus. Jacob moves lethargically. It seems incomprehensible that something so small as a virus could be so powerful, especially when I reflect that this same scene is going on in hundreds of thousands—millions—of beds throughout the world this very moment.

Miriam has brought a toy, a plastic cash register, for Jacob to play with. He hits the keys, making it ring.

"Kazi nzuli. Good job," Miriam tells him.

I lean closer. Jacob's breathing sounds like the gurgling noise of a coffee machine—air bubbling through viscous fluids in his lungs. Ruth tells me he has tuberculosis.

As we leave, Miriam says to me in her raspy voice,

"I was once in there."

"The nursing room?" I ask.

"Yes. They called it the 'death room' then. I was so sick, my skin was coming off with my clothes."

"But you got better."

"Jesus saved me." She looks at me, waiting for me to challenge her. I don't. She laughs inscrutably. I wonder if she is now having a go at me in retaliation for my comments about Jesus a few days before.

Jacob is dead within a week. We bury him in a field near his grandmother's home. His mother is at the funeral as well, but she is confused, childlike. A staffer from the orphanage informs me that she suffers from HIV dementia. The grandmother could not care for them both, so Jacob was sent to the orphanage. His grandmother stands by the grave in a head wrap, thick cardigan sweater, and skirt—the uniform of Kenyan women of a certain age. She holds her daughter by the arm. She has lost her grandson and is losing her daughter to AIDS. In a society where so much of a person's self-worth, identity, and life's work are tied up in offspring, I can't imagine the sense of loss the old woman feels. As the coffin is lowered into the slot of earth, women in T-shirts and colorful skirts form a circle and begin to sing. Jacob's grandmother walks a few steps away into the garden and collapses to her knees amid a few potato sprouts.

That night I can't sleep. It is November and the rains have come. Rain water drops incessantly from the ceiling into the half dozen pots and jars that I have placed about my room. I cannot turn on my lights because the rain causes termites to swarm. Attracted to light, they will exit their burrows, crawl under my door, and swarm through my windows by the hundreds, only to shed their wings, curl up, and die upon my floor.

I light a candle and pick up a notebook, the water dripping in the pots around me, thousands of more drops drumming on the roof. I have decided that I will write an article about Jacob, about his suffering and his family's suffering. Perhaps it will touch people back in the States, making them realize the need here. I want to draw a straight line between eight dollar mocha cappuccinos, flat screen televisions, and gas guzzling SUVs, and the privation here. I want to use Jacob to do it. I want to shame the people who don't know, who have more. I want to make them do something. But I can't. I get two lines into my opus and stop. I put down the pen and watch the rain water drip into a coffee mug. Everything is just too complicated.

On my resume it says I have worked as a freelance journalist. The staff members think this means I am a professional. If professional means having all your stories rejected, never having phone calls returned, and having to pay your bills waiting tables, then I'm a professional.

What they want is simple enough though. They ask me to write the newsletter that is sent to American donors. I say sure, I'll do anything they need.

My first assignment is Sofie Waceera.

She is five. She speaks no English. I go to her cottage and color with her. I ask her house mother, Agnes, what she is like. Agnes is a tall, fierce looking woman with her hair plaited into cornrows. But her appearance belies her loving nature. She smiles as she describes Sofie, telling me that she is one of the most well-behaved children in the house. I write it down. I look at Sofie's drawings. She's done a couple of flowers with green petals and yellow stems.

A driver takes me to Kangemi, the slum where Sofie used to live. He shows me down a dirt track to a shack made of corrugated tin. It's locked up. Beside it is a butcher's shop. The ditch in front is littered with bones, ashes, corn cobs, and plastic bags. Across the track is a high stone wall lined with razor wire. I ask the driver what is on the other side.

"Hillview," he says. "It is where many ministers from parliament live."

I walk around the wall to one of the gates. There are two security guards with automatic rifles waiting on the other side of the bars. Beyond them I see two-story homes, grassy lawns, Mercedes, and BMWs.

I am supposed to talk to one of the social workers at the Rainbow Children's Kangemi Clinic. It is across a four-lane divided highway from the slum. I suggest we walk, but the driver will not let me. He says the road is too dangerous to cross on foot. We have to drive.

I see what he means. Cars and lories race down the road at well over eighty miles an hour. There are no guardrails, no shoulders, and the kiosks of the market pile right up to the roadside. I notice as we pull out that the grassy median is crisscrossed with paths worn by foot traffic. So clearly people do cross, but at great risk. I am not allowed. I sense it is because I am a visitor and somehow, my life is more vulnerable.

Once across the highway, at the clinic I meet with a social worker. She tells me Sofie's story.

Sofie's mother's name was Judith Waceera. Judith and Sofie's father had three children, Sofie being the youngest. Judith had never been with any man but Sofie's father; however, as it turned out, he had had a girlfriend or two. From one of these women he contracted HIV, which was how Judith became positive.

All three of their children were positive as well. Judith and the oldest boy became sick first. When Judith's husband realized his wife might have AIDS, he left her.

Shortly after, Judith's oldest boy died. The middle child died soon after. Judith was left only with Sofie.

It is Moi day, just weeks after I arrived in Kenya. I am with Hannah. Hannah and I met in Ghana, we were both recent graduates on our first trips to an African country, me from the States, she from Germany. We had signed on for a paid trip out to a remote village where we helped to build a primary school: a "voluntourism" trip if there ever was one. But we both wanted more. Now she is in Kenya on her gap year between her A-Levels and University. Since we are the only other people that either of us know in this continent full of strangers, there was never any question about us seeking each other out in Kenya. After a week or two there is really no question about us sleeping together either.

Hannah grew up in the German Democratic Republic—the eastern side of the Berlin wall. Therefore she takes nothing for granted. She splits toothpaste tubes open to get the last bits of product inside of them. She does the same with hand lotion containers. Her only luxuries are her CD player and her camera. She has an uncanny sense of lighting when it comes to photographing Africans, once explaining to me that one must account for the fact that their skin "eats the light," whereas ours, as white people, reflects it.

Her own skin and hair is fascinating to the children. She is fair, with blond hair that she wears in locks. In Kenya she has chosen to keep her hair under a wrap. Her clothing of choice consists of ankle-length skirts with African-style prints on them. It's a weird inversion of cultural expectations, with her Kenyan counterparts striving to look more western in blue jeans in order to appear sophisticated, worldly, and cosmopolitan, while Hannah adopts a more "traditional" look that might penalize an African woman as "backwards" or "from the bush." As a white woman, Hannah can put on this "Africanness" as a costume, and take it off when it suits her. There are dynamics of internalized, Eurocentric ideals of beauty and cultural appropriation going on, that as a white, heterosexual male, only recently living in a predominantly black, formally colonized country, I'm embarrassingly oblivious to as I march around in my floppy bush-hat, cargo shorts, and sandals—my own clueless version of an ugly western stereotype.

Hannah is volunteering at an orphanage as well, but it could not be more different than my own. Malaika Children's Home receives few donations from the West. Instead of flowers and trees, they have a muddy courtyard. In place of a playground, they simply have a large field. There is no staff; the older children take care of the younger children, and the woman that is "mother" to every child is Mama Seraphina.

Mama Seraphina is an enormous Kikuyu woman with a gravelly voice. She is a force unto herself. While undergoing heart surgery in 1990, she died while on the operating table. The doctors had given up hope when her heart restarted miraculously. Mama Seraphina had been resurrected.

She decided that she had been brought back for a purpose, so she began opening her home to orphans. Today there are over a hundred and forty that live with her. There are so many that there are frequent days when there is not enough food to go around. But Mama Seraphina, Hannah tells me, knows every single child as if she had given birth to him or her, herself.

Since today is Moi day, about twenty of the children have been invited to perform at the ceremony in Ngong town, celebrating the current President Daniel arap Moi.

President Moi has been in power for twenty-four years. In that time he has held on to power by inflaming tribal rivalries to the point of violence, bribing cronies with funds meant for development and relief, and by torturing and killing any political dissidents. Before I arrived in Kenya, a white Jesuit priest that had been criticizing the president was found dead with seven gunshot wounds to his head. The death was ruled a suicide.

Recently, however, international pressure has forced Moi to announce that he will not run for president again. With the election looming just a few weeks away, Moi has become a lame duck. Today, on the state holiday he created to celebrate himself, the parade ground, where, in previous years, hundreds would gather, is desolate and empty. There are more dignitaries in the dilapidated review stand jockeying for position than civilians on the grounds.

We are on the grounds with twenty children from Malaika— the older ones reading pieces of a newspaper they are passing around—as well as a dozen Maasai women that will perform a ritual dance, children from an orphanage called St. Jude's, and then a few curious local boys with a soccer ball made from trash bags and packing twine.

The review stand, on the other hand, is packed with local "big men," in khaki suits and pith helmets. Upon seeing Hannah's camera, they ask her to take their photo, which they line up for in a row, each man standing rod-straight with his riding crop stuck beneath his arm.

The festivities officially begin when a Mercedes pulls up. A man in a military uniform, sparkling with medals, steps out, inspiring Hannah to comment in her clipped accented English,

"Ah, see, the crooks in Kenya, they drive German vehicles."

The official climbs up onto the reviewing stand and reads a long statement printed and distributed by the State House especially for this occasion. His reading is monotone and unrehearsed. He seems as bored as we are. The children continue reading the newspaper. When the official has finished reading, there is an obligatory smattering of applause—most fervent from the men in the pith helmets. The official sits down in a wooden chair with a high back. One of his assistants gives Mama Seraphina the signal that the children may now begin entertaining.

The children line up in a row facing the review stand. They stand patiently in the sun while Mama Seraphina carries over a decrepit stereo. Two children carry over the mismatched speakers. Mama proceeds to twist and cajole wires from the stereo and the speakers together, causing no small amount of static and pops which are so loud that even the military official flinches and makes a displeased face.

But Mama Seraphina is unashamed. She is a prophet sent from God, as she has told Hannah, and she saves children.

Hannah walks over and helps her with the stereo. In a moment it comes fully to life and the children jerk into a lockstep dance. I am surprised—they are coordinated, their expressions animated, their smiles wide. Their moves are a combination of traditional African steps and Jackson Five choreography. They are amazing. I say as much to Hannah and she laughs. "Of course they are. They are beaten by Mama Seraphina if they are not."

There is one child, Andrew, who has a particularly attractive face with pinchable cheeks, wide eyes, and a wider smile. He is younger than the other dancers but it is his job to run in front of them and do cartwheels. However, by the second song he is dizzy and finds it difficult to run in a straight line. By the third song his cartwheels wobble over and end with him on his back or his face. But each time he brushes off the dried grass sticking to him, runs, and starts again.

While the performance proceeds, Mama gets a call on her mobile phone. An Indian woman has donated two dozen large bags of rice to a church in Nairobi. The pastor wants to give the rice to Malaika. Can Mama come get it?

She says yes and leaves Hannah and me to watch the children. She says she will be back to return the children to the orphanage at the end of the ceremony.

The Malaika Children finish their performance. They have ingratiated themselves sufficiently with the dignitaries. The military official even invites Andrew up to the review stand to shake his hand. Andrew does so, climbing up the stairs on all fours, still dizzy.

Next the Maasai women perform. There is a brief moment of tension as one of the Malaika children, Latia, recognizes her mother in the group of Maasai. Latia is eleven and her parents had wanted to marry her off to a seventy-year-old man. She had run away and Mama Seraphina took her in. Now she was hiding behind Hannah. Fortunately, besides a few longing, pained looks from Latia's mother, a woman in a blue and orange robe, with a shaved head and long drooping ears, no conflict ensues.

The Maasai women finish then leave the grounds. The children from St. Jude's are next, but their dance is hardly as refined as the Malaika children's. When they finish, the ceremony is concluded. The official climbs into his Mercedes and is driven away. The rest of the local dignitaries disperse.

Only the Malaika children remain. Mama has not returned. If the parade ground was desolate before, there is no word for the abandonment of the place now. It is past noon and the sun is beating down on all of us. The children gravitate toward the review stand and sit in the shade beneath the places where the roof is intact. No one has eaten since breakfast and the children are all listless, although none complain. Bored myself and eager to get my mind off my own hunger, I walk over to a nearby ditch where I find some string and an old shoe. I tie the shoe to the end of the string and start a game of helicopter with the children.

Initially they join the game with enthusiasm, leaping and diving over the shoe as I spin it around just a few inches off the ground. However, they drop off one by one as they grow tired. Soon I'm left with only one child.

I remember her from the performance. She had been placed front and center. She has a vibrant face and an infectious smile. Her hair has been pulled into two braided pigtails on either side of her head. When she danced she seemed to have possessed more energy and speed than the other children. That holds true even now as I try to devise a two-person game to entertain myself and her.

Her name is Agnes. Her English is excellent. I teach her how to spin the shoe around perpendicular to the ground then release it to send it flying. Once we have established how to throw it, I teach her how to catch it by grabbing the string alone. Soon we are lost in a game of foxtail. When Mama finally shows up I am surprised to realize that an hour has passed by.

Agnes shows few signs of tiring, although even I am exhausted and light-headed with hunger. The children pack into the back of Mama's pickup truck. They have to squeeze and wedge themselves between bags of rice, with the older ones laying the younger children across their laps.

There is not enough room for Andrew and Agnes so they sit up front with Hannah, Mama Seraphina, and me.

The shoe and the string have won me Agnes' devotion and she begs to sit next to me. As Mama drives us homeward, Agnes' energy finally ebbs. She curls up against me and falls into a slumber that is undisturbed by the bouncing of the truck.

At one point her arm flops over onto my lap. I notice that her wrist is layered with scar tissue. I roll the sleeve up further and see that the scarring circles her entire wrist in an irregular band that is two inches wide at its narrowest. I examine her other wrist and find the same scaring.

Hannah is already looking at me. She answers my question before I can ask it. "Her stepfather did not want her. He tied her wrists together, hung her from a tree, then beat her with a stick. He left her for dead. Three days later someone called the police to come collect a dead body. The officer, she is a friend of Mama's, found Agnes. She was still hanging by her wrists. There was a huge pool of blood beneath her, but she was still alive."

Mama Seraphina added, yelling across the cab of the truck, "And look at her now. She is so beautiful. Sometimes she still has dreams in the night that her stepfather is coming back to take her. She comes to me crying and I let her sleep with me. When she first arrived she had to sleep with me every night. A few months ago her cousin showed up and asked for her back. He said he wanted to take care of her, but I could tell from the way she ran from him that he had been cruel to her in the past. Later I found out that he had promised to sell her to an older man for marriage."

I am a little stunned. I can't reconcile the outgoing child drooling on my sleeve with a child hung from a tree like a piñata and left for dead. The abuse seems incompatible with a child that could play games with a man who was a stranger to her then fall asleep on his shoulder afterwards. But I need only look at the scars, thick like putty with pointed spurs reaching up to her forearm and hands, if I want proof.

I have to admit, Mama Seraphina must be doing something right.

Chapter 4

On Being a Fraud

While living at Rainbow Children's Home and even the years afterwards while in graduate school studying global health, despite my efforts, I couldn't write the book about the children or my experiences with them in Kenya. It was not a question of writer's block. I wrote plenty. But I had no handle on the material. It was overwhelming. In the States I had worked with children who had access to antiretroviral treatment (ARVs); their prognoses were generally hopeful. I had worked with risk groups that were relatively small. I was not ready for the horrors of sub-Saharan Africa's generalized epidemic, where millions of adults were dying, leaving a generation of children with the physical, emotional, and mental scars of abandonment. There was so much need among the children we cared for at Rainbow and our outreach program *Eleza Familia* (Lift a Family) that I did not have time to be a journalist and chase down every story of interest that I came across. Nor did I have an editor or mentor to coach me through the issues, political, professional, and otherwise. After living with the children for two years, I was hardly objective either. And frankly I was in the way. The character of me in my stories, my own needs for recognition, for praise, my own narcissism and self-righteousness skewed everything. I was not objective about the children and I was hardly objective about myself and the hero I thought I was.

How did Sebastian Junger do it?

Then in 2006 I came across Binyavanga Wainaina's article *How to Write about Africa,* in a 2005 edition of Granta magazine. Wainaina is one of Kenya's best known journalists and authors, a winner of the Caine Prize for African Literature and a brave advocate for gay rights in Kenya and beyond. His essay skewered the hackneyed tropes, clichés, and self-serving narratives white authors had been writing about Africa—for centuries. It was a long and ignoble tradition stretching to include Karen Blixen to Kuki Gallmann and Aiden Hartley (whose book *Zanzibar Chest* was one of my favorites). Wainaina shone a glaring spotlight on how these works, even written decades apart, fell back on the same sweeping characterizations of Africans, inevitably portraying them as stereotypes and caricatures, at once as insulting as they were infantilizing. Africa was either a sweltering war torn tragic-scape of starving figures and mass graves or a misty Garden of Eden populated by noble savages, imperiled children, and majestic beasts. But in either case, these settings were to serve as backdrops to the heroic white protagonists who parachuted in and, after an initial period of culture shock, would shed their naiveté and triumph over adversity, recognizing the siren call of fate that called to them . . . *to save Africa.*

Wainaina's essay was eloquent, witty and—most importantly—completely right.

What a mirror he had held up to me. I looked at my pieces, drafts of book chapters, long form pieces, even short articles that I had written over the years. Each smacked of the very clichés and peddled the same tropes Wainaina's presented. My ego was knocked down a peg. Africa would be just fine without me, fine without another book on vulnerable children and a privileged, white, liberal expat come to save them. I set the writing aside to contribute in less self-aggrandizing ways.

After two years at the orphanage, I went to Emory's School of Public Health and earned my Masters in Global Health, with a focus on child psychosocial development. I landed a job at the development agency, CARE, based in Atlanta. I worked on children's issues throughout the world, traveling all over Africa and Asia. I was another cog in the international social work machine. It was thankfully, and finally, less about me and more about children. I thought I had finally escaped the egotistical, fame monster that I had almost become.

In 2011 when Greg Mortenson was accused of feeding the public lies about his adventures, for the sake of his cause, I saw myself—in his good works and bad. I saw in myself the same neediness, the yearning to be relevant, to make a difference that would earn the admiration of others stateside—a home where a sensitive idealistic man can often feel undervalued, invisible.

By then there were other players in the field, and train wrecks as well. Invisible Children, a foundation catalyzed by the short film by the same name made by three young film school graduates, Jason Russell, Bobby Bailey, and Laren Poole, became a national sensation, with supporters camping out in public parks all over the (developed) world to raise money and awareness of the children in Northern Uganda—the Night Commuters—who had to sleep en-mass in cities and towns in an effort to flee kidnappers who would make them child soldiers.

But when Jason Russell, one of the most outspoken founders of Invisible Children, had his very public breakdown in 2012, again I followed the story with the sense that I could be in his place. A journalist describing the original video that Jason and his friends made that began the Invisible Children movement said you could sense the film makers naiveté and the moment where they come up against the hard truth that the world is not fair.

"And this has been going on for how long?" says one of them. "If this happened for even one night in America, it would be on the cover of Newsweek magazine!" You can feel their self-absorbed, righteous teenage outrage at suddenly realizing that the world is fundamentally unjust and unfair, and it's this sense of outrage that somehow they have managed to keep hold of and harness.

That was me. I had long ago learned that the world was unfair and unjust, but I did not think that was any reason not to try to make it less so. Had I been a charismatic film major I might have done the same thing as Jason and his friends. Instead I had tried to use the form of writing, and since that medium was slower or my talent less than that of Jason, Bobby, and Laren, I had been spared success and becoming a public figure before I was ready.

And the casualties, so to speak, did not stop there. November 12, 2012, David Oliver Relin, the professional journalist who had helped to write *Three Cups of Tea* in partnership with Greg Mortenson, committed suicide by stepping in front of a train near Portland, Oregon. He had been diagnosed with depression. As the criticisms and controversies grew around Mortenson and his alleged deceptions regarding his work in Afghanistan, it was too much for David to bear.

Over the years I had experienced an intense rush when speaking on behalf of the orphanage. I saw the mixture of awe, respect, and romanticism in the faces of those who listened to me— the guy who lived with orphans. People thought of me as a modern-day saint—I think on some level, people look for celebrities, aid workers, etc., to vault into these positions—it gives them hope. Back in Kenya I was treated with respect and deference that can only come to a white man who is perceived as rich because of his skin color. In the Peace Corps they call this the "zero to hero" effect. It's intoxicating. Why not keep it going with a propaganda that paints you as a hero? Why not make yourself the center of the story, the film, as Jason did? Your story is certainly exciting. Why not stretch the truth, as Greg did—it's for a good cause.

Why not start believing your own press? Why not start believing you are a saint? It's a nice place to be, for a time.

I was becoming aware of the degree to which ego, insecurity, and self-seeking enmeshed itself into my ambitions to "help." Something I had seen all too often with "Great White Knight" charity workers who journey to impoverished nations and attach

35

themselves to a cause. Greg and Jason were accused of this as were countless other charismatic activists. Africans themselves can often be the harshest critics. One could argue that it was, sadly, Relin who paid the price for Mortenson's alleged inaccuracies.

Beside my own ego and insecurities, I had reservations about a book based on the children for a second reason. They had shared with me, allowing me to take notes, even tape record them, without any respectable form of consent. I was not aware of the constraints and restrictions on researching children until I was at Emory and learned that my use of their stories, which they had shared with me as a friend whom they trusted, could just be another form of exploitation and violation. Reluctant to be another purveyor of hunger porn—photos or articles about undernourished, malformed, abused children used to elicit donations without the consent of the subjects—I withdrew from my writings even further.

I remained at CARE for a number of years, contributing with other well-meaning individuals who found their identities in being part of a team, a movement. I had escaped being a Great White Knight, or so I thought. I was not the face of the cause, CARE was. But the politics and realities of non-profit life defeated me. I worked long hours, traveled to dozens of countries, losing time with loved ones back home—but the next promotion, the next raise was always out of reach. After five years and the financial crises of 2008, I, along with a third of CARE's staff, was laid off.

For me, it was devastating. As much as I thought I had become enlightened and tamed my ego to become the "aware" development worker, deep down, I still harbored a sense of entitlement. After all, I had gone to school, college, even graduate school. I had worked tirelessly for good causes. Where was the recognition, the reward, not to mention the salary, that I had *earned* for being so full of self-discipline, selflessness, and self–awareness?

But the world doesn't really work that way and I was waking up to that.

Chapter 5

Belts

Miriam saw her first *mzungu* at the market where her mother worked.

Miriam loved the market. She loved helping her mother, who sold avocadoes, mangoes, papayas, potatoes, passion fruits, tomatoes, onions, peppers, bananas, and of course *sukuma-weki*. Miriam's mother always said that she was a very helpful child. She helped with everything, carrying the food, arranging it, stacking up the tomatoes, cutting the *sukuma*. The only thing she did not help with was fighting and bartering with the *mhindi* man that came to the market each morning and sold Miriam's mother and the other market women their goods. He was always trying to charge too much for his fruits and vegetables, and it took strong women to get the right price out of him. This was to be expected because all people from India were thieves and liars.

Miriam liked the other market women. Having them around her mother's stall was like having many aunties. Miriam fancied that her mother was their leader and lately she got special attention because she was pregnant. Miriam was known by all the women because she was trusted to run and get change for the ladies whenever they needed it. They also liked her for this job because she had long legs that she could run fast on like a Kalenjin.

There were other children around the market and sometimes Miriam would play with them, digging up bottle tops, or finding water bottles and throwing them at geckos in the grass or dogs that sniffed around the trash piles.

The first time Miriam saw a *mzungu,* she had noticed that some of the women were talking quickly and softly, which always meant that something interesting was happening or about to happen. They also were looking in one direction, but trying hard to appear like they were looking in the other. Miriam looked in the direction that their attention was actually focused.

She saw the ugliest woman ever. Miriam felt sick at the sight of her. Her skin was the color of the plastic wrap they laid on the roof of their house to keep the rain away. There were a number of children laughing and giggling, calling out *"Zungu nipa sweet."* Miriam said nothing to her. She did not want a sweet. She did not want anything from her.

Miriam wondered if she should hide, but seeing that her mother did not move, she remained fixed in place. To her horror the *mzungu* stopped at their booth.

Her hair was wrapped in bundles that reminded Miriam of the hairballs that cats coughed up in the alley behind their house. Her skin was even more disgusting up close: there were splotches of pink and red on her face and back. Miriam felt terribly embarrassed for her: her clothes were like underwear—they covered her hips and her breasts but left her legs and belly bare. Her belly button was strange too—it was just a slit, as opposed to the nubs Miriam and everyone else she knew had. It looked like she had a metal ring stuck inside it as well. Miriam wondered if she should point it out to the woman, but decided not to. It probably hurt her.

Over her eyes she had dark spectacles with orange lenses that were so shiny that Miriam could see herself and all the market reflected in them. Miriam could not see the woman's eyes, but she realized she was looking at her when she said,

"Jambo."

Miriam was afraid to answer and afraid to look at the woman, for fear that her skin would change to the same color. Her mother smiled and answered in her sing-song voice.

"Sijambo."

They were speaking Kiswahili, not Kikuyu. The *mzungu* asked for two oranges and two avocadoes, but she did not know her numbers very well. Miriam was surprised to hear her mother speak suddenly in *Kizungu,* which seemed to make the *mzungu* happy because she smiled after that.

Her mother smiled a great deal as they spoke and the girl gave her mother a one hundred shilling note for four pieces of fruit. Miriam was surprised when her mother pocketed it and did not ask her to run to find change. The *mzungu* did not seem to care. This was when she realized *wazungu* were all rich. The ugly woman smiled, said *"Asanti sana,"* and walked away. Miriam wanted to laugh when she saw how the woman's thighs jiggled as she walked, but she knew it was not nice to laugh at people who were misshapen.

Once the *mzungu* was gone the other women came over and began to talk excitedly about how she was dressed and how outlandish she looked, clicking their tongues disapprovingly. When the conversation came to a lull, Miriam asked her mother why the *mzungu* had covered her eyes the way she did.

The other women clicked their tongues again. Miriam's mother shrugged and answered that many *wazungu* wore glasses like that because they had weak eyes that were not used to the sun like *wafrika.*

Miriam nodded, then she folded her hands, closed her eyes and thanked God she was not as ugly or as blind as a *mzungu.* She never wanted eyes that she had to cover or skin that turned red and spotted. The women laughed uproariously. Miriam's mother smiled too, but then stroked her head and told her she did not have to worry.

It did not occur to Oliver that his mother had been sick for a long time until Christmas Day. They were sitting down for dinner at Babu's—Babu had needed to remind Oliver to remove his red knit cap, he had taken to wearing it often—and his mother had a

coughing fit. She had to go lay down until it passed. It was then that
Oliver remembered the same thing happened the previous Christmas.

He noticed other things after that, like how her face was now
thinner than it was in many of the photographs Babu had around his
house. Most of his mother's friends still came to visit, but now their
visits were to cook food for Oliver and his mother, or to quietly
drink tea, which his mother never finished. His mother and her
friends no longer stayed up late laughing and giggling. Oliver took
careful note of which ones still came. Adrianna, who often came
over with everybody, or sometimes alone just to paint her nails with
Oliver's mother, never came any more. They had not seen Lucille
for a long time either. When Oliver asked Pricilla about them, she
said that Adrianna was simply too busy, but then she clicked her
tongue, which Oliver knew meant that Pricilla did not approve of
whatever "busy" meant. Lucille did not come to visit because she
was sick. Oliver asked why. Pricilla simply said, "Everybody gets
sick."

So when Oliver got sick it did not seem, to him, to be
unusual. He began coughing like his mother. He often felt weak and
feverish. He found it difficult to pay attention at school because he
wanted only to put his head on his desk and rest. For the first time he
got answers wrong on a test. This upset him greatly because he knew
how proud his mother was that he had been first in his class for two
years in a row and that he was even a grade ahead of the other
children his age.

He knew he would have to pray to God to get better. Since
she had become sick his mother prayed more. She knelt down beside
the bed every night and asked God to give her strength, wisdom, and
guidance. God answered her prayers, for most days she still was able
to get dressed up and go to work. She was still too tired, however, in
the evenings to help Oliver with his homework. Most nights she
would change out of her work clothes, sit down in front of the
television, and fall asleep. Many nights she would forget to eat

dinner. Babu had asked Oliver to remind his mother to eat. Oliver knew she did not always like to because she had diarrhea often.

Eventually Oliver went with his mother on one of her trips to the doctor. The doctor examined Oliver as well. A nurse stuck him with a needle that made him bleed into a glass tube. Oliver cried but his mother took his hand and told him he had to be brave. After that visit, he and his mother both took medicines. Oliver's cough got better but his mother's did not. He asked her why and she said,

"Perhaps mine likes me too much. It does not want to leave. But people live a long time with coughs. Old men always cough."

Oliver asked her if he would cough when he was an old man. He did not know why, but his mother almost began to cry. She went to her room and closed the door. Oliver knew he should leave her alone so he went to his room and read one of the books Pricilla had given to him. It was one he had already finished so it was not very interesting. He could not focus very well on it and he found himself reading much more slowly than usual.

Eventually his mother came out of her room and hugged him. She sniffed like she was still crying. She told him he would be fine and that his cough would go away. But she made him promise to always be brave and never to be afraid, like he was when the nurse had taken his blood, even if she was not around to hold his hand.

He said he would be and this made her happy. Then she told him to get his shoes; she was taking him to Nando's for dinner.

Ivy's father had just beaten her mother. Ivy knew it was important to beat children if they misbehaved, otherwise they would be lazy or play all the time and they would not do work around the house or in the *shamba*. She guessed that the same must have been true for adults, however, as far as she knew her mother was always working. It was her mother who went to market. It was her mother who cooked their food, made their tea, and gathered charcoal and sticks for the *jiko*. It was her mother that swept the house and took care of Ivy's brother Maurice. Ivy helped whenever she could, but she knew she would not be able to do these things on her own. That was what a mother was for.

Ivy sat in the corner and tried to make herself very small. She thought of herself as a fighter, she was often getting in fights with other girls and boys. She nearly almost won. But tonight she did not want to be beaten. Her father was so much bigger and he had a weapon this time. Father usually beat her and Maurice with a reed, but tonight he was beating her mother with his belt, flailing the belt buckle down on her like a carpenter beating a nail with a hammer. When he grew tired of that he used his fists. Sometimes when Ivy's mother beat her, she used her slipper, so at first when Ivy saw her father remove his belt to beat her mother, a part of her laughed because his pants—which had grown too big for him—nearly fell down.

But now she was scared. She knew the belt would hurt, especially the buckle. Ivy found herself trying to imagine ways she would try to counter such a weapon if ever used against her in a fight. Her mother had not figured out a way, except for cowering. The belt buckle made a loud, heavy popping sound on impact. Her father seemed so angry it was as if he might do anything. He was speaking in *Kizungu,* which was harder for Ivy to understand, but he seemed to be accusing her mother of bringing sickness into the house. He called her Jezebel, Delilah, and Salome, which were names of bad women from the Bible. Ivy knew this from church.

But Ivy's father was sick and old, so he did not beat his wife too long. Her mother used to laugh when he would beat Ivy with the reed. She would say that because he was so old and tired that his beatings were softer than when she beat Ivy. Ivy agreed that mother and her slipper were usually worse than father and the reed, but the belt was a different matter.

Ivy's father was weak. He would breathe very heavily when he walked too fast and he often coughed at night. Mother coughed too and so did Ivy, but not as much as her parents. Her father was so old that he had white hair and mostly walked with a cane very slowly. Many people, when they first met him, thought that Ivy's mother was actually his daughter and that Ivy was his granddaughter.

Her father did have daughters from two other marriages—his other wives had died. His other daughters and sons were all older than Ivy's mother. To Ivy they seemed more like aunts and uncles than her own brothers and sisters. Ivy's mother was always very kind to them and made them tea and biscuits when they visited. However, Ivy knew her mother did not like them. When her own friends would come over and they would sit outside and sort rice, Ivy's mother would complain to them that her husband's other children were bossy to her and treated her like a child.

Eventually her father did grow tired and stopped beating Ivy's mother. He coughed and spat. After that the only sound in the room was her mother's coughing and sniffling. Then her father announced that he was hungry and asked her where dinner was. She silently got up, blew on the *jiko* coals and went to cut potatoes. Ivy immediately got up to help, grabbing the knife and *sukuma weeki* that she knew they would need to cut as well, but then her father bellowed, "Don't make the children do all the work."

This was in *Kizungu* so Ivy froze for the moment that it took her to interpret it. Her mother was quickly beside her, taking the cutting board and knife away. Then she told Ivy to go outside and play.

Ivy put on her slippers. She knew she should take Maurice with her, so she took his slippers as well and went to her parent's room, where she knew her brother was hiding. He always hid there when father was angry but she knew father would be even angrier if he found Maurice in his room. Ivy found him behind the chair in the corner. Maurice was almost four. He had light brown eyes that

43

women cooed over, full cheeks, and an ever present smile. But he was not smiling right now. He sat on the floor with his knees curled to his chest. Ivy checked if his pants were wet because sometimes when father was angry, Maurice would pee on himself. This time they were dry.

Ivy told him he was a good boy. She put his shoes on him, then they walked, without a word, past their parents and went outside. It was already growing dark. Normally they would not be allowed to go outside, but she knew tonight they had to go out for a while. As long as she was there to protect Maurice, she knew there would be little danger. So they grabbed some sticks and drew pictures in the dirt by the lantern light that shone out from windows and the cracks between the corrugated metal walls.

By now most of the neighbors were shunning Judith. People assumed that her husband had left her because she had been unfaithful. No one wanted to help her. No one wanted to catch AIDS.

Judith, who was already tall and lean, lost weight. She looked like a skeleton. She had chronic chest infections as well as Karposi sarcoma lesions on her legs. Her boss at the seamstress shop where she worked fired her. She could no longer afford to pay her rent in their apartment, so she and Sofie moved to a shanty house in Kangemi.

Judith looked for work, but no one would hire her. Around this time the lesions on her legs grew worse. They became so painful that she could not walk. She stayed inside all day. She could not afford to send Sofie to school so she let Sofie play outside in front of the shack, where she could watch her from the doorway.

Sofie was very outgoing. She would greet neighbors as they walked by, but they never acknowledged her. Instead they simply hurried past. Judith noticed that the other children would not play with Sofie, except for the *chakoras*—the street children, orphans that wandered about with crushed, discarded water bottles filled with cobbler's glue. The vapors from the glue made them high, eliminating their hunger pains, but after too much use the children would become as dumb as animals.

Judith became feverish. The day came when she was too weak to sit up and watch Sofie. She asked the wife of the butcher to care for Sofie, to at least give her some food. The woman only made a sign with her hand that meant she was trying to avert a curse.

Judith knew she was going to die, but she could not bear the thought of Sofie being abandoned. She could not bear the thought of Sofie becoming a *chakora,* wandering the streets begging, growing up—if she grew up—to trade sex for food.

Judith would kill Sofie, then, herself. She took one of her belts, called Sofie to her bedside and wrapped the belt around her neck. Sofie cooperated as if her mother was prepping her for school, buttoning her school uniform or rubbing *mafuta* on her skin.

Judith could not pull it though. She was too weak. She wept and then she lost consciousness.

Chapter 6

Mickey Mouse, Donald Duck, Missionaries, Jesus, and other objects of my Disenchantment

After Jacob passes, a second child who is seriously ill is placed in the nursing room. She is ten and her name is Valentine. She is a lanky girl who would be tall if she were not always in bed. She is from our outreach program in the slums that surround Nairobi. Her mother is still living and is also HIV positive. Her condition is not as advanced as her daughter's. Valentine is asleep or comatose for most of the time. Weena, a fourth-year medical student from the States, takes turns with the Kenyan nurses providing Valentine round-the-clock care. Weena is brilliant and is constantly teaching me little bits of medicine and techniques of hospice care. She is training to be a pediatrician and one of her mottos is, "Always look at the test numbers and play with the kids." Although she can run few tests here at the orphanage, she does play with the children every chance she gets. They love her for her sunny disposition and the playful sounding name. "Weeeeeennnaaahhhhaaaaa," they sing when they see her. She admits to me that she never cries on the job, even after losing child patients; however, whenever she gets home after a tiring day, she will put a Disney film in the DVD player and only then be able to cry her eyes out watching Bambi's mother or Simba's father die.

Weena monitors Valentine's vitals, feeds her through a nasal gastric tube, and holds her over a bed pan when needed. As she changes the sheets around Valentine, I see for the first time that the mattresses are wrapped in a covering that makes them waterproof. It is needed, for shortly after Weena has changed the sheets,

46

Valentine—without waking up—vomits up the nutrient rich liquid Weena has just eased down the tube that snakes through her nose, down her throat and into her stomach. I'm sitting next to Valentine as she does this. The motion is automatic and strange, as the rest of her body remains inert. It is an involuntary reflex, one of which Valentine is not even aware. Soon the frothy stuff is sinking down past Valentine's folded hands, across her pillow, and onto the new sheets. Weena groans. The entire vomiting reflex motion brings to mind something inanimate, machine-like, such as a fire extinguisher discharging its load or a clogged sink burping.

Maybe it's from Weena's medically informed explanations, or just all the sickness we are surrounded by, but I've become keenly aware of the metaphor of the body being a machine: the long-short-short gasping of Cheyne-Stokes breathing of dying children, not unlike a broken down car engine coughing to a stop; the leakage from my students' ears and from other orifices when the children die; the cotton wads used to plug their noses and ears like gum on a radiator. So many bodily processes going wrong while an immune system is rendered broken by a virus smaller and simpler than the most basic of human cells.

Weena is there, with Valentine's mother, when she passes away during the night. Her mother weeps uncontrollably, holding her dead child. Weena moves discreetly to the far side of the room while mobiles of Mickey Mouse and Donald Duck whir overhead.

Malaika Children's Home consists of one main building. The central room has mismatched furniture lining the walls. It is lit by a single, dim overhead bulb, and it is often smoky from the kitchen that is one room over. Opposite the kitchen is the girls' room: a room that smells of urine-stained sheets, tightly packed with bunk beds, but military in its neatness and order.

The boys' room is the same but the door to it is located outside, away from the girls' sleeping quarters, in order to make midnight trysts more difficult.

As the sun sets at Malaika, the darkness I always associate with the mystery of Africa arrives. This is not Joseph Conrad's implacable, brooding darkness, but rather a darkness more mundane, one from a lack of electricity and/or light bulbs. In the Ghanaian village where Hannah and I met while volunteering, with the setting of the sun, open spaces became dim and the insides of huts became dark as pitch, making this most basic abode of the Africans mysterious and impenetrable to us. Additionally, the dark complexions of Africans made their expressions that much harder to read in the dark (although I imagine our faces could be as perplexing to them at times).

It would be easy to let imagination fill this void created by miscomprehension and allow ourselves to conclude that the Africans are just alien and impossible to ever understand.

But as Hannah points out, this is simply laziness.

When I visit Hannah, we spend the night in the house where she boards, a place owned by a family that is friends with Mama Seraphina. As we lay on our roll up camping mattresses, light from the setting sun fills the room. A breeze that I imagine has crossed the jungles of Congo, climbed up to the Great Rift Valley, tumbled down the side of the Ngong Hills, and over the vines of fuchsia bougainvillea along Hannah's windowsills, tugs gently at the mosquito net draped over the bed. Lizards scramble along the rafters in search of their insect prey. It is moments like these that we are both certain in our knowledge of why we have come to this continent.

Hannah shares the house with the family that owns it. The matriarch is Teresa, a tall Luhya woman who is a mother of two children in primary school. She supports the family with her income. Their house is large by Kenyan standards—about the size of a single family home in the United States. It is unfinished though. Teresa's husband, Tom, had worked for a bank where he had been stealing money in order to finance the house. When he was caught and fired, the construction on the house halted. Now he spent most of his days drinking with friends while Teresa worked extra hours in order to feed the four of them. Many times she had confided to Hannah that she would have to get a new job, since as a Luhya in an office run by Kikuyus, Teresa had little hope of getting a promotion, much less a raise.

Wires hang out of the walls in the house where fixtures were supposed to have been placed. The walls themselves do not reach the ceilings, so any impression of privacy is deceptive. From Hannah's room we can hear everything in the house. When we make love we must maintain some type of inane conversation, one of us raising our voice, talking about grocery prices or news of home, to cover up the sounds of the other gasping. All this in order to sound like two God-fearing Christians, as opposed to two foreigners alleviating their isolation and loneliness.

In the world of safari tourism five animals are considered must-sees: buffalo, lions, elephants, rhinos, and leopards. They are referred to as the "Big Five." The term goes back to when a safari was less about telephoto lenses and more about rifle calibers. The big five were the most ferocious animals on the savanna when cornered and so they made the best trophies for adventurous hunters. Nowadays they make for the best pictures mounted on the walls of adventurous travelers.

At the orphanage some of the volunteers and I cynically begin to call AIDS orphans the sixth member of the big five. No one is hunting them, thank God, except to take photos—thousands of photos.

UNICEF actually has recommendations in the Convention on the Rights of the Child (the CRC) on respecting children's privacy. The convention, as described by UNICEF, is "a universally agreed set of non-negotiable standards and obligations. These basic standards—also called human rights—set minimum entitlements and freedoms that should be respected by governments and individuals."[1] In the spirit of the Convention it is generally frowned upon to take pictures of children without permission from their guardians. At our orphanage, permission is always granted. Those of us who live there look down upon the tourists (often from our own home countries) who come passing through in safari vans, clicking away pictures of "our" children.[2]

There is a tinge of exploitation on the part of tourists, who decked in beads, dressed in khaki, and sometimes pith helmets (really), snap pictures of the "poor AIDS orphans." But then again, there is no small amount of snobbery on the side of us volunteers who in the tourists see ourselves and wish to distance our "authentic experience" from those just passing through.

Truth is, we're all just passing through and as Alexander Fuller writes, "Your perception of a third world country is often dependent upon whether or not you are free to leave it."

But some visitors get me more twisted than others. I'm in my room reading on New Year's Eve when I hear a commotion in the orphanage's quad in front of the schoolhouse. A few safari vans worth of American missionaries from California have arrived. Now, before I criticize missionaries, I must first recognize I have no legitimate ground to stand on, having attended Catholic high school, and college, and now I volunteer at an AIDS orphanage run by nuns and founded by a Jesuit, a missionary visa stamped in my passport.

---

[1] The US and South Sudan governments are the only United Nations member countries not to ratify the CRC.
[2] This is no longer the case today, as the privacy of the children, of the institution Rainbow Children's Home is based on, is well protected.

But there is something about the zest of Americans on week-long "missions" that tweaks me in a certain way.

In front of the schoolhouse the leader of the mission trip is speaking through a bullhorn while next to him stands a man in full clown regalia—blue-and-white-striped pants, red suspenders, polka-dot shirt, and a wig of rainbow-colored hair. The mission leader, a man in his fifties with a coach's air about him, tells the group of high school students to sit down with the kids from the orphanage for a magic show. Seating is tight on the lawn, as the Rainbow kids are outnumbered by the Californians in cargo-shorts, T-shirts, and crucifixes.

The clown introduces himself as Mr. Small. He is at least 6'2" but he points out that compared to God, the creator of the universe, he is very small. Miriam is sitting with two white girls who are older than her but hardly have the burden of experience she does. It's a little amazing to me that the thirteen-year-old sitting between them has already buried her parents, cared for dying children, almost died, and experienced more heartbreak than the average American will in a lifetime. I wonder, who is really the child among those three? Miriam turns and looks at me, as if she knew Mr. Small would irk me in my secular agnostic sanctimony. I roll my eyes and she shakes a finger at me as if I'm one of my baby-class students misbehaving, then she turns back to the show.

It is a decent magic performance, if you don't mind the heavy-handed religious themes: Mr. Small puts two handkerchiefs—one labelled SATAN, the other JESUS—into a sack, which he turns inside out to reveal that only the JESUS handkerchief remains, implying that Jesus banishes Satan. Thank goodness, I think to myself. I have an answer if one of my own bags needs to be exorcised.

To be honest, I like magic shows, religious themes or not, but this one would be shitty even in the US. Our kids eat it up though. Their faith is unwavering and it helps them, sometimes, in their suffering. But at the same time, they are a captive, vulnerable audience and it seems as if the urge to be a good Christian is coercive. But it is not as striking as some situations I've been in.

Once while in a slum called Kangemi, the outreach staff and I had set up a clinic in a dusty school room. Dr. Alex, a UK doctor, fresh out of med school, was seeing patients, while I took notes, held kids while we took blood, and directed patients to the waiting area. The line was out the door and there was absolutely no privacy as Dr. Alex conducted histories. One woman whose fourteen-year-old son had begun to experience seizures sticks in my mind. Perhaps it was the concern in her face, or the way she shared so many intimate details of their family life, and health history, in hopes that Dr. Alex would be able to do something more than refer them to a hospital for further tests they could not afford.

Our nurse that day was an American missionary, driven by kindness, compassion, and a need to bring Jesus into people's lives. While the line extended to the next block and Alex skipped lunch—because how could he eat in front of these waiting people—the nurse asked me if she could try to convert some of the patients. I was shocked. According to the demographics of Kenya, and personal experience, I knew most of them already were Christian. But what struck me most was the coercive nature of the conversion. Here was the only medical attention they could receive. I imagined they would tell us they believed in Baal, Zeus, or Thor, if we—the ones holding power over their health—asked them to. I personally knew I would choke a puppy as a sacrifice to Mickey Mouse if the only doctor available to treat my child asked me to.

Needless to say, I said no to the kind nurse.

Back to the show. Mr. Small continues. Things go awry at the end when he begins to create balloon art for the boys of Cottage Red. Mr. Small is partial to making peaceful crosses for the children, but the boys immediately turn them into swords and begin to beat the holy-hell out of one another. He switches to hats after that and the missionaries eagerly place them on the heads of the children. Their leader announces on his megaphone that they have eight minutes before they have to depart, so they should make friends with the children quickly.

Here sheer numbers become a problem as there are still more visitors than kids. I see children literally lifted off their feet while missionaries pull on either arm. I search for Miriam. She looks happy as she shows a group of high school girls Cottage Yellow. Meanwhile I watch as two girls place a pink balloon hat on a bewildered Edison (my frat-boy student with the pot belly who likes to chew rocks), plop him on one of the swings for the older children, and set him swinging. Their cameras flash, whir, and click. I chide myself for my cynicism as Edison smiles and begins to kick his stumpy legs back and forth. He enjoys the attention. Who am I to judge?

I follow the girls on tour in Cottage Yellow. Miriam poses for pictures, her sweeping, photogenic cheekbones on full display, holding her Barbie doll (with blond hair, blue eyes, and white skin if you are wondering). I ask one of the visitors what their trip is about.

"God," she says, between chomps on her gum. She's young, wearing sandals, cargo shorts, and a white T-shirt, her brown hair pulled back into a ponytail.

I ask her to elaborate.

"We're here bringing God to the people of Kenya."

When I point out to her that the kids are already Christian, she corrects me and says this is irrelevant. "We're here to bring them love, compassion, and donations from home."

I can't object. I ask her what their plans are tonight for New Year's.

"We'll go to a concert in this stadium and we'll pray with other missionaries and Kenyans. It will be, like, awesome."

She peels away to take more pictures of Miriam who I can tell is doing her best to ignore my sourpuss expression. I swear I get a look from her that says, "Don't bother me while I'm working." And that is the uncomfortable part about it. Sure the visitors will give the children attention, expose them to new culture, and even bring donations; their lives may be altered by spending a few minutes with a child living with HIV. But on such a day and others, when white CEOs from multinational companies show up with wipe-away check-boards to display their generosity to the poor of Kenya for the newspapers, I feel we are in a certain kind of business. We're selling the opportunity for people to look good or feel good. Our kids are our product or at least our sales force.

The missionaries, keeping to their schedule, board their safari vehicles, open the windows, and hold out their cameras for last minute pictures of the children waving good-bye. Amid the clamor I hear a child crying. I follow the sound to the playground where Edison has been abandoned in the big-kid swing. He is turned around, his face red, his shirt askew, his balloon hat crooked, as he dangles over the edge of the swing, trying to let himself down from a height that is too great for him. I help him down and carry him to his cottage where his house mother is waiting.

Chapter 7

Dambisa Moyo Tells It to Me Straight

Career-wise by 2011 I was already frustrated with the fruits of my labors and doubting the choices I had made. I had followed my passion, and what I thought were laudable values, leading me to work with the children at the orphanage, to pursue a service-related degree at Emory, and accept a job at CARE. But where had those choices left me? I had chosen a career that had not paid well, I was saddled with student debt, and I was now unemployed at thirty-four. Around this time I received a bit of a lifeline, however, in the form of a full scholarship to attend Georgia State University to earn my MBA.

I should mention that I had already enrolled in the MBA program while at CARE. It was a result of what I had learned in the field, heard from villagers, and even children themselves: that people needed economic opportunity as much as they needed a safety net. "Clinics and schools are wonderful," one Zambian told me, "but we need jobs." Truly, the most successful programs that I worked on at CARE whether health, education, early childhood development, or gender empowerment, had an economic component built into them. African countries needed credit ratings as much as they needed mosquito nets. Income generating skills for parents, value chain management, access to capital and markets, produced the gains that ultimately made schools, clinics, and women's shelters possible— and sustainable. Furthermore, I had found the writings of Dambisa Moyo, author of *Dead Aid*, persuasive. Aid, in many cases, had hindered the very development it sought. Dependency on the state and local levels could cripple the necessary institutions and skills needed to truly improve the standard of living in the long term. The good intentions behind aid (and the aid industry) are not enough to protect against unintended consequences and even the perverse incentives that could create a self-sustaining cycle that, in some cases, perpetuated poverty rather than eliminating it.

There will never be enough charity in the world to solve the problems of poverty, while one has to admit, capitalism has raised the standard of living and life expectancy, and lowered infant and maternal mortality, for—literally—billions. Was economic growth the best public health intervention in history? What I was asking was anathema in some aid circles, but Dr. Moyo's writings encouraged me to look at aid and the industry of jobs and livelihoods that had arisen around it in a new light. I realized the "good guys" are as vulnerable to mistakes, group-think, bias, and prejudice as much as anyone else; our assumptions had to be questioned, just like anyone else's. Had capitalism brought environmental devastation? Yes. Exploitation? Certainly. Inequality? Yes, Yes, Yes. But it was hard to deny the good that had come from it as well. I began to realize that the solution for poverty was not an issue of charity or business, but both/and. There would always be a need for social safety net programs. *Always.* But we should not mistake them for long-term solutions. We need economic growth, even with its unfortunate by-products: pollution, inequality, and exploitation. It's a contradiction, a paradox that must be managed.

But none of that was what I was thinking on September 25th when the handle of the knife found its way into my hand. I was thinking I was a failure. I had led with my heart and where had it gotten me? In debt, unemployed, and too poor for anyone to consider as a partner, much less a parent. Meanwhile my peers who had not tried to save the world in their twenties were buying houses, starting families, and contributing to their retirement funds. I was back in school, with students ten years younger than me. What better proof was there that I had made all the wrong choices?

Worst of all I had never done what I intended to do—write a story about the children. Much less set the world on fire and see my face emblazoned across the back covers of best-selling works. I had given up on it for all the reasons listed earlier—I was too flawed myself, too clichéd, and the problems were just too great to make a difference with a book. It was easier to be a faceless cog in the international development machine. And how could I reconcile that with the insecure, fame hungry, narcissist with dreams of grandiosity who went to Kenya in the first place? I couldn't. Both existed within me and I was wary of feeding the beast.

Yet I had nothing else to hold onto. Having lived in five different cities between moving from volunteering in Nairobi, saving money for school in the States, and finally enrolling in Atlanta, I had a thin network of good friends. I guess my own sanctimonious nature resulting from my work did not endear me to people much either. Also, I had lost much faith in, well, faith. Watching so many of the children die had done that. One night, while holding Jacob as he died, I had asked Weena, "Is the world a good or bad place?" She had looked up at the ceiling and answered, in an oh-you-are-so-naïve-you-are-precious tone, "Ted, it's just a place."

So nihilism set in. Along with social isolation, financial troubles, and self-criticism. My self-esteem eroded, replaced by a toxic self-hate that grew into self-loathing. It was amazing how effective my own mind was in crafting arguments about my own abject failure and utter worthlessness. The evidence was all around me: in my thirties, in debt for a degree without the earning power to pay for it, living in a basement apartment, unmarried, little savings, and a car I had to ask my parents to help pay for.

My intellect's favorite pastime became reinforcing these messages, my own focused nature turned on myself. Some observers have said that depressives are actually quite rational individuals, who are free of the rose-tinted self-deception that everyone is able to engage in, due to religious faith, willful ignorance, the proper balance of serotonin and dopamine, or all these things. My reasoning "helpfully" reminded me every day that I didn't really matter. I never had. If I died at thirty-two as opposed to eighty-five, the world, the universe in its vastness, would not notice in the least. After all, I had seen so many people—children—die and the world had not noticed.

Chapter 8

School

At dinner Miriam had once said she wanted to grow up to be a market woman, or maybe even a fisherman. Jesus and the apostles were fishermen, she knew, but they were also carpenters. Like good *wafrika,* they had many jobs—*kazi ni kazi,* work is work, as the saying went.

But her mother had become quiet, her face like a stone, which was what she did when she was angry. Her father became quiet as well. Not angry quiet but scared quiet, for everyone in the family knew to be quiet and scared when mother was angry.

Her words finally came forth: Miriam would not be a foolish market woman, nor would she be a fisherman struggling to make money and smelling like dead fish. She would go to school. She would be a teacher, a nurse, or even a banker.

That was why this day was so important. It was Miriam's first day back at school. She was nine. The year before, when she was eight, she had come to school as well, but they had sent her away, saying she was not ready yet. Now she was dressed in her uniform once more. Her skirt was blue and her sweater green. Her mother had re-braided her hair just the night before. Her skin was clean and shiny with oil and her father had helped her to polish her shoes.

Her mother was wrapped in one of Miriam's favorite wraps today. She had decided not to go to the market and instead to come with Miriam to school. Now she stood and spoke to the headmaster. When they finished talking, her mother walked over to her while the headmaster waited in the doorway of the school. "Be good and work hard," her mother said.

Miriam promised she would, even though just then she wanted to jump up and down and shout with happiness because she realized that this meant she had been allowed back into school, that she was ready. But she knew good girls would not make such a disturbance, so she quickly walked over to the headmaster, greeted him and thanked him politely.

He nodded then led her to her new classroom. She noticed that the other children in her class were much younger than she, but upon reflection, she decided this could work to her advantage: if she was older she might be smarter than they were. Maybe she would be allowed to be prefect.

The teacher told her where to sit and once she was in her desk she sharpened all her pencils with a sharpener that Patrice, one of her mother's friends from the market, had given her. She placed the pencils in a straight row beside her exercise book. The other children did not have sharpeners, so Miriam sharpened their pencils for them.

She behaved well in class. She never spoke to the other children when the teacher's back was turned. She copied the letters he wrote on the board very carefully. She would even do a few extra copies of each letter just for additional practice. When the teacher walked by, she hoped he would notice her extra work, but instead he would point out to her how she had copied a number of letters backwards.

Reading remained her worst subject. When it came time to practice reading aloud, Miriam would just repeat what she heard the other students saying around her. She did this each day, until one day, when they had to take turns reading aloud to the class alone. When her turn came she could not sound out the words that the other children had read so easily. After stumbling over the first two words, making the rest of the class erupt in giggles, she simply stopped.

The teacher stood up, walked over to her desk, and asked her if she had fallen asleep.

She said no.

Then what was she doing?

This was not a question she really understood. She was sitting. She was looking down at the floor. She had been trying to read. She had been trying to do what her mother said to do in school: learn.

"I am learning," she finally ventured.

"How can you be learning if you cannot read?" the teacher said.

This was another question she did not know the answer to, but the teacher did not seem to need one. He walked back to his desk and told the girl next to Miriam to start reading. Miriam hated the other girl for the ease with which she began pronouncing the words. Tears came to her eyes and she wiped them away with the back of her hand.

At the end of the week the headmaster called her to his office and told her she should go home and not to return since she was not serious about learning. Miriam was sure her mother would be angry. She was so sure that she debated not going home right away, but then she decided her mother would be even angrier if she came home late.

Her mother listened and was very quiet for a while. Then, she went to the kettle, poured some tea, and replaced the kettle on the *jiko* overly hard. Miriam told her that she had tried her hardest. Then to Miriam's surprise, her mother said that she knew. She knew Miriam was a hard-working child and that Miriam had tried her best. It was the teacher's problem, not hers, she said. They would find a different school.

Oliver's cough did not go away. He made sure to wear his red knit cap as well as his sweater to stay warm in the cool mornings, but the cough persisted. He was afraid it was because he was not praying enough. So he prayed in the morning and the evening too, like his mother, that he would get better. He accompanied his mother on all of her trips to the doctor now. Sometimes afterwards he would feel better, other times he would not.

One day when his mother and he were coming out of *Uchumi,* they saw Adrianna. She did not appear to see them, even though she was quite nearby getting into her car. Oliver called her name and waved to her. He knew she heard him because she looked up, but then she turned away, got into the car and drove off.

Oliver did not understand. He knew his mother was angry though because she did not speak for the entire walk home. When they did reach the apartment she called Pricilla, took the phone into her room, and closed the door.

One day, when he arrived at school, Oliver's teacher asked him to go to the headmaster's office. He was afraid because he knew children only went to the headmaster's office when they were in trouble. Although the one time he had been called to the headmaster's office it was because he had received an academic award, so perhaps he would get another—although he thought this unlikely because they only gave out awards at the end of the year and that was a long way away.

The headmaster was not even in his office. Oliver had to wait in the hallway outside. When he arrived, he greeted Oliver. He asked Oliver how he was, and how his mother was, and how his grandfather was. Oliver said they all were fine. The headmaster nodded, told Oliver to wait, then went into his office and closed the door.

Oliver waited. A long time passed. He did not seem to be in trouble, but it did not seem like he had done anything that merited praise either. Most of the morning had passed. Oliver wanted to ask if he could go back to class, but he was afraid to knock on the headmaster's door. Near noon, when Oliver was wondering if he would be allowed to go and eat lunch with the other children, Babu appeared in the doorway.

Oliver was happy to see him, but he was surprised as well. It was not one of Babu's days to pick him up, and he was hours early anyway. Babu greeted him. Oliver asked him if he had done something bad. Babu told him that he had not and he would fix everything so he could return to class.

His grandfather went into the headmaster's office. They spoke for a long time in lowered voices. Oliver could not hear much but he could tell that they were talking about his coughing.

When they were finished, Babu emerged from the office, and called Oliver to him. Oliver followed and was saddened to see that Babu was not leading him back to class, but rather, home. Oliver wanted to ask what had happened, but like his mother, when Babu was angry he was very quiet.

Ivy and her family lived in Kariobangi. Kariobangi was a nice place during the day. There were many children to play with, but Ivy did not like Kariobangi at night when there were noisy people, drunk from local brew, that would hurt you if you went outside.

But otherwise Kariobangi was a place to call home. Ivy and Maurice liked to go down to the stream and throw in plastic bags, to watch them flow along until they disappeared in the tunnel that went beneath the road where all the *matatu* stages were. When she had been younger Ivy thought that this hole led to hell and that if you went down it you never came back because the devil was waiting for you there. However, one day when she had gone on a trip with her mother they had walked to the other side of the road to catch a *matatu* and there Ivy saw where the stream came out and she realized it did not go to hell, at least not here, but just kept going along on the other side of the road. She looked to see if any of their plastic bags were still there waiting on the other side but none were. Her mind raced with the new horizons that this represented: if the bags were not still there and they were still floating they would be thousands of miles away by now. Ivy could not even imagine what the world would be like so far away. There might be places like Kariobangi but with completely different people, names, and *matatus*. Maybe far enough down the stream it turned into a river and that was where wildebeest would cross and get attacked by lions and crocodiles—she had seen that on a television once.

She and her brother had to be careful when they went down to the stream because sometimes there were *chakora*—scavengers— there. Scavengers, street boys, could be very dangerous. They would stand in the water sometimes looking for metal to sell to the metal collectors. Or sometimes they would be so high on glue they would just be confused and try to drink from the stream, but they might fall down and drown. One time one of Ivy's friends, Winnie, threw a stick at two street boys and they chased after her and beat her. Then her family came and beat the two street boys until one was dead and the other they put a tire around, filled the inside of the tire with petrol, then lit it on fire. He kept calling out for water until he fell down and died. Ivy saw both their bodies—their faces looked funny, all swollen so their eyes were tiny slits. Their skin was covered with mud and rocks. Sometimes she saw the burned boy, his skin red and black like burned chicken, in her dreams.

So when there were street boys around, Ivy kept Maurice away from them. She knew she could beat up regular boys that might decide to disturb them, but street boys were a different matter. They were crazy like animals and did not know pain, because of the glue they sniffed. That was likely why crowds had to burn them.

Ivy walked alongside Maurice when they went to school. However, lately she had been feeling tired and sick like her mother. Some days Ivy's friend Anne would have to accompany Maurice to school. Once Ivy's mother took her out of school for a whole term so she could rest. It had helped but when she had returned she got very bad marks because she had missed so much. Plus, she did not like the idea of Maurice being alone at school without her to look out for him.

When Maurice was sick he was taken to the doctor and often got better. Ivy would never get as well as he did. She wondered if it was because when you got older you were weaker—her parents certainly seemed weak. When Ivy asked if she could go to the doctor, her mother often told her the doctor was too expensive and she would just have to be strong.

Months passed and Miriam was not sent to a new school. She continued to help her mother in the market, but each day when she saw the children walking to school in their ironed uniforms and polished shoes, she felt jealous and ashamed.

But she did not bother her mother. Her mother was too busy with the new baby, Miriam's sister Purity, whom Miriam loved very much. Miriam thought that Purity deserved love and attention, just like she had had as a baby, so she did not want to interfere.

But one night when Purity's crying had awoken her, and Purity cried a lot, Miriam unfolded her school uniform and tried it on again. To her horror she realized it no longer fit. The sweater's neck was so tight Miriam could hardly move, the sleeves were comically short and the skirt was an inappropriate length that was just above Miriam's knees.

Miriam began to cry. She realized she would never go to school again. She tried to be quiet, but her mother heard her and came to see what was the matter. Her presence was announced by her coughing. Miriam looked up to see her in the doorway. Miriam should have known she would have been awake, with father sick so often and Purity as well, her mother hardly ever slept. The women in the market helped her and reminded Miriam that she needed to help her as well. They joked that her mother had two sick babies to take care of, Purity, and Miriam's father.

Miriam's father was not a baby, but she had never argued the point. He was sick. He was always coughing, but he and her mother had coughed as far back as Miriam could remember. It was just what adults did, Miriam thought. She knew their coughs like she knew their voices: her father's deep slow coughs with long pauses in between, and her mother's that were many at once. But lately her father's coughing fits were always followed by spitting. Miriam would find her father's spit in tissues, crumpled newspapers, and old bottles. Sometimes it was dark brown with blood. Some days he could not work as a result. This made Miriam's mother very quiet. This was not angry quiet, but worried quiet, for it never erupted in words. Miriam thought this silence was even worse.

Now Miriam was sure her mother would be angry. She asked Miriam if she was sleep walking and Miriam said no. Then why was she dressed for school? Miriam said she was afraid that with the new baby she would never have a chance to return and she had tried on the uniform to see if it still fit.

Her mother swooped down on her and picked her up in her arms. Miriam cried anew, almost from relief that her mother was not angry but was suddenly full of soft loving words. Since Purity had been born it had been a very long time since her mother had held Miriam. Miriam realized now that she had missed it. She also realized that her mother's body had changed. No longer was it soft and round, but it was hard and bony, not like she remembered it before the baby.

She put Miriam on the bench, lit the lantern, and found one of Miriam's exercise books. She pointed at words and asked Miriam to pronounce them. As she did so Miriam noticed that her finger nails were cracked and brown colored, but she said nothing as she was eager to try to read.

However, when she looked at the words on the page they seemed to tumble away under her own gaze. She could not fix them on the paper in front of her. Her mother's finger tracking alongside helped, but still, they would spend a few minutes saying a word, move on to another, then return to the previous one and Miriam would have no recollection whatsoever.

Her mother grew frustrated and tired, although she tried not to show it. Finally she held Miriam close to her and said it was best they both went back to bed. Things would be better in the morning.

Oliver's mother was not quiet when she learned that Oliver had been expelled from school. She stamped her feet, clicked her tongue, and shouted. Babu did everything he could to calm her. Eventually she stopped, but first she went into her room and closed the door.

She emerged sometime later, after Oliver and Babu had played two games of chess. He was glad because he was hungry. She made them dinner and offered to let her father sleep in her bed and she would sleep on their sofa. He said he would not, saying that she needed a good night's rest. So after dinner he left.

The next morning Oliver's mother woke him up early. She was already dressed for work. She was in one of her black suits that Oliver liked a great deal because it had gold buttons on the front and on the sleeves. Her hair was still in curlers but she said she wanted him finished with breakfast and ready for school by the time she took them out.

He was and then she walked with him to St. James. They arrived at school much earlier than Oliver was used to. There were no students there yet. The schoolyard and the classrooms were strangely empty and quiet except for a *cucu* who was bent over sweeping leaves from the playground. Some of the teachers were around drinking *chai* and eating *mandazis*. Oliver was very proud of his mother as she walked past them in her Nairobi suit. He was sure now they would allow him back.

Oliver's mother told him to wait outside the headmaster's office. Oliver sat down in the same chair he had waited in the day before. Then his mother was allowed in to see the headmaster.

Unlike Babu, she was not quiet. She was loud and forceful, as she sometimes had been when her friends became too rowdy at night. She spoke in a mixture of *Kizungu* and *Kikuyu*. Oliver heard her say that he was the smartest student in the school. She said that he deserved an education. She said Oliver would grow up to be a great man. The noise she made attracted the attention of other teachers, who walked slowly past the door to listen to what was being said. Many times Oliver felt like coughing but he stifled it as best he could since he understood now that was why he had been kicked out of the school.

As his mother's voice went on, he heard the headmaster less and less. Soon the headmaster was only speaking in short, low sentences. This seemed to make his mother even louder. Finally the door swung open. The headmaster walked out. He went by Oliver without greeting him.

His mother followed and told Oliver in a loud voice to follow her and that she was taking him to a better school.

Oliver did. They crossed the school yard. Oliver noticed that his own teachers did not greet him either. They stared at his mother who was walking very fast. Oliver struggled to keep up with her. She continued her pace until they were a good distance away from the school, then she sat down on a bench beside a kiosk where she began to cough.

She coughed harder than he had heard her cough in a very long time. It scared Oliver terribly. There were other children walking by now, wearing the same uniform as Oliver, on their way to school. They were staring at his mother. A few even stopped. Oliver turned his back to them so they would not recognize him. He was embarrassed and his face flushed hot with shame when he saw the bright scarlet blood when she moved her handkerchief away from her mouth. He moved in front of his mother so they would not see the blood spreading on her hands or the sleeves of her suit.

Now Oliver just wanted her to stop. He wanted them to leave so the other children could not see her. Was this his fault? If he had not been coughing they would not be here on the side of the road attracting attention. He did not know what to do except to put his hand on his mother's shoulder, tell her that he was sorry, and pray that she would stop coughing and they would start moving again.

One of the owners of the stalls came out and told Oliver's mother to go away. She stood up but had to lean against one of the kiosks first. There was now a wall of children they had to walk through. Oliver did not look up at any of them—he hoped none were his classmates.

When they got home, his mother did not go to work. She lay down and coughed the rest of the day.

Judith was delirious with fever for days. When the fever broke she woke to find herself in clean clothes and clean sheets. There was a pot of cold tea beside her bed.

Sofie was gone.

Judith called out for her, but Sofie did not appear. Judith tried to sit up, but each time she tried her limbs collapsed with weakness. Her head spun violently. But her daughter was still missing. After an eternity she sat up.

She noticed the belt she had wrapped around Sofie was sitting on the floor beside the bed. So were a pile of sheets that smelled of urine and feces. She called out for Sofie again.

No one came.

She lay back down. It was daytime. Perhaps if she rested she might build up enough strength to go to the door and look outside for Sofie before dark. Maybe she could ask the butcher if he had seen her.

She rested for what seemed an hour, but still could not get up. Sitting up once had drained her of all her energy. Then the door opened.

It was Sofie. She was carrying a plate of hot *ugali* and some *sukuma weki*. She lit up seeing that Judith was awake. Judith asked her where she had been.

"Getting food," she said

Judith asked her from where. Sofie said that she had found a woman down the track that would give her some food. Judith asked her how she had found the woman. Sofie said that when Judith had not woken up that she had walked from house to house saying that her mother was sick and that they needed food. She had found that some people would give food only once, others gave a bit every day.

She asked Sofie who had changed the sheets and her clothes. Sofie said she had. Judith asked where the tea had come from. Sofie had brought it from one of the neighbors.

Judith asked how many days this had gone on. Sofie counted on her fingers and said four.

It went on for a few more days. Sofie even found a bucket that her mother was able to use as a toilet, which Sofie would empty in the nearest pit latrine. The neighbors, however, were growing tired of giving food. Sofie had to go farther each day. One night she came back with some *githeri*, and announced to Judith that she had heard of people that would help them.

Judith asked who. Sofie said they were doctors. Judith asked where. Sofie said that they were on the other side of the road—the highway.

But Judith could not walk that far. She could not even walk to the toilet.

The next day when Judith woke, Sofie was gone. Sofie usually left to beg for food mid-morning. By the temperature and the light Judith could tell it was still early. Maybe she had gone out to find hot tea. Maybe she would be back in a few minutes.

But Sofie did not return. Judith waited. The sun rose, the air grew warmer. Soon it was tea time. She could hear the butcher and his friends conversing as they always did in the next room over—always oblivious to her. She could smell their fresh tea.

Tea time ended and still Sofie had not returned. The shack became hot. Usually around this time Sofie would be there to open the door or the window. Judith decided she would try herself. She pulled herself up from the bed. This time her head was not spinning. The food Sofie had brought had helped. She put her feet in front of her then stood up. Pain shot through her legs, but it was only one step to the window. She pushed it open. Light and air flooded in. She did not see Sofie. She was too weak to remain standing. The pain was too much.

She lay back down and began to weep. She had lost her husband, two of her children, and now her last child was taking care of her. She was a curse. She almost wished Sofie had run away, so at least she would not be burdened with herself. She suddenly wondered how she would pay rent. She knew the landlord had not been by to collect simply out of fear of catching AIDS. But she knew her time was short. He would not come himself, but he could pay a few older street boys to come and throw her and Sofie out. They might kill her. They would probably rape her and Sofie too.

Perhaps they already had taken Sofie. Perhaps that was why she was gone now. Panic welled up inside her. She called out for Sofie. Her voice was hoarse and shrill, it did not sound like she remembered it. She began to cough, but she fought it as much as she could, calling out Sofie's name, screaming to the point that she heard the butcher cursing her in the next shack.

"Where is my daughter!" she cried out. She knew he could hear her. He had ignored her all these months, but she would not let him now. But he did, only turning up his radio so it drowned her out.

She fell back on the bed, breathing hard, as if she had just run a sprint. Her heart was pounding. The room stank with the smell of her own breath. Her mouth was full of sores and opening it to scream caused her throbbing pain. She was still panting hard when the door opened. A tall figure stood there, blinding light shining all around. Judith squinted as her eyes adjusted. Perhaps it was the landlord. Perhaps he had finally come to throw her out.

It was a woman. She called Judith's name and continued into the room, sitting down beside the bed. Judith did not understand. She asked for Sofie.

Sofie answered. Judith looked over to see her daughter in the doorway. There were two more people behind her, a man and a woman. These were not neighbors she knew. Their clothes and faces were clean. They smelled fresh, of soap, disinfectant, even perfume. Their faces wore expressions of concern and sympathy.

"Judith," the voice beside her was saying in her mother tongue. "Judith, I am a nurse, we are here to help you."

Chapter 9

Aliases

I am not alone, of course, at the orphanage, accompanied as I am by a number of well-intentioned foreign volunteers. For one particular month when the children are out of school the need for volunteers is intense. So I am joined, among others, by a team of six Canadian college students, all women, who have already acclimated to living in Kenya after spending a semester traveling to the national parks in a massive Land Rover and taking courses on ecology, biology, international law, and economics at night, in their makeshift camps, from their guides, who when they are not traveling are professors back in Canada. Aside from being amazing with the children, they are great company to hang out with, play board games, and watch movies. One night we compete to see who can clip the most clothespins to their face. The winner, Ainsley, displays an amazing ability to endure a total of twelve pins pinched onto her cheeks, ears, nostrils, lips, and eyelids.

There is Helen with whom I teach preschool. Helen is from the UK. She is soft spoken, gentle, and consistent with the children—basically the opposite of me, so she is a good teacher. She is constantly finding ways to make art projects from bottles, egg cartons, toilet paper rolls, and cereal boxes. She also has a prescient way of always being right about what the kids will want to do next, leading me to coin the unofficial Rainbow Children's Home rule, meant with full sincerity, "Helen is always right."

Melissa is a volunteer from my church back home in Northern Virginia. She is a school teacher and makes me realize that even I need practice at long division. One night I get the losing end of a deal with Melissa. The children had just finished watching a movie in the schoolhouse and Rachel, a new girl still adjusting to the diet and medications of the orphanage, has a case of explosive diarrhea in the schoolhouse bathroom. Melissa asks me if I'd like to take Rachel to her cottage and clean her up or if I would be willing to clean the bathroom. Without seeing the bathroom I agree to clean it, feeling that it would be more appropriate for Melissa to strip Rachel down and stick her in the shower.

There is a scene in the Eddie Murphy movie, *Daddy Daycare,* wherein Eddie Murphy, having set up his own daycare must confront a similar situation in his own bathroom. As the audience, we never see the actual damage to the bathroom, instead the camera fixes on Murphy's face as he looks in, capturing his reaction to the carnage. His eyes examine the toilet, the walls, and even the scatologically-stained ceiling.

I can assure you such things are not just in the movies. While the ceiling was spared, the rest of the bathroom looked like a trichromatic Jackson Pollack painting. I cannot even enter, the best I can do is haul in the garden hose and spray down the entire room from outside.

For those readers expecting page after page of unmitigated tragedy, I can promise some relief, as it is impossible to have one hundred children living in one place without having ridiculous shenanigans.

Most amusing to me is the children's tendency to personify everything. A toilet is not backed up and gurgling, it is talking. My shirt is not faded and tattered, it's tired. When the soles begin detaching from my shoes, leaving them to flop beneath my toes, my shoes are not ruined, or old, they are just smiling. The creative language does not end there, neither does their directness. After considering my acne for a few moments and mistaking my pimples for mosquito bites, Josephine, a ten-year-old says to me, "Ted you would be much more handsomer if the mosquitos would stop kissing your face."

One Saturday we take the kids to see *Spiderman* in a theater where the management wanted to provide a treat. We have the theater to ourselves. I sit in back letting the kids sit as close or far from the screen as they want. During the scene when Toby McGuire bursts into the frame chasing after his school bus around eighty children turn around simultaneously and say, "Ted, it's you!" To clarify, no one in my entire life has ever mistaken me for Toby McGuire but just as whites are accused of acting as if all black people look the same, the reverse might also be said of Kenyans, or at least these children. No matter the differences I see between me and Toby, to the children, with my lean frame and glasses, I'm a dead ringer for Peter Parker—even though his face is blessedly free of acne.

For the following years that I know the children they often refer to me as Peter Parker. It is one of my nicknames in addition to Ted D. Bear and Ted *Ushumari* (the Kiswahili word for nail since my last name, Neill, sounds similar). I lose count of the children who want to examine my wrists to see where the web comes out and/or fold down my middle two fingers and back away, expecting webbing to issue forth.

Harry Potter is a close second to Peter Parker when it comes to my aliases. One of my favorite memories is taking some of the boys from Cottages Red to see *Chamber of Secrets* and watching them lean forward in their seats as Ron's family car comes roaring to Harry's bedroom window, levitating in the air. The boys were enraptured and amazed and I've never been more convinced of the magic of the big screen. After that, the children regularly check my forehead for a lightning bolt-shaped scar.

I am in a field hospital in Mesano, in the far west of the country, where HIV rates are the highest. I am accompanying the doctor—an American missionary—on rounds. I see things that will haunt my dreams the rest of my life. A woman with an infected C-section incision that is yellow and purulent, another woman with AIDS whose chicken pox has advanced to the state that massive sections of her flesh have turned to festering sores. She looks as if she has been flayed. Another man lies in a bed reduced to nothing but a skeleton, a figure of death, prone on an altar of white with a gaping mouth, pleading eyes, and a death rattle.

But by far the case that strikes me the most is the story of an eleven-year-old girl. She is sitting alone in the children's ward, nothing beside her except a plastic cup. She sits with her feet hanging off the side of the bed, her hands folded in her lap. Her shoulders are folded inward, her head down. The doctor explains to me that she is HIV positive and from Mombasa, on the country's east coast. Her parents are dead; her relatives, tired of taking care of her, and convinced her case was hopeless, bought her a one-way ticket to the far side of the country to be rid of her.

Now she sits waiting to die in a hospital ward where she knows no one. To even contemplate her plight gives me an ill feeling in my gut—and yet I'm all too aware that I am the observer here, a voyeur to suffering I could never imagine and have avoided by sheer, unfair, dumb luck and a level of privilege that is utterly unmerited and, on some level, built upon centuries of exploitation of millions of black and brown bodies like hers. If she were a middle-class eleven-year-old where I come from, likely she would be entering seventh grade. She'd be consumed with her friends, pop stars, and fluorescent head bands and charm bracelets. Maybe there would be a boy she had a crush on, maybe two. Maybe some would even have crushes on her, her emaciated face shows signs of high cheekbones and clear, light eyes, and long lashes.

But none of those things will be for her. Instead she is here, in an alien part of the country, with no one but strangers to keep her company while she dies.

Randolph is a quiet fourteen-year-old street boy who originally came to Rainbow Children's Home after police arrested him for stealing. He has deep soulful eyes and a tentative but bright smile. He is a lanky kid but it still seems sudden to me the day I look up from playing hopscotch with the kids and I see him outside Cottage Red, thin, skeletal. I freeze.

Randolph is dying, I think to myself. *But how?* He's been a healthy kid, responding well to antiretroviral treatment. However, I learn from his house uncle that he has tuberculosis that has spread to his stomach, making it difficult, if not impossible, to eat.

It's not long before he is moved to the sickroom.

Chapter 10

"It's not like the movies."

Mental illness is insidious. You can't see it necessarily like a rash or hear it like a cough. But it does become physical. You do *feel* it as it manifests in the body. I can't exaggerate the pain of it. For me, it was analogous to the pain you would feel if you knew a huge ogre were standing behind you about to slam a cinderblock, covered in razors, on your head. The physical blow never comes, but that instance of dread in anticipation of its painful impact lengthened from an instance to an eternity for me. The tensing of muscles, the pinched shoulders, the cringe and rush of adrenaline and cortisol that come with the bracing for imminent pain, was a 24/7 state for me. I could not concentrate. I could not sleep. The lack of sleep kept me from being able to be fully awake. But awake, I moved in a distracted and trembling daze. It became worse and worse. I had days that I didn't tell anyone about, where I would curl into a ball on the floor of my apartment in a fetal position, as if I were protecting myself from that very ogre. I would remain there until the panic would pass, or until I *had* to leave the house, for class or my job as a research assistant. I would force myself through hour by hour, presenting a mask of normalcy and calm but leaving me beyond exhaustion at the end of the day.

Then there was the morning it didn't pass and I couldn't manage to eat or even shower. I remember writhing that day, as if in pain from electrodes on my body, even if it was all in my head. I guess it can be hard to imagine unless you have actually experienced it. But I took the position of a prisoner in a torture cell, begging for it to stop.

Then I realized I could make it stop.

I stood up and picked up a steak knife from my counter. It was easier to slit my wrists than to continue on. The knife had a wooden handle and a serrated blade. It was one that I had taken from my parents' knife set when they had replaced it at home. The knife had followed me from apartment to apartment in the past years. I had picked it out of the dishwasher and placed it in the silverware drawer as part of my daily chores countless times growing up. How strange, that the innocuous things, things that accompanied us through childhood that were as familiar to us as a mother's face or a childhood bedroom, can come also to be the instrument of our undoing. I held the handle in a tight fist and turned the serrated teeth towards the underside of my forearm where I could see the blue of my veins through my skin.

I guess it is a measure of how much pain I was in, how sick I had become, that it was *easier* to slit my wrist than to continue being alive, to continue suffering. I had heard someone on the radio once say that being depressed was like having your hand slammed in the door, over and over, but without even the relief that might come when the door pulls back for another swing. It's that moment of impact, shock that is prolonged, interminably.

And it only seemed rational to end it.

I threw the knife across the room just before cutting myself and recoiled from it as it clattered in the corner. Sadly it was not a sense of connection to others, a sense that I would be missed, or even an awareness of any love others had for me or that I had for myself. I was beyond feeling any of those things, such is the sickness of mental illness. I think, in that moment, I was just scared, if nothing else, of the pain of rending open my own flesh.

I managed to put some clothes on and make it out to my car. I fought the urge to swing the steering wheel into oncoming traffic the whole way to the Georgia State University Counseling center. I remember begging to see a therapist. I remember curling up in a fetal position on one of the chairs in the waiting area. I was still wearing my shoes and the student volunteer working at the desk came out and asked me multiple times to put my feet on the floor. I kept trying, but even that was too hard. When the available therapist finally called me back into her office, I simply took my shoes off upon entering and curled up in the chair for her clients.

I told her about the knife. But I also told her about the thoughts that had flashed in my mind with growing frequency over the past year: of filling the bathtub, plugging in my space heater and dropping it in with me; of how I had taken measurements of whether or not the hose my landlady left in the side yard would reach from the tailpipe of my car to the driver-side window; about how I even had a place picked out, near Stone Mountain park where I would go to run the engine and simply drift off. The place I had picked was the corner of a church parking lot, just under the shade of some elm trees. I told her I had been there a number of times already, just thinking about how peaceful it might be to end things that way.

I was deemed a danger to myself. Georgia State University police and the therapist herself accompanied me to a mental hospital just outside the city. It took an entire afternoon to admit me while insurance forms were processed, doctors evaluated me, and phone calls were made. Finally, I was told I could enter Cottage Green, as they called the ward for adults. A part of me shrank from the very name, just another terrible reminder of the origin of some of the sadness, loss, and nihilism I was fleeing.

The ward was a beehive of quiet activity. The staff had an area to complete paperwork and read files. A wooden railing separated them from us, the patients. A common area with deep cushioned chairs was the heart of the ward. A dining area was off to the left, next to it were windows into the small office where medications were prepared and at certain times we patients would line up to receive our drugs. For my first half an hour I sat under observation with an African American teenager Calista—she had just turned eighteen so she had "graduated" from the adolescent ward. Her wrists were bandaged from a spell in which her body dysmorphia and self-loathing had overwhelmed her. A white guy in his twenties, Ian, also sat in the observation section with us. He had lived with ADD and anxiety disorders successfully for years, but his new psychiatrist had adjusted his medications and he had been unable to sleep for four days. He sat, his knees pulled to his chest while he wiped away uncontrollable tears. "Please," he pleaded with the ward aids, "tell the doctor I just want to sleep."

I was sharing a space, a label, and the stigma that came with mental illness. I met others who hoped to become stable enough to be allowed to stay in the halfway house, at least, and out of lockdown. We were from all backgrounds: Pablo, a former army officer in his fifties who in a state of despair and disassociation even deeper than my own, had gone through with sawing through the flesh of both his wrists, tendons, arteries, and musculature, leaving both forearms thickly bandaged and many of his fingers immobile. Cora was a white woman, an alcoholic, and had a Mensa-level IQ. She was depressed with the life of a housewife and had been arrested after picking up her daughters from school while intoxicated. She spent her first hours weeping in shame in the corner on the phone with her husband, apologizing for putting their daughters at such risk. There was also Henry, a black man in his seventies who after decades of alcoholism had checked himself into the hospital in an attempt to get sober. The combination of delirium tremens and the medications he had been placed on caused his hands to shake so much he could barely feed himself. Humiliated, he had to ask us to help him eat. At dinner I also met two doctors, one a cardiologist, the other an emergency room physician, who were struggling with alcoholism and addiction to drugs, respectively.

My first night I slept in my clothes, waking up multiple times as staff members would enter our rooms to shine a flashlight on us to make sure we were still alive. In the morning we lined up again to have our vitals checked. Rob, a kind staff member in a polo-shirt, took my blood pressure and recognizing that it was my first time waking up in a psychiatric ward, wearing the same clothes as the day before, tried comforting me.

"Don't worry, it's not like the movies."

Chapter 11

Fire

Ivy's mother survived so many beatings from her father, even the beating with the belt, she was sure that her mother could survive the illness that had infected her chest. Ivy told her brother Maurice that their mother was a strong woman, a fighter—which was where Ivy got her pugnacious spirit from—and that soon their mother would grow well and be back to normal.

But Ivy had been wrong. Their mother could not defeat her sickness. Ivy cried when they buried their mother in the ground next to father's other two wives. Many of their father's other children came for the funeral and one of them, Bahati, never left. She moved in and began to take care of Ivy, Maurice, and their father. People thought she was a new wife but Ivy's father had to explain that she was one of his daughters from his second wife.

Bahati thought that Ivy and Maurice should be in school so she took Ivy to the doctor and bought her medicine (she could because her husband had a good job). In a few days Ivy was feeling better and she started attending school again, but for a while her marks were not very good because she had missed so much. She was also very tired at the end of the day and often did not do her homework. The teachers would hit her knuckles with a pencil if she did not do her homework, but this did not bother her much—it did not hurt nearly as much as punching or being punched by someone. She would try to do her homework, but often she just wanted to go to sleep when she got home. At the end of the year they even told her she would have to repeat the grade. This did not surprise her but she was still very embarrassed.

When the next school year started, Ivy was already sick again. She was repeating it just like the year before, she realized, with the sickness and everything. She wondered if she would be fifty and still in standard four. The good news was that Maurice was the top of his class, so if she was not a good student and failed out of school, she was not too worried, since she was sure Maurice would grow to be smart and get a job to support both of them.

It was while she was in her second year of standard four that her father died. Maurice would not play or talk for several days after. Ivy did her best to distract him, to comfort him by reading to him, and buying him sweets, which he unwrapped and ate, without his usual smile. Ivy was also sad, but more so because Maurice was. She did not think she would miss the beatings from her father. She was more afraid that their father's ghost would come back and haunt them or that they would become poor. Many people came for the funeral, more people than for her mother's funeral. Because Bahati was around there was lots of food prepared this time. Bahati did not even go to the burial; instead she stayed home with her friends and finished cooking the food.

Ivy's father's other children remained the next few days for the reading of his will. When it was read, there was great fight with lots of yelling. People were very upset. Then they left very quickly and soon it was only Bahati, her husband Raphael, and her baby Emanuel left in the house.

Ivy knew better than to ask right away what the commotion was about. The next day, however, she learned.

Charity, another daughter from Ivy's father's second marriage, a full sister of Bahati, wanted Maurice. Her son had died the year before and she only had daughters. What she wanted more than anything was a new son. She had begged for Maurice, but the will was very clear.

Ivy and her brother were to stay together. They had not been left to anyone in the family, but rather to the parish priest.

Miriam's sister, Purity, died. At the burial, Miriam's father had to lean on her brother Peter, who worked for Kenya Bus and had returned from Nairobi.

Miriam knew something was not right with Purity one morning when she was feeding her and she noticed bumps on the baby's cheek. She had showed them to mother. Her mother had taken Purity to the doctor the next day, but he did not know what to do for the bumps. They soon spread all over the side of Purity's face.

Then she died.

Other things were not right and Miriam's brothers Peter and Joseph pointed them out. They tried to speak in *Kizungu* so that Miriam did not understand, but she had picked up some *Kizungu* and *Sheng* from the children at the market.

Her brothers were worried about their mother and father's coughing. Both slept fitfully now because of it. Miriam realized that neither Joseph nor Peter coughed in their sleep, making her worry that indeed something was wrong with her parents. One day Miriam had noticed that her mother's fingernails did not even look like fingernails anymore—they were broken and looked the way an old paint can looked after it began to rust and turn brittle.

There were long days, one after another, when her parents would only leave their bedroom to go to the toilet outside or to get some food. Miriam lost track of what days were which. She had to see what other people were wearing to figure it out: on weekdays the children wore their school uniforms. On Sundays people were dressed in their church clothes.

Her mother's friend Patrice would bring them food sometimes, but Miriam thought it was strange that she saw the market women so little. Miriam finally felt hopeful when Aunt Evelyn appeared. She lived in Nairobi near Peter and he had gotten her a ticket on Kenya Bus to come and help Miriam and her parents.

With Evelyn around there was someone to make food, do wash, and even to braid Miriam's hair. Evelyn was very good at telling stories and she would sit in the sun with Miriam sorting rice and entertaining her. Miriam would sometimes tell stories herself. Evelyn said they were very good stories and one time she asked why Miriam was not in school. Miriam said it was because she had not learned to read. Evelyn said she would speak to Miriam's mother about it. For the next few days Miriam waited for Evelyn to say something further on the topic, but she never did.

One afternoon Miriam wandered down to the old market— since Evelyn had arrived they had been going to a different market that Miriam called the "new market." It had been a long time since she had seen the old one, so she thought a visit was long overdue.

She was shocked at what she found: her mother's booth had been burnt. There were only bits and pieces of boards left. They all were blackened and broken. She saw Sofie, one of her mother's friends. Miriam ran up to her and asked her what had happened. Then she became confused, because the woman looked just like Sofie, but she seemed to be deaf. She would not respond to what Miriam said. Miriam walked in front of her. The woman, Miriam was sure she was Sofie, looked briefly at her, then away again. Miriam did not want to press her further. Then she felt something hit her back and scatter to the ground. There was a cloud of dust rising about her. Someone had thrown dirt at her. She turned around. She saw many of the faces she was used to seeing in the market, women whom had gathered around her mother and herself many times. Women she had fetched change for, but none would look at her now.

She went up to Beatrice and greeted her. Beatrice spoke loudly to one of her friends, drowning out Miriam's voice. Miriam was about to speak again when she felt even more dirt hit her from behind. It fell over her shoulders and spilled onto the bright red tomatoes on the stall before her.

She turned, thinking it was some child, but there was Sofie, right behind her, reaching down for another fist full of dirt.

"Get away. Get out of here!" she said and threw the dirt right in Miriam's eyes. She coughed. Suddenly all the women started to cry at her to leave and get out. Dirt hit her from all sides. Miriam was blinded. She ran with her head down, bumping into stalls. Now even men were yelling at her to watch where she was going. Harder things than dirt were being thrown at her. She heard a rock hit the wall of a shack as she ran by. Children were following her now, throwing water bottles, throwing bottle caps.

When she got home she was weeping. Evelyn took one look at her and asked her what happened. When Miriam started to explain, Evelyn covered her mouth, took her outside and said in a low angry voice that she should never go to that market again and that she should never ever speak of it in the house in front of her parents or anyone else.

Miriam nodded. Evelyn told her to clean herself up and to be quiet because her parents were resting.

A few nights later a noise woke Miriam. She tried to fall back asleep but she heard voices outside. Many voices. Wide awake voices. She looked through a gap in the wall and saw a flame pass before her eyes. At first she thought that someone was burning rubbish, but she knew rubbish was only burnt on the ground. These flames were moving higher than that. Some were now fixed upon the roof. Miriam smelled the acrid odor of burning plastic.

She sat up and screamed, "Fire!" Evelyn woke up with a start. Something was dragged across the ground just outside their house and slammed against their door. Miriam thought someone would come inside, but no one did. The door stayed shut, only it was pressed inward more than usual. Smoke was creeping in from the roof now. Evelyn ran about trying to find water. She pressed on the front door but it did not open. She cried for help and for mercy. Even though Miriam heard voices outside, no one answered. She did not understand what was going on. Were these the same people that had burnt her mother's stall?

The door to her parent's room swung open. Her father was standing there, leaning heavily against the wall. It had been so long since Miriam had seen him out of bed, she had forgotten how tall and imposing he could be. He crossed the room, like an old man, leaning on the table, coughing, and limping. He tried the door, but it did not budge. The room was filling with smoke now. Miriam was choking. Her mother was screaming now as well. Miriam called her father and said to him she did not want to die.

His eyes, were larger and deeper than she remembered. He almost looked like a skeleton to her. But then he turned to the door and leaned his body into it. Miriam thought of the strength he once had to carry things at the truck depot and somehow he summoned it now. The door moved and something very heavy fell away to the ground outside.

Evelyn came out with Miriam's mother leaning on her. Miriam ran to the cupboard, grabbed their family's Bible, then ran outside.

Her father was standing in the center of the road. There were men all around with torches. Evelyn yanked Miriam to her side by her night shirt. Miriam looked back at the melting plastic of the roof. Burning sticks were crackling. The corrugated metal was making loud popping noises.

Her father was wheezing but speaking in gentle tones like he always did. He asked the men politely to just let him and his wife die in peace. He swore to them he meant them no harm. Then he called their names, for they all were from the community. Even Miriam knew some of the men her father named and she hoped that because they knew Miriam and her family, they would leave them alone. These were the husbands of her mother's friends at the market, the fathers of Miriam's friends. Even one of her brother's friends was there. She saw him holding a torch and a petrol can, but she could not believe he would burn down their house with them inside. She guessed he had just been doing what his father had told him. Maybe his father was drunk, maybe they all were. People did things as tricks at night when they were drunk that they would never do during the day.

Her father spoke of Jesus and how Jesus treated lepers. Miriam was now glad that she had brought the Bible in case her father would want to read from it.

But he did not. He stopped speaking, except to say please, please leave them in peace, to have mercy on them as Jesus would want.

They listened to him. The torches and the men disappeared.

Once the torches were receding, a figure came running up with water that he doused the flames with. It was Patrice's husband. Patrice was there in her nightclothes, as were many other people who had been awoken by the commotion. But they slowly began to disperse. Miriam thought that Patrice would come over to them, but her husband led her away. As she turned she said, "Sorry."

Oliver and his mother moved back to Babu's house. Oliver understood that other people would now live in his mother's apartment and they would send her money to live there. It felt strange to Oliver to think about other people living in what he had come to think of as his home. He was happy to be living in Babu's house again even if his mother was so sick now that she could not get out of bed.

Oliver did not begin school right away. They decided he would wait until next term. Pricilla brought him a few exercise books that he would work on in the mornings. In the afternoons he would play outside in the fields and the yard.

One day Babu called to him and asked him to sit with his mother. Oliver went into her bedroom. He knew the person lying in the bed was his mother even though she looked more like a skeleton. He told himself that even if she looked like a skeleton, his mother was inside. It was like a story he read in one of his books where a man's brain was transplanted into another man's body. On the outside he looked different, but on the inside it was still the same person.

Oliver sat beside his mother's bed and held her hand—which was more like Babu's hand because he could see and feel the bones inside. His mother was breathing very hard. Her teeth stuck out of her mouth. He wondered if she knew he was there. He decided to tell her a story about a man named Ndegwa who had to climb a mountain to find his water gourd.

When Oliver was finished, Babu told him that his mother needed to rest. He was not sure how Babu knew since his mother did not seem able to speak. She only breathed very hard and loudly. But he obeyed, went to his room, and went to sleep.

In the morning when he woke, he heard strange voices in the house. When he came out of his room he saw two *cucus* go into his mother's room and close the door. His grandfather was sitting in his chair. He called Oliver over and held him on his lap. He told him that his mother had gone to be with Jesus and that they both would see her again someday when they met Jesus. Oliver knew this meant she was dead because when Pricilla's aunt had died his mother had said to Pricilla that her aunt was with Jesus, but when they were alone his mother had said to Oliver that Pricilla's aunt was dead.

Oliver sat with Babu a long time. Finally one of the *cucus* came out and asked for Babu. Babu went into Oliver's mother's room.

Oliver was left behind. He waited a while and when the door did not open, he walked outside into the yard and sat down underneath his bush.

When she was supposed to be sleeping, Ivy had overheard Raphael and Bahati talking. They were surprised and also insulted that Ivy's father had left the children to the priest. It was highly unusual. Why not leave them for the family?

Ivy was surprised herself. When she had asked Bahati what might happen if her father died, Bahati had said that they would simply go to other family members.

Ivy wanted to stay with Maurice, but she was afraid that they would be separated to different daughters of their father, so in a way she was glad they had been left to Father David.

Father David was a very nice man. He was also a priest, so he had a nice house that was up the hill from the church. It was made out of stone and had a metal door. It also had electric lights.

But Ivy was surprised to learn that the entire house was not his. He shared it with many people and only two rooms were his. This was his explanation as to why he could not take Ivy and Maurice.

Bahati and Raphael did not like this news. They could not keep Ivy and Maurice either—at least that was what they said. They also had to be leaving Kariobangi soon because a son from the first marriage had been left the house and he wanted to move in soon.

So Father David said Ivy and Maurice could stay with his mother. But that meant they would have to say goodbye to the home they had known all their lives. That night, Ivy told Maurice wonderful stories of how nice their new home would be, even though she had no real idea. She just wanted to keep him from crying so he could sleep. When he finally drifted off, she buried her face in her own pillow so her sobs would not wake him.

Chapter 12

Night Commuters

We shouldn't have favorites but we do. Miriam is of course one of mine. Anika is another, if for no other reason than she plays hard to get.

Anika is nine and scary smart, as smart as Miriam is emotionally perceptive. Working with orphans attracts a wide range of characters but common to all of us, I suspect, is a desire to be liked, even loved; the open arms of children desperate for connection and attention is a comfortable place for us in our codependence. Anika, however, sees through us, or at least the foreign volunteers. She spends her energy on her relationships with the Kenyan staff, as if she knows we are just passing through, as if she recognizes our neediness and she is too smart to set aside her own needs for ours.

But this does not mean Anika does not like any foreign volunteers. At one point I bring in a cadre of female Canadian college students who turn out to be my best volunteers ever. Anika takes a liking to them like no other. One of them, Amy, teaches the children a song, along with dance steps, that goes like this:

Pick pick pick pick banana
Peel peel peel peel banana
Eat eat eat eat banana
Go go go go bananas

It is accompanied by picking, peeling, and eating motions. When you "go bananas" you spin in a circle with your hands in the air. The children love it and I watch Anika responding to Amy with such genuine fondness that I'm actually slightly jealous. I try to

92

teach her a song as well, but she remains uncooperatively still, narrows her almond-shaped eyes, and simply comments, "Ted, you are stupid."

Like a scorned school boy, I just want her to like me more.

Hannah goes on a sightseeing trip to Uganda with three American men fresh out of college. They have come to Africa looking for a story to film. They have been to Sudan, but finding nothing but stomach bugs, empty desert, and footage of them, in a screaming panic, killing a large snake that had slithered into their campsite. They turned back to Kenya and then Uganda. Hannah says she can understand them easily because their accents are as horribly American as mine.

They pass through Northern Uganda. One evening as they are riding in the back of the truck they have rented, Hannah notices long lines of children walking along the road, all in the same direction. The lines go on for miles. Hannah asks the driver what is going on.

The driver explains that the children are the night commuters. For twenty years, the Lord's Resistance Army, the LRA, headed by a man named Joseph Kony, has been terrorizing Northern Uganda. Joseph Kony preaches that he is the new Messiah. He and his followers want to install a theocratic government in Uganda in order to save their countrymen from the forces of evil. In twenty years, twenty thousand children have disappeared in raids conducted by Kony's men. The children are used as child soldiers, sex slaves, and servants. Often they are made to beat their own friends and parents and relatives to death, then eat their flesh or drink their blood. Children that try to escape are often killed in the same manner. If they are allowed to live, their lips, noses, hands, breasts, or entire limbs are amputated as punishment and warning to other children that might try to escape.

Since most children are taken in night raids, as soon as the sun begins to dip down near the horizon, any child that is old enough to walk makes his or her way out of the villages and towards the towns where they can sleep in relative safety. They sleep in the streets or, if they are lucky, under the eaves of a building.

Hannah asks the driver to slow down. She climbs out of the truck bed and begins taking pictures. Some of the children stop, studying her warily. Some ask for food or money. Hannah is able to get one young girl, with an even younger girl on her back, to stop and pause for a close up. Children form a knot around her, tugging on her clothes and reaching out with open palms.

But the driver thinks he hears gunfire. He tells Hannah to get back inside and they drive down the road, leaving the children behind.

I find Judy sitting on the porch of her cottage looking miserable. She is seven, light skinned, freckled, and usually very articulate. I ask her what is the matter. She says,

"I am having bad thoughts about my mother."

"Do you want to talk about it?"

She glances at the other children around her and shakes her head no. I have crayons and paper in my hands that I was planning to use for an activity with some of the older children. Judy takes a piece of paper and a box of crayons. She writes,

I don hav my mum I don wat tub a lon

She draws a house, two figures, a red figure, her mother, and a blue one, herself.

Our house Judy is two years Mum issma ilen

The Mum laek to play with children and she laek to stay with them

I ask her, who plays with her now.

One Le children
What is the difference between mothers and children?
One Le mum kan kip me in her arms
I love her so much
I am so sad
She puts down the crayon as if she has suddenly realized something. She turns to me.

"I will die soon."

"Judy, don't say that."

"I will. Do you know why?"

"Why?"

"Because if you think of your mother too much, she will come and get you."

The children I am closest to are six girls in Cottage Yellow: Miriam, Josephine, Ivy, Tabitha, Jamina, and Winnie. I call them collectively, the Gremlins. I read to them every night. The orphanage has a wide selection of donated books and the most popular by far, the one that produces the most squeals, hoots, and peals of laughter is a comic book series about a portly, balding middle-aged high school teacher who has Superman-like powers but a costume that consists of nothing but a pair of underwear—briefs to be specific. His name is Captain Underpants. And years later the Gremlins tell me their favorite book was always Captain Underpants.

I also teach the Gremlins how to play mafia, a card game where the card you are handed gives you a role. Numbered cards are townspeople; a jack is an informant; a queen is a medic; and a king is the killer. With the help of a facilitator (me), the killer in the bunch has to kill the other players while they try to figure out who it is before they are all dead. It's a game of lying, cheating, and deception, and at times earnest protestations of innocence. Needless to say, the Gremlins love it and ask to play it every night. The irony of course is that they know each other so well and are such unsophisticated liars, that the killer is often correctly identified and caught in the first two rounds—short by the standards of the game but it does not diminish the kids' enjoyment.

Hannah is leaving. The trip to Uganda, the night commuters, the LRA, the over-the-top American boys trying to make a film, not to mention the endless tragedy of the children at Malaika, it's all too much. She's seen enough. She wants out of this "God-forsaken place." She has university to attend. A life to live. The sense that I will be all alone in a country without anyone to understand me begins to overwhelm me, yet I tell her I don't think I can keep what we have going over long distance. Selfishly I touch her and hope that at least she will make love to me once more before she leaves, but she is uninterested.

I decide not to go to the airport with her. I don't think it would matter much to her anyhow. She gets into a car with Mama Seraphina. It is late April. The long rains have come. It is pouring like it only does in the tropics. Nairobi is a mile above sea level, so the rain is also cold. I kiss my hand and blow it towards Hannah.

But I'm not sure she can even see me through the fogged window. The car pulls away and disappears down the road. Later when I lose my temper with the children over something exceedingly minor and I send them crying back to their cottages, I turn to find Miriam glaring at me, her arms akimbo. She takes a few steps towards me and shakes her finger.

"When you speak to young children, you must keep the angry words inside your mouth, Ted."

☼

It was Sofie that had crossed the highway to the clinic to find someone to help her mother, Christabell, the social worker, told me. When they realized Sofie had crossed the road herself, dodging between the traffic, they were horrified. When she led them to her house where they found that she had been taking care of Judith, they were astounded. Sofie was not yet six.

"She is a genius," Christabell said.

I ask what happened after the nurses came to Judith and Sofie's house. She tells me that with some networking, they found some distant relatives of Judith that were willing to take her in and give her hospice care. Sofie was admitted to the orphanage on a temporary basis. The tentative deal was that the family would take care of Judith until she died and then they would take in Sofie.

I ask Christabell if she had heard from the family. She tells me no. Does she know how Judith is?

"Probably dead."

"Then why have they not come to get Sofie?"

"They probably do not want her. They took care of Judith as she died, they probably don't want to do it again for a child. And after all, Sofie is comfortable at the orphanage."

I write a story for the home's newsletter about Sofie and Judith. After which I write a short-form story and send it to the *Washington Post*. I tell them I don't even want any money for it. Three months later they run it.

I guess I'm a writer now.

Chapter 13

Cottage Green

There was a nurse in Cottage Green, psych ward, who dispensed medications, named Hunter. He was in his twenties and in the same public health program that I graduated from in 2005. We had taken the same classes and experienced the same professors. We talked about some of their quirks and idiosyncrasies. He had done work in Haiti as I had done in Kenya. On a few occasions he came out from behind the window to sit with me. He was a kind person, but I knew he was also trying to figure out what went wrong with me. Our profiles were similar: sensitive and empathetic guys in glasses with penchants for helping people and a love of travel. He wanted to support me, but I also sensed a thread of fear in him, as if he might come to the same fate as me.

In group therapy sessions I learned more about the people in the ward with me. There was Grant, a singer in a metal band by night, post office worker by day, who since he was a little child had impulses and fantasies, of slashing open people's necks. It was his obsession and he hated himself for it, so he tortured himself with negative self-talk and suicidal ideation, even though I saw him using a cup to catch a spider so he could toss it safely out the window. His therapist tried hard to convince him he was a good person.

"You may think about killing people, but have you ever hurt anyone?"

"Never. I've nearly fallen in a pool trying to rescue a drowning butterfly."

"Then stop torturing yourself, you are a good person."

My roommate was a six-foot-five, three-hundred-pound manic depressive. He was courteous to me and my first night there, my only complaint about him was that he snored. But by the second night he had a manic episode, attacked a staffer, and ended up screaming, strapped to a board for the next twelve hours. The seclusion room was across the hall from my own and even with the door closed I could hear him. So again, I couldn't sleep.

I made my way to the common area with my blanket and my pillow and tried sleeping in one of the cushioned chairs. Not long after I settled in, a man was admitted who would not relinquish his cell phone. Three staffers had to wrestle him to the ground. Afterward I was too agitated to sleep.

It was about this time that Pat, an old drunk who with his beard and short stature resembled Gimli the Dwarf, came into the common area leaning on his cane, his hair still wet from the shower, and sat down next to me.

"Boy if it isn't dark out. What time is it?"

"Two thirty."

He laughed, a nice hearty, unselfconscious laugh, a welcome noise to me. It turned out that when the staff came in to check if he was still alive—as they did with all of us every hour—he thought it was his wake-up call. I asked him why he didn't go back to bed.

"Won't be able to sleep now," he said.

I told him about my ordeal the past few hours and he took sympathy on me. "How about you get some rest and I'll sit up and keep watch. There are some old National Geographics in here that I might read."

When I woke in the morning, he was still there next to me, a pile of Nat Geos on the table next to him.

Another patient, trying to quit a drug habit, after overhearing me talk about my time in Kenya, confides to me that he contracted HIV when he was a teenager after a brutal rape by a gang of men. The resulting trauma was one of his triggers for his drug use.

"Why are you telling me this?" I ask.

"I don't know. You don't seem crazy. You don't seem like you would judge someone for being HIV positive."

Chapter 14

Forgetting

Father David's mother, Susan, was a giant fat lady. She had taken a few other children that were not her own into her house. Ivy shared a bed with a girl named Rebecca and Maurice shared a crib with a boy named Edison. An older girl named Ruth lived with them too. She had once been a street girl and could be very mean. Ivy was afraid of her.

But Susan lived in Kariobangi as well, so for a while things were the same as always. Maurice went to school. Ivy went when she was not sick and when she was sick, Ruth and Rebecca would take him to school—times like these Ivy was happy Ruth was once a street girl because then no one would try to disturb Maurice.

Susan finally took Ivy to the doctor. This was a different doctor than the one Ivy was used to. This one was in a large hospital that was very far away. One of the nurses there took Ivy's blood. Then she came back with a piece of paper that she showed to Susan and they went into an office and talked for a long time without Ivy. When they came out the nurse was very nice to Ivy and told her that she would see her again.

Ivy did see her again when they came back with Maurice. He cried when they took his blood. Ivy had not cried when they took hers, but she wanted to when she saw her brother so upset. Once they were done she held him on her lap, which she always liked. Having her brother so close to her made her feel whole, calm, and peaceful as if she was doing what she was meant to do as a big sister. They told Ivy they would need to take her blood again.

That night Father David came over to speak to his mother. When she was supposed to be sleeping, Ivy tried to listen to their conversation. She heard the word *ukimwi* many times. She knew it was a very bad sickness. She also knew they were talking about her and her brother. David kept saying, "Their father's wish was to keep them together. They should be treated the same."

Ivy was not sure what this meant.

Miriam knew this noise. She had heard it before, this whimpering, coughing, crying. But it was lower now than ever. They all kept their voices low since that night of the burning, as if to try to make themselves as inconspicuous as possible to their neighbors.

At first when she heard the sound she was scared. She thought it was Purity crying and that the baby had come back from the dead to bite her. But that was not the case. Evelyn was not on her sleeping mat. The lantern was burning in her parent's room. Miriam entered.

Her mother was weeping with a low moaning sound, interrupted by her coughs and sputters. Evelyn had her arms around her shoulders. Her father was still. Miriam knew this stillness from when Purity had died. She also knew it was a great change from the quick shallow breaths her father had been struggling to make the past few days.

She went in and stood beside her mother, who held her hand.

Her brothers came home for the burial. Joseph left after that to return to school. Evelyn insisted he go, saying it was what their mother would want, if she had been strong enough to say so. Peter stayed. One morning Peter took Miriam for a walk and when they returned, Evelyn said her mother had died. Miriam asked to see her but she had already been taken away.

Miriam wondered if perhaps her mother was alive. She even wondered if she was dead and she might come back to life in three days. But in three days they had the burial, and when Miriam saw the coffin loaded into the back of the pickup truck, she knew her mother was not coming back. And it was her mother inside, Miriam had checked the little window on the top. It was her mother's face on the body below. Her eyes were closed, but her mouth was stretched open over her teeth that seemed to protrude from her face. She looked like she was crying.

Evelyn shut the cover over the window and pulled Miriam over to her side. A woman came up and said to Miriam, "Don't feel sad. Just pretend you never had a mother. Many children don't. It is better to forget."

Even though Babu was dressed in his best suit, the headmaster would not allow Oliver back into Busura Academy. He said that there were not enough spaces. He also said that he felt that Oliver would find the classes too slow now that he had been to St. James for two and a half years. Oliver did not understand either of these reasons since four children could share a desk. Oliver even said that he would not find the classes too slow because he had been out of school for a while now and he was sure he had fallen behind.

But nothing swayed the headmaster. Oliver wondered if it was his coughing that was the real problem.

He went with Babu to a few other schools in the area near Babu's house, but none of them would take Oliver. He and his grandfather began taking longer trips to children's homes. Oliver knew that these homes were for orphans, which were children that had no parents. Babu said they were visiting the homes because some homes had schools and one might accept Oliver. But still none did. Oliver would try very hard not to cough when they were meeting with the managers or headmasters of these homes, but inevitably he could not help it.

Traveling with his grandfather was not terribly different than traveling with his mother when she had grown ill—his grandfather walked very slowly and had to stop to take long rests. Oliver did not mind this because often he was tired and had difficulty breathing himself after walking a long distance.

Finally one day Babu took Oliver all the way into Nairobi. When they first arrived, Oliver was afraid that his grandfather would not be able to find his way, but Babu reminded him that he once worked downtown in Nyanyo House.

Babu led them, slowly, to a bus stop where they joined the queue. While they waited, Oliver saw a young boy leading an old blind man with a stick and a cup. The man came along the queue and people dropped shillings into his cup. Babu gave him a few as well. His grandfather had leaned heavily on Oliver a few times that day already and Oliver wondered if a day would come when he would have to lead Babu like a blind man.

When the big blue bus pulled up Oliver recognized it as a Kenya Shuttle, just like the one he and his mother had taken the time they went horseback riding. He and Babu boarded. Oliver sat beside the window and soon realized that they were going along the same road they had taken when they went to ride horses. Oliver asked Babu if that was where they were going but Babu said no.

When they alighted Oliver recognized the same petrol station and the same market. He looked in the direction of the stables but could not see them through the traffic and the trees.

Babu asked a few people for directions then they walked for a while until they reached another *matatu* stage. They boarded a tired-looking *matatu* with plastic bags covering where the windows should have been, then waited a long time for all the seats to fill up.

They did not ride the *matatu* long before Babu tapped the tout and the tout slapped the roof, telling the driver to stop. Oliver and Babu had to climb over many people since they had been some of the first to board.

When they got out Oliver realized they were at another children's home. This one had a long driveway with trees and grass along it. It was very quiet—he could not hear any children. They walked all the way down the drive until they reached a few buildings. Inside the first one was a receptionist that asked them to wait. They did. There were many people around. There were nurses. There were some *wahindi* and a *mzungu* lady that walked by and smiled at Oliver.

Eventually the receptionist said to Babu that the chief manager was ready to see him. Babu asked Oliver to wait then followed the receptionist.

While Oliver waited he finally heard the voices of other children. One little girl came in crying because she had cut her knee. The nurse, who seemed very nice and had a sing-song voice, put a plaster on it for her.

The receptionist was very nice as well. She gave Oliver some biscuits and tea and told him she liked his red cap. He mentioned that his mother had given it to him. The receptionist did not ask him where his mother was. Before Oliver had finished the biscuits, Babu returned with the chief manager, a man named Bonaventure. Babu said that Bonaventure and the very kind people at this home had agreed to let Oliver go to their school, but he would have to sleep over here. Oliver did not want to stay here. He did not want to leave Babu but he knew Babu wanted him to go to school, so he said he would stay.

Then Babu did something Oliver had never seen him do before, not even when his mother had died—Babu wept. Not a lot, but just enough that he had to wipe his eyes. He took both of Bonaventure's hands in his as if they were close friends. He thanked Bonaventure and said that God would bless him. Then Babu bent down beside Oliver and said,

"I will come to visit you. Show them what a good boy you are."

Oliver said he would.

Chapter 15

Adoption

William is a six-year-old boy with a pointed face and ears that are too big for him. I call him rat boy. He asks me what it means. When I explain it to him he kicks me in the shins. But he runs off flexing his arms and screaming, "I am Rat Boy!"

A few months later he goes to bed with a headache and never wakes up.

At an outing to a museum with the kids I take a picture of Anika. She is wearing a multicolored knit cap layered like the bands of a rainbow and is smiling while she looks off to the side with her almond-shaped eyes. The picture is nothing short of perfect. But the camera has limited memory and I have to delete the photo to make room for others.

It's all right, I tell myself. There will be other opportunities to take pictures of Anika.

In the morning staff meeting the next day, Ruth, the nurse on duty with the sing-song voice gives the names of children who are sick and not going to school. There is always a headache, stomachache, or a case of conjunctivitis. This morning she announces that Anika is ill. I go to her cottage (purple) and find her stretched out in bed, the blankets pulled up to her chin while her house mother brews some tea. I offer to keep Anika company, read to her, drink tea with her, whatever.

"No," Anika says, an impish grin on her face. "You are stupid."

Randolph, the teenage boy whom I noticed weeks before who had become so emaciated, continues to wither, his flesh melting away. He refuses to eat. Kenyan staff members take turns in endless progression, holding a bowl of porridge or fruit to his face, telling him to eat. He doesn't. He withdraws further from everyone, except one volunteer nurse. Her name is Monica. She is visiting from Germany. She does not tell him what to do, she simply keeps him company and asks him what he wants.

He wants to die.

I'm not close to Randolph, so I don't crowd him in the sickroom. I feel bad for him, with endless visitors cajoling him to eat when he has clearly made a decision. I do note the light on in the sickroom each night indicating that someone is on the nightshift with him.

It is perhaps overly romantic but I picture Randolph in the warm light of that sickroom on a journey towards death, his body existing there as well as on some subterranean path towards a river you only can cross once, turning more and more skeletal as he nears some border between whatever life is and whatever is after. No one has accepted his choice to go willingly except Monica and so it is she whom he chooses to accompany him to the end.

I am placed in charge of all the foreign volunteers at the home. Doctors, nurses, social workers, recent college grads, anyone that has decided to come and stay at the home, driven by some desire to help sick kids, must answer to me. It is a relief to the Kenyan staff that uniformly profess frustration in dealing with the *wazungu* and their strange ways. Bonaventure, our chief manager and my boss, is a thoughtful and intelligent man. We call him "Bonava" for short. I ask him if he finds me as strange as the other *wazungu*.

"Yes and no," he tells me. "Yes, you must be strange because you want to live in Kenya and not in America which is your home. And no, it is easier to understand you and communicate with you because you understand us Kenyans."

Some of the volunteers are helpful, others more of a hassle. One thing they all have in common is that they leave. There is no one that has pledged to stay on for two years like myself. As a result, I have no permanent companions. Any friends I do make end up leaving me behind.

With so many foreigners coming and going I am increasingly in downtown Karen emailing prospective volunteers. I try to screen the bad ones out. I try to inform the good ones which shots they need.

I am the internet café's most regular patron. After a while the two young women who work there know me by name and I them.

There is Jossy. After finishing high school she came to work at the internet café because she had some computer skills and she thought it would be decent money—especially since it was located in Karen where there were many *wazungu* that were willing to pay the café's exorbitant price of five shillings a minute (in downtown Nairobi it is only one shilling a minute).

The other employee is Eve. She is strikingly beautiful, enough that a number of volunteers remark upon it to me. Having attended a strict boarding school in rural Kenya where there was often no electricity, Eve did not have any computer skills when she applied for the job, but she learned them quickly. Industry is in her character—days she spends at the café, evenings she spends in night school taking classes towards her BA in business management.

One day while surfing in an international chatroom at the café, Eve mentioned that she lives in Kenya. One of the chat participants remarked, "That is in Africa, right? Where everyone has AIDS." Eve clicked her tongue and closed the window.

Shortly after that incident she sees me at the shop nearby trying to buy phone credit. I'm wearing a floppy hat to block the sun, a shirt that does not fit me, and patched cargo pants. I think I look like I'm set for whatever adventure Africa is about to throw me. Eve thinks I look ridiculous. I'm speaking in broken Kiswahili, even though the girl at the counter speaks fluent English. But I am trying to practice. Both she and Eve are dressed in jeans and blouses that fit them better than my shirt fits me. Eve interrupts, completes the transaction in English, then leads me outside into the hallway.

"I think it is time we adopted you, Ted."

Being that all my volunteer friends eventually return home, leaving me lonely for the company of peers my own age, I'm not against Eve's offer to adopt me. I ride the *matatu* to Ngong with her, walk down a few narrow dirt lanes, and arrive at a gate that leads to her house. Inside waits a beautiful white and blue house with terra-cotta tiles, balconies surrounded by a lush garden and fuchsia bougainvillea waving in the breeze. Her house is about the size of the home I grew up in but it feels more solid. Lumber and sheetrock walls are replaced by smooth brick walls that are cold to the touch.

Inside I meet her younger sisters, Chiru and Chloe, both students at college and living at home, as well as her older sister Meredith who works downtown at one of the many mobile phone shops popping up all over Nairobi. The sisters are beautiful, affable, and cosmopolitan. They read *Vogue*, *Newsweek*, and *O* magazine and listen to Coldplay, Jay-Z, and Rihanna. They are dressed no differently from any college students or young working women I might meet in the States—if anything they are a bit more formal. Eve introduces me, slipping a few times into *Kiswahili* wherein she replays some of the ugly stereotypes that she feels whites have of poor, sick, warring Africans. Chloe snorts while Chiru laughs. In the kitchen is a dried coconut husk sliced in half. Chiru puts a half on either breast and says smiling, "Ted, is this what your friends think we are dressed like here in Kenya?"

"Well, minus the jeans and replace them with a grass skirt and you might be getting close," I admit.

Eve's mother, a police officer, arrives home after dark. She is doting and welcoming, insisting that the girls make a good dinner for me. Her father, a *matatu* company operator, arrives home and is similarly gracious, even if he is not as confident with his English. We have a dinner of *chipatis,* vegetables, and potatoes and we watch episodes of *The Young and the Restless* and *Smallville* on television. The living room is not so different than living rooms I've been in back in the States, with throw rugs, fluffy couches, and easy chairs. Pictures on the walls depict high school graduations, family portraits, and outings to parks and tennis courts. The women tsk and huff at some of the characters in *The Young and the Restless* and Eve and Chloe sing along to Coldplay's "In My Place," which plays during the credits of *Smallville.*

Eve and her sisters are all so striking, beautiful, and sophisticated, I feel a bit self-conscious hanging out with them in the raggedy clothes I usually wear around the orphanage—something that is not lost on Chiru. One evening after dinner and TV at their house, Chiru pinches the edge of my second-hand shirt while examining my floppy hat, patched cargo pants, and dusty hiking boots. She turns to her sister. "Eve, can I take him shopping?"

In one trip with Chiru I am transformed. A few visits to vendors downtown and booths at Toi Market near Kibera, with the aid of her furious negotiating tactics, and I'm outfitted with an entirely new wardrobe. My shirts fit and are professional looking, my cargo pants are replaced by respectable trousers and slacks. Chiru even finds just the right shoes for me, they are durable and thick soled, but look somewhat dressy. The clothes are not so nice that I'll be afraid to walk on a dusty lane or jump on a greasy *matatu*—required if you are a resident of Nairobi—but they are nice enough that I feel some pride in my appearance and I notice people, especially Kenyans, treat me differently. I look less like I'm about to go camping and more like, well, a Kenyan.

"You see the people coming out of Kibera," Chiru says to me, Kibera being one of the largest slums in Africa. "How do they look?"

I reflect upon it. "Actually pretty neat, clean, and polished."

"That is right, because most of the working population of Nairobi lives in a slum. It's like the apartment complexes that you'd find on the edges of a big city in the States, just not quite as . . . permanent."

Considering that most of the houses are made of sticks, mud, and corrugated metal, she's right about the permanent part, but she is also right about the industry, ambition, and professionalism of the people who live there. Not just a place of misery, disease, and despair, Kibera is a place of hope for people coming from the countryside to find work and improve their lives. It's not as if the privation, injustices, and humiliations of poverty do not happen in the slum—they do. But both realities exist side by side in a more nuanced community than many outsiders realize.

And in the end, it's a good place to buy a shirt too, especially with Chiru negotiating on my behalf.

Judy—who had drawn with me on the porch of her cottage who was afraid if she missed her dead mother, she would come for her—looks as if she has gained weight. This has caused some people to remark that she looks more healthy.

It is otherwise. She is in heart failure. Her lungs have not been able to clear her infections. Clogged as they are, her heart cannot produce sufficient pressure to force her blood through them to be re-oxygenated. As a result, when her heart beats, blood flows backwards. She has a pulse in her veins. In her capillaries, where arteries break into thousands of tiny branches and then turn into veins, fluids are backing up.

A Belgian film crew has come to the orphanage. They are doing a documentary on children orphaned by AIDS. The producer tells me that she would really like to speak to the children about their parents.

"A lot of them don't remember their parents," I say.

"What about the ones that do?" she asks.

"Why do you want to talk to them about that? It's traumatic."

"Well, if we could get a child to cry on camera, it would be really powerful."

I feel sick, but the powers above me have given these people permission to interview the kids. I look around at the kids on the playground and call over Sofie Waceera. I ask her to tell them her story.

She does. When she finishes, the camera crew is weeping. Sofie is bright and chipper. She is resolute. She adds in English, which she has picked up quickly:

"Me, I try to be a good girl. Me, I take my medicine like the nurses tell me and do my chores and read in school. I hope that if I am being a good girl I will see my mother again."

I tell her she has done a very nice job telling her story and that she can go play. The producer says she probably has enough footage. I'm relieved. She asks me how Sofie's mother is.

I tell her that Judith Waceera is dead.

Chapter 16

Psychic Injury

Kenya was a place to stop believing in God. I had gone there somewhat religious, but after seeing so many children die, so many children pray for relief only to suffer, I had let go of the notion of an all-knowing, all-powerful, benevolent God. It was too much like Santa Claus to me.

My therapist suspected I had a certain level of "psychic injury" that had put me at higher risk of depression, anxiety, and suicide. I asked him what that meant. He explained that psychic injury was a loss of hope, security, and trust in self or others, often as the result of close experience with injustice or wrong doing. It was often associated with, even mistaken for, post-traumatic stress. After witnessing traumatic events it was not unusual for a patient to abandon his or her religious beliefs. I told him how I had stopped believing in God because of my time at the orphanage and a litany of children whom I had sat next to while they wasted away in a crib or bed. I had seen too many small graves, the red oxidized soil shaped into a short pile, as short as a child's coffin. I had heard too many children pray to a God, any God, to stop the pain, that pain only stopping after an excruciating process of dying.

And weren't psychic injury and post-traumatic stress for rape survivors and war veterans? I could understand if some of the kids I had worked with had experienced trauma themselves, but I had never thought of it affecting me. I didn't think what I had gone through could be characterized as such. I had a hard time accepting any of it until my boss from my work study position at Georgia State came to visit me at the hospital. He was a professor of ethics in the business school and widely admired as an expert in his field as well as a charismatic teacher.

He told me that he had worked with a number of students who were veterans and had their own version of psychic injury. He also participated in a group called Veteran's Heart, wherein civilians work with veterans to try to help them readjust to civilian life. Psychic injury, even post-traumatic stress, were problems of personal narrative, he said. Oftentimes either condition can result from having to kill others or watch others die. A person can't reconcile their self-image of being a "good" person with that of having killed or let someone else be killed. I see his point. I have struggled with the fact that I left the children behind, that after my two years, I returned to the States. Just another two-year wonder on a jaunt of voluntourism. Meanwhile after I returned to my life of privilege after "slumming" it, so many still suffered.

"You can still be a good person though," he tells me. "Even if you did not save the children from dying. Even if you are not saving them from dying this very instant."

It sounds like a bit of a contradiction. I feel guilty. I just feel unable to accept their suffering especially from my place of comfort.

"I can't find a way to reconcile it all," I said.

"You never will."

Chapter 17

Family

Harmony and her mother had just been arrested. She and her mother had been hawking sweets and cigarettes, which they got from a church for selling on the street. Actually only Harmony's mother had been hawking; Harmony had Loraine's baby Michael on her back and was begging for shillings. There were lots of *wazungu* around Moi Avenue, especially around the queue for the Kenya bus. They felt more sorry for children than most *wafrika* and they had more money. They felt even more sorry for children with other children on their backs. But they were the most sorry if you were crippled or blind. Harmony had pretended she was blind once but nobody believed her. Her mother said next time she would have to wear a blindfold over her eyes if she wanted to be convincing. Instead Harmony had tried singing. This actually worked well, as people would stop, stare, and listen, telling her that she had a beautiful voice. Her mother had always told her this, but she was surprised when other people said so. So she made a point of singing often and earned more than most children did begging for change.

There were now new laws forbidding hawking on Moi Avenue, so the police had come and confiscated her mother's candies and cigarettes. Then they put her in the back of a dump truck with other hawkers they had picked up. With all the hawkers gone, Harmony had never seen the pavement along Moi Avenue look so clear.

Harmony had been lucky. She would not have even noticed her mother had been picked up if she had not been following a *mzungu* that had gone into Kenya Cinema. When she saw her mother being led away she ran up to her. Loraine was there too. She had

avoided being arrested since she had been around the corner
hawking on Uhuru Way. Harmony stood next to her watching as the
police led her mother and other women caught in the round up into
the back of a truck they were using to transport them to the police
station.

Harmony's mother yelled at her from the truck, where the
other hawkers were all sitting quietly as if they were asleep. She told
Harmony to stay with Loraine until she came back. Then she asked a
policewoman—one wearing army clothes—when they would be
released. She replied that since this was a Friday and that there was
no one to process them on weekends, they would not be released
until Monday. Suddenly all the quiet hawkers became very angry.
Harmony knew that other children had lost their mothers when they
had not seen them in over a day. Harmony knew that she and her
mother had remained together a long time because Harmony did not
let her mother out of her sight for long, so she took Michael off her
back and returned him to Loraine, then she climbed into the back of
the truck.

Her mother clicked her tongue.

"They are taking us to the jail," she said. "We will be there
until Monday."

"Then I will go with you," Harmony said. She would rather
be in jail with her mother than lose her forever. Her mother said she
was foolish, but she said it in such a way that Harmony knew she
was happy that they would be together. Harmony knew she would
never have let her mother go without her. They had made it this far
by sticking together.

The house seemed empty. Miriam and Evelyn still slept in
the front room. Neither of them went into what had been her parent's
room, even to change.

Miriam felt sick a lot of the time now herself. She stayed on her sleeping mat most of the day. Evelyn took her to the doctor who had one of his nurses stick Miriam with a needle and fill a tube with her blood. A few days later, Evelyn left Miriam alone in the house while she went back to get the results of Miriam's test. When she returned, Miriam asked if she had passed the test. Evelyn said she had done fine.

Miriam watched the children walk by her house on their way to school each day. She could not imagine walking so far now, as tired and weak as she was. One morning as she woke up she touched her face. There were bumps there. She kept fingering them throughout the day but Evelyn told her not to. As time passed Miriam tried to ignore them but she felt more each time she checked. When Evelyn left for the new market one morning, Miriam went into her parent's room to find their mirror.

The room was not the same without them. All the furniture had been removed and the place was empty, dead. Miriam looked around for the mirror that was once on the wall but it was gone.

The next week Evelyn woke Miriam up and told her to get dressed. She had laid Miriam's first communion dress out beside her. Miriam obeyed and put it on although it did not fit as well as it once did. Miriam noticed that Evelyn had opened all the drawers of the dresser and had placed a number of Miriam's clothes in a bag. Looking around, Miriam did not see her school uniform anywhere.

After a breakfast of *mandazis* and *chai,* Evelyn said they had to be going—they had a bus to catch. Miriam followed her, but felt dizzy as she stood. Evelyn was dressed in her nicest traveling clothes. She fastened her head wrap, turned to Miriam, pulled her veil down over her face, and told her not to remove it until she said so.

Evelyn wanted to walk fast but Miriam could barely keep up. Eventually they reached the *matatu* stage. Miriam was afraid she would have to stand up as they rode, but Evelyn was able to get them both seats.

They alighted at the bus station, and Evelyn sat Miriam down with their bags then went to the ticket window. She returned with two tickets and said they were going soon and that she would need to go to the toilet because it was a long ride.

Miriam wanted to ask where they were going but her head hurt and her mouth tasted badly. She did not even want to get up to go to the toilet because the walk and the *matatu* ride had tired her so much. She did not want to move from the seats the rest of the day.

But Evelyn insisted. Miriam got up and step by step approached the toilet. Many people walked by her as she did. She kept her face down. A woman said she looked beautiful in her dress. Miriam could not see her through the veil.

It was inconvenient to squat while wearing the dress. Miriam was sure to bunch it up to keep the ends from touching the ground. When she had finished and was walking out, she noticed a mirror on the wall. She looked at the entrance. No one was coming. Evelyn was still outside. Miriam took a few steps towards the mirror. Her face only appeared at the very bottom. She took a last look around, saw that she was alone, then lifted her veil.

She saw them: clusters of bumps all along her jaw, fat like peas, swelling, and spreading up her jaw onto her cheek. Just like her sister.

She pulled the veil down. She knew that wherever she was going now, she was going there to die.

A few weeks later, after Ivy had taken more medicine that made her feel stronger, Susan put Ivy and her brother in their best clothes. Ivy asked if they were going to church. Susan said yes but it was not just any ordinary Sunday. This Sunday David would find them a new family.

Ivy, Maurice, Ruth, Rebecca—the street girls—and Susan sat in the front row of the church this Sunday. Usually they sat in the third row beside the window, which Ivy liked more because the breeze would keep her cool. This Sunday she felt very hot and uncomfortable. She could even see sweat on the side of Father David's face as he read from the gospel.

David's sermon was about the holy family, Jesus, Mary, and Joseph. He talked about how they were refused room at the inn when Mary was about to give birth to Jesus. He said that there were people in our community today that needed shelter. He talked about how it was God's plan to care for these people. Then he talked about how Jesus loved children and always wanted children around him. Finally he talked about the poor and the sick, and how Jesus said good Christians must take care of them.

Then he said that two children who were in need of help were with them that morning. That was when Susan made Maurice and Ivy stand up. Ivy did not like staring out at all the people and feeling them stare back at her. When Maurice started to fidget, she stepped on his toes and told him to stand still. When he looked as if he was about to cry, Ruth intervened by telling him to be quiet. He obeyed immediately.

Susan spoke next, saying that Ivy and her brother were very nice children. They were very good children too. She said Ivy was always helpful and that both worked hard in school. Ivy was happy she did not mention the fact she had been forced to repeat a grade and that she still did not go to school often when she was sick.

Father David asked someone to come forward that would take care of Ivy and Maurice because even though he had been left them, he could not take care of them. He talked about Ivy's father. He mentioned how her father was a respected member of the community. He said that Ivy's father had even helped to build this very church.

The room remained silent. Ivy noticed people looking around at the walls. She looked at them too. She had been unaware that her father had helped to build the church. She pictured a younger version of him lifting boards, hammering nails, and pushing up the corrugated walls.

The people looked around the church as well. They examined the walls, the ceiling, the floors.

None were looking at her.

They would not look at Father David either. Father David said nothing. He was waiting. But the silence went on. Children made noise playing outside. A baby inside cried. A few people coughed.

But no one stepped forward. Ivy examined the crowd carefully, looking for a pretty woman that might be her new mother, but all of the ones she liked remained silent.

Ivy's legs were getting tired. Her mind drifted. She stared at a sunbeam and the dust floating in it. Maurice sat down on the ground.

Finally Father David spoke. He said he had faith in God that a home for them would be found.

Oliver now lived in a cottage with many other children and with a woman named Amelia that all the children called "Mum." Oliver was supposed to call her Mum too. Bonaventure, or Bonava as everyone called him, had said that she was Oliver's new mother and that she would love him very much. She had short hair, not long hair like his mother. He thought his own mother had been much prettier.

The other children ate with their fingers and with their mouths open. They did not always say please and thank you. Oliver found them very impolite.

The oldest girl in the cottage was the bossiest. Her name was Miriam and she would yell at the other children when they did not clean up after themselves, when they would not sit down for dinner, or when they made noise. She even yelled at Oliver once and when he cried, she yelled at him for crying, which made him want to cry more. Mum Amelia finally told her to be kind to him, that he already was a well-behaved boy.

He missed Babu. He asked Mum Amelia when Babu would be coming to visit but she said she did not know. He did not have much to remember Babu or his mother by, but he did keep his red cap, wearing it whenever he could—he knew it would be easier for Babu to pick him out when he did come to visit.

The home did have a school, but it was not like the schools he had gone to before. They did not wear uniforms and there were many children in the same classroom of different ages. Oliver was at first put with the younger children that were practicing tracing letters. He copied letters like he was told, but he already knew them all. When the teacher came by and saw that he had written his name on his own, she asked him if he could already write. Oliver said yes. She asked him if he could read. He said yes. She gave him an exercise book and asked him to read it aloud. He did. It was easy because it was at a level he had read two years before. Then the teacher asked him, in *Kizungu,* if he knew *Kizungu.* He said yes. She moved him into the next room.

Even in the next room he could read better than all the other children. Soon the teachers were making special lessons just for him.

He could not wait until his grandfather would come to visit. Oliver knew he would be proud of him. Mum Amelia was and so was Bonava. But Babu did not come. It occurred to Oliver that perhaps Babu would not come often and that it might be a long time before he saw him. Oliver decided that he would have to make better friends, so at night he found books on the shelf in the cottage and read them to the other children. He did what his teachers did: he would read a line then ask one of the children to read; this way he could teach them. In doing this he discovered that Miriam, even though she was one of the oldest, could not read. She would struggle to sound out words as if she were in grade one. When Oliver would be reading to himself, Miriam would sit down beside him and read books that were for very little children. If she became stuck on a word, she would show the word to Oliver, and he would tell her how to say it and what it meant. Then he would ask her to pronounce it herself.

Whether or not she did it well, he always told her, "Good job."

The back of the dump truck was not comfortable. The floor was hard and there was nothing to hold on to, so whenever the truck went over a bump or made a sharp turn, all the hawkers would lean far over, and some would fall. Harmony held on to her mother's hand. They sang a few songs to pass the time, the other women, as always, complimenting Harmony on her voice. After a while though, Harmony was hungry and too tired to sing. She said so to her mother. She and some of the women joked with each other that at least they would get meals in the jail.

Harmony's mother's best job had been in *Nakumatt*. Before then she had been a hawker. But the *Nakumatt* job was the best because her mother would bring home lots of food and sweets for her. But then she got sacked and went back to hawking.

They had lived in many places since then, Gigeri, Kangemi, Kariobangi and others places that were only named for the *matatu* stage. They were always moving, moving. Mean landlords evicted them, or *cucus* asked them to leave. Or they would tell them that Harmony could stay but her mother should leave. But her mother had always kept them together. She would have rather moved than separate herself and her daughter, which was why Harmony would follow her mother even to the police station.

One time they had gone to Harmony's grandmother's house in Kericho. It was a nice place. They had taken a very long bus ride to reach Kericho. The place was very green with lots of tea fields and few buildings. There were not many cars like in Nairobi and the air was clear so you could see the sky. This was the only time Harmony ever heard her mother speak about Harmony's father. Harmony's grandmother had brought him up and so Harmony later asked her mother about him.

She said that he was a mean older man with two other wives. She had run away from him when Harmony was little.

One morning they had to leave Kericho without saying good-bye to Harmony's grandmother. Harmony's mother said it was because her father was coming.

They never went back.

When things had been very *very* good, Harmony had been sent to school, but that had been a long time ago when Harmony had had a completely different set of clothes that she had out grown since. That had been before hawking sweets and cigarettes, before they had come to live with Loraine beneath a sheet of *mbati* set up between a green grocer and a mechanic's shop. Loraine had been living there because her sister, whom she had been living with, had died. Loraine was a good friend to have because she had a *jiko* made out of an old paint can and would cook when they could find food and enough trash and wood to burn.

But Harmony preferred living in a house. It was more comfortable, warmer, and there were also no street boys. Street boys were very dangerous because they sniffed glue and would steal from you and if they could, they would kill you. Harmony avoided them. She remembered one time she saw one try to steal a light off of a car. Then a mob came and beat him. They punched him and kicked him and wrapped his arms and legs together with barbed wire. Then they beat him more. Harmony laughed when he tried to walk and fell over.

But then, after a while, he did not move and he was very red from blood and so was the street under him. It was sad because he had died. His face had also changed. He did not look like he looked before: his face had gotten big and his eyes were narrow, almost like he was Chinese. Harmony could not remember what he looked like before but she knew he had not been Chinese.

Finally the police came. The only people left were a few street boys with their bottles of glue to their noses. They had gathered around in a circle to stare. They stood staring, some crying, until the police took the body away.

Chapter 18

Thieves

Anika, who I could never get to like me enough and preferred to call me stupid, the girl with the almond-shaped eyes and the impish grin, is in the nursing room most days now. For a time, when treated for tuberculosis, she had seemed to recover. She even returned to school where, despite missing so many classes, she was number two in her class—a testament to her intellect.

But one day she took a turn for the worse. Her recovery was short-lived and she is sent to the nursing room for twenty-four-hour care.

The day finally comes that I see a tall, light-skinned woman standing outside one of the cottages—Sofie Waceera's cottage. The woman looks like Sofie and when I glance across the playground, I see that Sofie is being led out of school by one of the teachers.

Sofie's mother has died. This is a relative come to tell her, I'm sure.

I return to my preschool class. At the break I visit Sofie's cottage to see how she is handling the news. I enter to find Sofie seated at the table speaking quite comfortably, swinging her legs over the edge of her chair, while the woman listens. I stand there for a moment then introduce myself to the woman. She takes my hand and says,

"I am Judith Waceera, Sofie's mother."

The experience of seeing a ghost must be like this. My sense of reality is, for a few moments, pulled apart as I look at someone whose continued existence I had long ago ruled out as impossible. Judith was on her death bed when they found her. She had Kaposi sarcoma lesions all over her legs. I think back to what the social worker had told me:

"She is probably dead . . . ."

But in defiance of all that, here she was, Judith Waceera, drinking tea right in front of me. She is thin and bundled in warm clothes although it is not cold. Her eyes are sunken and bloodshot, her nails are brown and crumbling, but she is undeniably alive.

"You know," she says to me, "Sofie saved my life."

Funny, I of all people know. Now through the Washington Post I have told the story to hundreds of thousands of people back in the US, with the sad ending of Judith being dead. I notice Sofie is happy, but I could hardly describe her as surprised. Of course she isn't. She always believed her mother would return. I was the one who did not.

Judith starts coming to visit Sofie regularly. She explains to me that she ended up staying with an uncle who lived near the border with Tanzania. There was no cell phone reception there so she could not call or be reached. She said things became worse before they got better. There were weeks that she could not get out of bed. But she struggled, "fought," she said, by thinking of Sofie and all she had done for her. She could never give up after that.

Her uncle took her to the hospital where she received treatment for her KS. After a year the lesions diminished. Although it was still painful she began walking a little bit each day. Her muscles had atrophied so it was like being a child, learning how to balance all over again. But each day the thought of walking to reach Sofie drove her.

Looking at Sofie and thinking about what she has accomplished, it occurs to me that no matter how much I work to care for Sofie, no matter how much I support the nurturing environment of the home, there is nothing that would make Sofie happier than simply having her mother back. Games, attention, affection, toys, she would trade any and all these things from us to have this one person that is so vital to her, alive and in her presence. Realizing this, as Judith leaves that first day. I walk her to the gate and say to her,

"Judith, I'm going to do everything I can to keep you alive."

Rosa Maria has died. She was one of my volunteers and in the past few days as I've watched her deteriorate, I have done so with the knowledge that my actions led to her death.

Isabella, a seven-year-old at the home, asks me why Rosa Maria died. She thinks only children die.

"Then what happened to all your parents?" I ask her. A casual reader might be shocked at my candor, but many of the children, like Isabella, don't even remember their parents. The Rainbow parents are the only ones they have now, but they know generally that their birth parents are no longer in their lives.

Rosa Maria was a stooping woman with shoulder-length gray hair and skin that had been sunburned many times. Her eyes were sunken and rarely met my own gaze. She had a long nose that was as prominent as a shark fin rising out of the water. She usually wore jeans, a khaki vest full of pockets, and a baseball cap. She was clearly at that point in her life when attracting the opposite sex was somewhat low on her priority list. She dressed functionally. With that vest, she looked like another *mzungu* ready to take on the bush.

Rosa Maria turned out to be quite the eccentric. Her English was not great and she was unable to learn the names of the children except for one of the babies she took a liking to. The rest of the children she referred to as *cukculuku,* Kiswahili for "rooster," and the children called her the same name back. It seemed appropriate.

The staff loved her. Kenyans seem to have an appreciation for eccentricity or even sometimes outright silliness. It's a typical

Kenyan trait to look past anyone's faults as long as they make you laugh. I found it one of their most endearing national characteristics.

On paper Rosa Maria looked like the perfect volunteer. She was an Italian citizen. She was fifty-seven, retired, on a pension, and had worked as a UN volunteer in Burundi, Rwanda, and Kosovo, when those hot spots were at their hottest. So her resume made her look as if she was committed, flexible, resilient.

She was actually falling apart. She had a drinking problem. How long she had had it, I never found out. It never interfered with her work at the home. She would work from eight in the morning until five in the evening, often without a break. She would work in the kitchen, help in the nursing room, or dig in the garden. It was only three months into her six-month stay that I found more than two dozen wine and liquor bottles all thrown into the trash bin outside her room at once. One of her roommates noticed that she drank a glass of vodka like it was water before bed each night. She asked Rosa Maria why and she replied that after working in regions where there has been incomprehensible slaughter, she had nightmares about soldiers coming to kill her and mountains of dead bodies. The alcohol made her sleep more soundly.

Needless to say I was relieved when she finished her time with the home and I was distressed when she showed up a few weeks later just back from the airport, falling down drunk, insisting that she was back from Italy in order to volunteer *indefinitely.*

I'd heard that one was never supposed to fire a drunk. But I also knew I could not let her live in the home again with her drinking problem. I told her she could work at the home but she had to live elsewhere until she sobered up.

She found an apartment in Dagoretti living with some staff members from the home. For all intents and purposes she was a faithful volunteer.

Then one weekend she went down to Mombasa. A few weeks after she returned, she fell ill with a fever and chills. She said her joints hurt. We told her she needed to be tested for malaria. She refused. On a Tuesday I visited her apartment. She said she was feeling better, although I didn't believe her. I returned Thursday and no one answered her door. I tried to believe that she had gone to a doctor. The next day Eve called me and told me she had seen Rosa Maria in the internet café.

"She is shaking and delirious," she said to me. "She has malaria."

We went to Rosa Maria's house after that but she had locked her door and would not let us in. She screamed that she wanted to be left alone. We had to break the door down. We found her on her bed with a pool of vomit beside her. A blood smear revealed that her parasite count—a measure of the organism that causes malaria in her blood—was nearly too high to count.

We took her to a hospital and when that one was not good enough, we transferred her to another. On Sunday she went into a coma. She had to be placed in the ICU. Her hands and feet turned blue. She was curled up in a fetal position, a breathing tube down her throat. Her organs were failing one after another.

Now as they carry her coffin towards her grave I vacillate between anger and guilt. Guilt because I know if I had let her live at the home we would have been able to monitor her more effectively. Anger because I feel like this is such a waste of a life.

Then I reflect upon the fact that she had locked the door against us when we came for her. Perhaps she did not want to get better. Perhaps she feared we would send her back to Italy. Perhaps she preferred to die than go back. The picture we gained of her life in her home country was a sad one, no friends, one relative, a brother who when we called and informed him that she was dying said he wanted nothing to do with her and hung up.

I go through her file and find out that she worked as a tour guide in Italy. I picture her giving tours to Americans decked out in shorts and T-shirts. In my mind I see her showing them around the countryside, eating dinner with them in the hotel restaurants then remaining a bit too long in the bar or at the table, getting so drunk that she causes a disruption and the staff send complaints to her supervisors. Her tours run behind because she is so slow to get up in the morning.

From the myriad of tour agencies she worked for and for the brief amount of time at each one, I sense I might be on to some grain of the truth. So Rosa Maria turned to helping people. She went to Burundi, Rwanda, Kosovo. A closer look at her resume might have revealed the red flags that she should not be put in an unstable situation.

But AIDS orphans and war refugees must settle for what help they can get.

The refrigerators at the morgue were broken and the smell was horrifying. I did not see Rosa Maria's body but the volunteer that did identify her said she looked terrible.

The grave site was not much of an improvement. The graves are dug side by side each day with huge mounds of earth around them. The plot assigned to Rosa Maria was one in the middle of many, all empty, all open. Carrying the coffin was difficult since we had to negotiate between falling in holes and tumbling off the unstable mounds. The coffin itself was only closed with a hook and eye latch and my heart pounded with each slip we pall bearers made, afraid that one of us would fall in a grave, causing the coffin to drop and the lid to open revealing Rosa Maria's restless, putrefying visage staring out at us. Forcing us *wazungu* to ask the question of why any of us are here.

I look at the children and the adults all around us. Why are we drawn to a population of children that become dependent upon us? Children who readily give us affection because they have been deprived of it themselves? Why have we chosen to live among a population of citizens that look up to us as richer, smarter, in general, more influential?

Here in Kenya, we *wazungu* are notable. Back home, we enjoy hero status for the work we do. What insecurities are we fleeing to be "saviors" and "saints" over here in Africa? We claim to be here helping others but really we are helping ourselves. I am an unpublished writer and journalist looking for a story. Another volunteer at the home is a recently widowed woman looking for a family. Rosa Maria was a lonely and pathetic drunk looking for anybody. Here we are treated with deference and respect, simply because of the color of our skin. Even me, with my pimples and thick glasses. We all go from zero to hero. And to some, they can never go back.

"Why?" is a question few of us give much time to. Nobody really wants to look at how they are broken. We'd rather fix others, or claim to.

I think a lot of us are looking for a purpose and meaning. The younger volunteers certainly are looking for a righteous cause. Maybe I am too. But the suffering one encounters, the poverty, the privation, has a way of playing a cruel trick on you. It makes you realize that perhaps there is no purpose here other than to simply survive. The country office director of CARE Kenya tells me that their mission is sort of along those lines. "We are not saving people, we're building resilience to the next shock, be it economic or health." As they lower Rosa Maria into the grave I wonder how much it is chance that decides, when the next shock comes, if you survive or not. Good intentions are no protection.

I notice Eve is different than any woman I have ever known. Our differences are not African vs. American. They are the difference from one of us being raised in a resource poor country and another (me) having been raised without giving a thought to resources as a result of their abundance.

Eve does dishes by filling the sink and using the water there instead of leaving it running. She is so unused to running water that she hesitates before turning the spigot as she tries to remember which way turns the water on and off. A few times she turns it the wrong way and gives a playful yelp as it suddenly comes gushing forth.

She is not "backwards"—Kenyan's term for their own countrymen that are not modern or educated—although she often is concerned that she is, especially when we get into a debate over whether or not it is safe to eat an egg with a runny yolk. She says absolutely not. I say it is fine and make an insinuation that she simply does not know better. She yields to me simply because she is willing to believe that my education has been better then hers. I learn later that since there are not strict sanitary and health standards for poultry production in Kenya, eating an uncooked yolk can be very dangerous. Ironically it was illegal to serve one in restaurants in many US states until the 1970s.

From then on I eat my yolks cooked well, with a slice of humble pie.

Eve, like many twenty-something Kenyans, is an interesting mix of cultures. Kenyans her age may speak Kiswahili at home but their English is often better. Their grandmothers may dress traditionally, but the younger generation will wear basketball jerseys, baseball hats, and skull caps like their favorite American rappers. Eve may live in a house where she and her sisters must carry their water from a well to barrels in their kitchen, but she can disassemble and reassemble a computer with such confidence and competence that one would think she invented it. She can run software programs that I do not even know how to turn on. When the server in the café goes down, she falls to her hands and knees and manipulates the spaghetti plate of wires behind the CPUs until the correct lights blink in the correct sequence on the modem and the connection returns.

She also unknowingly displays a level of equanimity that I find myself admiring—mainly because as a high-strung *mzungu*, it is something I lack entirely. It is a steadiness I have found in many African women but never in a *mzungu* one. The best example was when a *matatu* Eve was riding was hijacked by gunmen. One gunman leapt into the seat in front of her and pressed the barrel of his rifle into her chest. He told the passengers that he would shoot if the others did not give up their mobile phones and wallets.

I met Eve at the police station where she and the other riders were making a report. She showed me the mark left between her breasts by the gun—a half-moon welt. Then, her mind already elsewhere, she asked me,

"Would you like to come out with my sisters and me tonight?"

Miriam is light-headed and weak. She's unable to even stand. Mum Amelia sends her to the nursing room but she is unable to even walk. I pick her up and carry her in my arms. She is surprisingly light. She leans her head against me. Knowing what I know of the children and their time in the nursing room, to say I am worried is an understatement. I want to hold her against me and tell her, "Don't die, not you, not *ever* you!"

As scared as I am at this moment, I have an utter certainty of purpose, knowing what my life is for—helping children, helping this girl right now. I never wanted to experience this moment with this child of all children, and yet now that it is taking place, I know there is nowhere else I should be.

Miriam recovers. Her symptoms a side effect to a cough suppressant she drank earlier in the afternoon. I am relieved. She is even able to walk back to the cottage and sleep in her own bed.

I sleep a lot better knowing that.

It's 9:37 p.m. Judy, who has struggled so much with her cardiac conditions as a result of her HIV status, sits up in her bed in

the nursing room. She has been laying half-conscious but now she is suddenly lucid and alert. She turns to Kate, a volunteer, who has been holding her.

"Kate, I am cold."

"Do you want me to close the window?" Kate asks her.

"Yes." Kate gets up. As she places her hand on the window's handle, Judy says, "I don't want anybody to catch me," then falls over onto the mattress. Kate asks her what she means. Judy does not answer. She's dead.

It's Friday night when Father McLeod and another priest are carjacked while pulling into the Jesuit residence on Ngong road. A car pulls in behind them while they wait for the gate to open and men with guns jump out of the bushes demanding that they get out of the car and hand over their keys. Father McLeod and the other priest cooperate and the thieves drive off, Father quietly confident that the car will be returned because of the kill switch installed beneath the seat. In about a mile, the alarm will beep and if the thieves do not know where to find the switch within a few moments, the car will die.

What concerns Father more is the premeditated nature of the robbery. The men lying in wait in the bushes, the car that pinned them in from behind, it all speaks of careful planning and preparation. He knows they had to be followed and he wonders if the other vehicles from the orphanage were as well.

He places a call to Bonava who is out with the children at a Diwali celebration. I've passed, choosing to catch some precious time away from the kids, but being Indian herself, Weena has accompanied the children.

It has been—by all accounts—a grand evening. There has been traditional Indian dancing, African dancing, and freestyle by the children, all accompanied by heaping plates of Indian food (more on this later). The children are in a merry mood as they ride home, that is until they are told that the bus must make a stop at the police station to get an escort because thieves are about.

The children immediately are somber and scared. The word *mwizi* (thief) echoes in hushed tones among them, traveling like an electric current. Harvey, the assistant manager of the home who is the chaperone that night, reassures the children that a police escort is just a precaution, but it is too late. Every sound, every shadow outside the bus is taken for a thief. There is no levity left in the bunch. Some children are whimpering and crying.

"Oh, we're going to be fine!" Weena insists, trying to reassure the children with her unrelenting California optimism.

"I wish Ted was here," Humphrey, a teenage boys says.

"Why is that? I am a doctor, if anyone gets hurt I can help them," Weena says.

"Ted knows *Tae Kwon Do,*" one of the girls points out while she huddles in a seat holding hands with two other girls.

Some of the younger children mention that I am also Peter Parker and that I could save everyone with my superpowers. Some of the older children insist that I don't *really* have powers, but the younger children disagree. "He does!" they insist.

At this point Weena resigns herself to her second-class status, medical degree notwithstanding.

The police take their time to locate a vehicle to use as an escort. In the meantime, the children grow restless. Their diet at the orphanage is rich in nutrients but kept very bland. The Indian food at the Diwali celebration was not. In reaction to the spicy food the children drank copious amounts of water. Only now are the consequences becoming clear.

The kids hold out as long as they can, but once one child admits to their unfolding emergency, a chorus of "Me too" erupts. For any kids who did not have to go, all the sudden discussion ensures that they too now need to relieve themselves.

It is decided that the children will go *susu* behind the bus. They are within the police station grounds, but the children insist on being escorted—the boys by Harvey, the girls by Weena.

The bus holds around fifty children, fifty children who have drunk a great deal of water. The boys are quick with their business and even go out three at a time, sharing Harvey as their guardian. The girls are not so brave and are cajoled one at a time by Weena. Some would rather hold it than risk being snatched by *mwizi*. Weena escorts each one to the back of the bus where the girls squat. One of the children, who had voiced a preference for my superpowers, Isabella, is too terrified even to venture around the corner of the bus.

"Weena, come with me," she says.

Weena steps around the corner of the bus but looks away to preserve Isabella's modesty. It occurs to her that she does not hear the telltale tinkling of Isabella relieving her bladder.

"Weena, come closer."

Weena takes a step closer. "Here?"

"No closer," Isabella insists.

Finally, at Isabella's request, Weena is squatting next to her, at which point Weena encounters the problem of finding a dry place to step as forty-nine other children have just relieved themselves in the same vicinity.

It's too late. She feels warm puddles splash over the soles of her flip-flops. Isabella finishes and runs back to the bus, leaving Weena to contemplate how unfortunate she is to have spent seven years studying medicine and yet still be without superpowers.

Chapter 19

My Name is Ted and I'm in Recovery

So it was drugs that helped me: Seroquel, Trazadone, and that old stand-by, Prozac. The drugs stabilized me and I was able to be transferred to the halfway house, still at the hospital but no longer in the psych-ward, no longer in Cottage Green. What followed was rewiring, self-examination through group and individual therapy. The intense lectures on my thinking, my assumptions, my habits, obsessions, negative self-talk, all in an effort to strip these learned behaviors and assumptions away and to replace them with tools and healthy coping mechanisms.

I was required to attend E.A. meetings. E.A. stood for Emotions Anonymous. It was a twelve-step program modeled after Alcoholics Anonymous. But for me, the meetings are only anxiety provoking—a bunch of people sitting in a circle venting about their lives did not exactly help me in my recovery. I actually just wanted to kill myself again. I told my psychiatrist and he urged me to attend A.A. meetings instead. "Some people don't like E.A. They say it is too negative and it triggers their anxieties further. Go to A.A., they have more fun."

I did. He was right. I quickly fell in love with the meetings. The members there welcomed me with a lack of judgment I had never experienced before. I was even allowed to share, disclosing that I was not an alcoholic but "in recovery," was more than enough. Especially since there was so much co-morbidity of mental health disorders and alcoholism, I was with a community that knew what I had been through.

The alcoholics and addicts in recovery were full of hope, love, acceptance, and support—not to mention humor. Despite myself, I even started to find some spirituality again, mainly due to the fact that the only thing keeping these people from drinking was their "higher power." I have alcoholics in my family. I know how hard it is to kick. But these people seemed able to live with their addiction. If I asked them how, they would just tell me it was a miracle.

They had phrases for everything. Let go and let God. Live and let God. Easy does it. Love lives here. One day at a time. If you want to be selfless, think about yourself less. When I take the "me" out of blame, all I have left is "bla . . . bla . . . bla. . . ." God always answers prayers, sometimes with "Yes," sometimes with "No," sometimes with, "You've got to be kidding." I talked to some alcoholics with years of sobriety about my loss of faith. I challenged them. I told them about the kids I sat next to as they died. Their demeanor was kind, but their answers firm: we can't control outcomes, that is just my ego wanting to tell God what to do.

In time, Rich, an older man in recovery for alcoholism, offered to be my sponsor and help me through the Twelve Steps. I reminded him that although I suffered from emotional and mental disorders, alcoholism was not one of them. He laughed and asked, "You really think the steps are about alcohol?"

Stumped, I answered, "Yes."

He explained to me only the first step was about alcohol and more precisely it was about control and surrendering our notions of it.

"What can I control?" I asked.

"You," he said. "Picture dropping a hula hoop over your head and letting it fall to the ground. Everything outside it is not in your control. Just worry about what is on the inside."

"That's me."

"Then let's do some work on *you.*"

The Twelve Steps, or variations of them, are at root a spiritual exercise, an unpeeling of your layers, assumptions, and the behavioral patterns they led to. You reflect on who you have hurt, and how your own insecurities and human failings—character defects in the lexicon of A.A.—contributed. It makes you aware of your legacy issues, the secondary gains of your most unhealthy choices. I saw my assumptions, my elitism, my entitlement, my neediness, insecurity, even my hurt, laid bare—all in a safe, loving environment.

As solipsistic as it sounds, the program is also deeply committed to community and relationships. The twelfth and final step is about turning to others and providing service to them, not because any of us need to play hero, but because it's only in service to others that we can save ourselves. Or as my alcoholic friends would say, "If you want to keep it [sobriety or sanity] you have to keep giving it away."

Rich and other recovering alcoholics and depressives did not hesitate to give to me. They told me I worried too much. That I wanted to play director when I'm just an actor on God's stage. I had to let go of any notion of control, it was an illusion anyway. If all this had come from anyone else, I wouldn't have believed it, but these folks, with their experience, their lows, their own depression and self-destructive behaviors of the past, somehow had credibility with me. Another phrase I heard in meetings that resonated with my experience and put lie to the pat, easy answers offered to me in my Sunday school version of faith was: "Religion is for those afraid of going to hell. A.A. is for those who have been there." Tom, the cardiologist whom I had met in Cottage Green on my first day and who was making progress alongside me, found many of the expressions trite and some of the optimism forced. He claimed to be an atheist, but—a little embarrassed—admitted that, "I believe in A.A."

Previously, I had rejected the advice and comfort of others because I felt they had not looked into the face of privation—evil—as I had. My friends in A.A. had a name for this too, "terminally special." It was the notion that an individual's problems were beyond compare or comprehension of anyone else, but really it was just another form of grandiose thinking.

Grandiose, that sounded familiar.

Most of the people in those rooms had experienced loss, trauma, and more than one night in Cottage Green—or the "it's not easy being green cottage," as they called it. And that was just it, these people had suffered, they had seen privation, even evil things, in their lives. Those things had left a mark, but those who recovered, did not take themselves so seriously that they couldn't find a moment to reflect and laugh—at themselves, at life. It was this self-effacing humor that I found particularly charming not to mention compelling.

I found myself sitting down and praying with these men, women, and others who did not choose a gender (for all were welcome), for the first time since I had left the orphanage. Honestly, a part of me wanted to rebel. A part of me thought I was too smart for it all. But there were others who showed me otherwise. Sam, a legally blind old-timer without an ounce of self-pity in him, but with thirty-six years of sobriety, worked with patients in the early stages of recovery. He'd been through drug addition, alcoholism, and depression. After sitting alongside me in a meeting, he turned and said, "Ted, your biggest problem is your big fat brain. It's a liar anyway; remember how it wanted to kill you?" As he spoke, I knew a part of me just wanted to turn off my thoughts and anxieties, to surrender, accept the mystery of it all, accept the paradoxes, the injustices, and leave it for God to sort out. I would focus on my side of the hula hoop (or as my A.A. friends would say, "just worry about keeping my side of the street in order"). God, he—or she—could make sense of the rest, not me. It was not my role to try to fix or save the world, just myself.

I did not listen without skepticism. As if he could read my mind, Sam laughed, put his arm around me and said, "If we can get you to stop taking yourself so seriously, Ted, who knows, maybe us drunks will end up saving your life."

Chapter 20

Drowning

Usually on Sundays women came over to Susan's house. They would eat, drink tea, and visit late into the afternoon.

But nobody came that Sunday. The house was much more silent than usual. Ivy asked Ruth if she should pack her things and Maurice's things together in case someone came for them that afternoon. Ruth told her yes.

But no one came except Father David.

A week passed. Another Sunday came around. This Sunday, Ivy, Susan, and the other children sat in their usual spot at church next to the window. They did not have to get up again, even though Father David mentioned them again.

Still no one wanted them.

Ivy tried to imagine what the trouble could be. She had been on her best behavior and although she had had to threaten a few children, she had not been in any fights since moving in with Susan. She wondered if it had something to do with *ukimwi,* the word she had heard the nurses and doctors saying in the low, hushed tones that adults used when they were being serious and did not necessarily want children to listen. She remembered when she had heard of *ukimwi* before. It was when a house down their street had been burned down. She had heard her mother talking to her friends about the cause. She thought *ukimwi* was something that started fires.

She was afraid to ask Susan about it. Instead she asked Ruth if the reason nobody wanted them was because of *ukimwi*.

Ruth would not answer.

One afternoon a man in a suit appeared at the gate. Susan greeted him respectfully. He was bald and had a narrow face and he was very nice to Ivy. Susan introduced him as Harvey. There was another woman named Christabell with Harvey. She was very pretty and was wearing an orange and blue skirt. They were dressed like important people. Harvey said that he and Christabell were there to take her on a picnic. She asked if Maurice could come. They said he could come on the next picnic.

Susan told her that she could go, so she followed them to their van, a red one, and climbed in.

Christabell was very nice. She asked a lot of questions about Ivy, where she went to school, how often she went. She seemed very interested in how often Ivy was sick. She also asked if she missed her parents. Ivy said yes.

They rode for a long time. They drove past many tall buildings and many *matatus*. They made a few stops at hospitals. Harvey would go inside with fat brown envelopes and come back with thin white ones. Ivy was hungry and was wondering when they would be stopping for the picnic but she did not want to be rude, even though the long car ride on an empty stomach was making her ill.

Finally, when they were driving on a road with lots of trees and grass along it, they came to a black gate. There were Maasai opening it. They smiled and waved at her and Christabell. Christabell told her she could wave back. Ivy asked if they were real Maasai. She said they were.

They drove down a driveway with lots of flowers and trees then stopped outside a two-story building. Ivy was led into an office with a big desk. Harvey sat down behind it.

Finally Ivy asked when they were going on a picnic.

Harvey said there was no picnic today. This was her new home, called Rainbow, where she would be living from now on.

Ivy asked where her brother would be. Harvey said that he would be at another home not far away called Malaika run by a woman named Mama Seraphina and her family. Harvey promised she and her brother would be happy in their new homes.

She cried that he was a liar. She said she and her brother had to stay together. She went to the door and Harvey got up to stop her, but she turned on him and started to punch him. She could tell by the way his eyes bulged and he crumpled that he was surprised at how hard she could hit. He had no idea how much practice she had. When he tried to restrain her again, she bit his hand and kicked him.

Then she started to cough. She had her hand on the door. She opened it and went out, but the exertion of fighting Harvey had made her so tired she could only take a few steps before she collapsed on a couch outside the office. She kept coughing, suddenly ashamed that she had grown so weak and lost her fighting edge. She looked to the door that led outside. There were three children staring at her. She wanted to tell them to go away, but she was coughing now too hard.

She lay down on the couch and cried. She heard Harvey pick up a phone and call for a nurse.

Harmony followed her mother from the truck into the police station. She had been in a station before when her mother had reported a robbery, but she had never been in the jail before. She was scared. Other women looked at her. Harmony's mother kept her hands on Harmony's shoulders. When a policeman asked how old Harmony was, her mother said she was fourteen—which was four years older than Harmony thought she was. But her mother whispered to her that if the police thought she was younger they would try to take her away.

The cell was very crowded with women. Many of them were hawkers that Harmony recognized from Moi Avenue. They had even arrested the old *cucu* who sold sweets, cigarettes, and mobile phone cases. Harmony liked her because she had given Harmony a sweet once, even when Harmony's own mother would not let her eat their sweets. In return, when Harmony had been given a piece of bread by a *mzungu,* she had split it three ways between herself, her mother, and the *cucu.*

The cell only became more crowded as more women were added. It smelled of sweaty bodies and unwashed armpits. Everyone had to keep shifting to make room for the new women, but when the women in the back started complaining that they were being pushed too close to the toilet, no one moved any more and the new ladies had to simply sit next to the toilet and no one wanted to do that. It was disgusting. It was overflowing with excrement and the smell filled the whole cell.

Hours passed. Harmony was tired and hungry. The police supplied the women with some bread and butter but it was not enough for everyone to get more than half a piece. But Harmony was with her mother, so she did not complain.

One woman was brought in with a baby. She was allowed to remain outside the cell. Another woman was brought in who was falling down from being so drunk. This made the policemen and the ladies in the cell laugh. She came in and did not seem to mind sitting next to the toilet because she fell asleep right away.

Some women had to urinate but when they went, it just fell onto the full toilet and spread onto the floor. It made Harmony have to go but she did not want to go in the cell. She tried to hold it but it became unbearable. She said so to her mother, who spoke up to one of the guards.

The guards were women, a very fat one and a very skinny one. They allowed Harmony out of the cell and let her use the toilet for the police. It was clean and nice. They shared their tea and bread with her. Harmony asked if her mother could have some they but told her no. They were still nice ladies though because they told Harmony she did not have to go back to the cell. They allowed her to sit with them and watch television. Harmony watched the news and then a movie. Periodically she checked on her mother—she had fallen asleep like many of the women in the cell. Harmony tried watching the TV longer because she did not usually have the opportunity, but she eventually felt tired herself and fell asleep on a couch. The skinny woman guard woke her when it was close to morning and told her she would have to get back in the cell. Harmony obeyed.

The second day was even more boring than the first. It smelled worse too because more women had used the toilet. The puddle had spread. The drunk woman's clothes were now wet with it. She was angry and mumbling at everyone.

They were given bread at lunch and some at dinner as well. This time there were two loaves to go around so they each had a bit more. After dinner the night guards came on duty. These were not the nice ladies again, but two men. They watched the TV with the volume very loud. The men had the TV angled so that the women could watch it as well, which many of them did to pass the time, but then after a few shows the men came to the cell. They told the women that if they wanted to keep watching they would have to give the men little presents. But none of the women offered anything. They all looked away.

The men went back to their table to watch the TV. There was a football match on. The men drank while they watched and became very loud so they could hear each other over the TV. When one man's team began losing, he came back to the cell and asked the women for *kiti-kidogo*. They ignored him again and he became angry, which Harmony knew meant bad things would happen. She tried to make herself very small.

But then she felt something poke her back. She tried moving farther away but the poking persisted. It was the guard. He had a club and he was poking at Harmony, calling after her, saying,

"Little girl, little girl."

Harmony was tempted to turn around and steal his club, but she knew that would only make things worse for everyone. She moved closer to her mother. She was scared now. Somehow the man extended his reach further and tapped Harmony hard on her head.

She started to cry. That was when her mother turned to look at the guard and told him to stop.

He spoke very quickly to Harmony's mother then, calling her bad names and telling her she made the place smell like a toilet. She curled her body around Harmony. Both men were at the bars now yelling at her and calling her a whore. They began to bang the bars with their clubs, saying they would do so all night so that the women would not be able to sleep at all.

Suddenly Harmony felt her mother fall backwards and let go of her. Harmony turned and saw that one of the men had reached in, grabbed the end of her mother's dress, and dragged her to the bars. She was screaming. Harmony grabbed her foot and tried to pull her back but her mother kicked her away. Harmony reached out for her again. At the same time one of the men raised his club up over his head. Then he swung it down between the bars.

The club hit Harmony's mother on the head with a clunk. Harmony screamed. So did all the women who suddenly leapt up to protect Harmony's mother, but the men beat at them as well. Harmony watched the club that was over her mother's head. When it came down and made a clanging noise, she was happy because the guard had missed and struck the bars. When there was no clanging noise, it was bad because there was a clunk from him hitting her mother.

Harmony and another woman tried pulling at her mother's feet, but they only succeeded in pulling off her shoes. One of the men had tied her to the bars with her scarf. Harmony's mother was moaning and had her hands up around her head, but she was no longer thrashing in resistance, but wailing quietly. Harmony got up and grabbed the arm of one of the men. He was amazingly strong because he could lift her up with just that one arm. He tried shaking her. She tried biting him, but he knocked her against the bars. At the same time one of the women grabbed Harmony and pulled her away.

Then it was all quiet. The women were saying nothing and the only sound was that of the men's breathing and Harmony's mother moaning and crying. She was crying like a baby and Harmony hated it.

Then Harmony realized why the men had stopped. The *cucu* was standing beside Harmony's mother. Her clothes were on the floor and she was naked. Her skin was sagging like it was going to come off her. Her breasts were flat and nearly touched her belly. The hair in her crotch was completely grey.

The men told her to put her clothes on. They told her she was disgusting. One of them laughed but the other looked away and started to leave. The other yelled at him and told him not to be "backwards," but it was too late. He was already gone, so the second guard followed him as well.

Harmony knew why they left: if a young man saw an old woman naked, it would curse him.

They went to her mother, untied her scarf, and put it on her head where she was bleeding. There was blood all over her clothes. Harmony kept telling her that she was sorry and held her hand and sang softly to her. Eventually her mother fell asleep.

In the morning, the two nice ladies had returned as guards. At first they thought that the other women had beaten Harmony's mother. But when Harmony told them it was the two men, they believed her. It took a long time to wake up Harmony's mother and for a while Harmony was afraid she had died. But she finally awoke. Once she did, the two lady guards were very nice to Harmony and her mother and let them both out. They helped Harmony's mother by finding bandages and cleaning her head. They even offered Harmony and her mother breakfast. Harmony took as much bread as she could and gave it to the women in the cell that had helped her mother.

That night they had to sleep in the cell once more. The next morning when Harmony's mother got up she said she was dizzy. She had trouble walking and when she spoke she did not make much sense. They were released from the cell and the women lined up to be processed out. Everyone let Harmony and her mother go first. The man that did their paperwork was very nasty and slow and didn't seem to care that Harmony's mother was hurt. Harmony hated him. But finally they were finished. A bag with their sweets was given back to them. The cigarettes were gone though.

Harmony did not know how to get back home so she waited for some of the women that had helped her mother to complete their processing. Once a few of them were finished, they came over and helped Harmony's mother onto a *matatu*. They asked where Harmony and her mother lived. Harmony told them between the green grocer and the mechanic's shop. The women found someone who was going in that direction. The *cucu* was going there as well as one of the ladies that held the scarf to Harmony's mother's head.

When they reached Nairobi, Evelyn did not take Miriam to her house. Instead they boarded a *matatu,* rode it for a while, got off, then boarded another *matatu* that was very old, rode it a short while, then got off. They alighted at a gate in front of a long driveway, which Miriam was not looking forward to walking down. The gate was opened for them by Maasai. Miriam knew about Maasai. She had seen them before. They could be very backwards but they were the fiercest of all the tribes in Kenya.

The driveway led to a children's home. Miriam knew what those were, they had them in Mombasa. But this one was nicer than the ones she had seen before. There were trees, grass, flowers, and three nice cars parked outside. A tall man in a suit seemed to be waiting for them. His name was Bonava. Miriam was afraid of him at first because he was wearing a suit, but upon meeting her, he immediately knelt down beside her and was very kind. He complimented her on her dress. He even tried to make her laugh but she was feeling too ill. Bonava suggested that they take Miriam to the nurse.

Evelyn sat with Miriam while a nice nurse named Ruth shaved her head and rubbed medicine on her scalp. She did not seem disturbed at all by the sight of the bumps on Miriam's face. Ruth gave her some small pills that she had to take with soda. Another nurse stuck Miriam with needles, but she was too tired to resist. Someone even brought some rice and green grams for Miriam and Evelyn to eat for lunch.

Miriam rested in bed and after some time Evelyn said she had to go. Miriam asked if she was coming with her. Evelyn said no. That was when Miriam knew she had been brought there to stay.

"Why not?" Miriam asked. She felt tears welling up in her eyes. Evelyn began to weep as well. She took Miriam by her hands and told her that she had a sickness called *ukimwi*. It was why they had taken her blood in Mombasa. It was the same sickness that killed her parents. Evelyn had brought her to this home because it was a special home for helping children with *ukimwi*.

Miriam asked if she would die. Evelyn said only God knew.

She remained a little longer. When she finally left it was getting dark. She promised Miriam she would be happy and that she would come to visit all the time.

Ivy's new home was not terrible. She lived in a cottage with eleven other children and a new mother. Her mother's name was Agnes. She was strict but could be very nice too. Ivy was one of the older children so she got to take care of some of the younger children, although she would rather have been taking care of Maurice.

They gave her medicines that made her feel better than she had in a very long time. Soon she was playing outside with the other girls. She could even play football with the boys. She got in a fight with one boy, Rashid, when he cheated at football. She punched him in the face. He ran away crying and when Mum Agnes found out, she told Ivy she would have to go to bed early that night. Harvey also spoke to her the next day and told her that if she misbehaved she would not be allowed to see her brother.

With this threat looming, Ivy made an effort to be as well-behaved as possible. She helped Mum Agnes clean the cottage. She made sure the children got showered and changed before dinner and she cleaned dishes afterwards.

Ivy was healthy enough to go to school. All the children above grade 3 went to an off-site private school that had green skirts for the girls, gray trousers for the boys, and red sweaters for both. Ivy was in standard four for the third time, but nobody except the teachers knew she was repeating. When people asked her how old she was she just lied.

One day when they came home from school, Ivy saw a white pickup truck parked outside the main building. On its side it said "Malaika's Children's Home." Ivy ran inside, hoping that they had brought Maurice to come and visit.

Harvey was in his office. When he saw Ivy, he called her inside and closed the door. There was a fat woman with a scratchy voice sitting across from him. She was very large, her thighs pressed against the chair's arms and the skirt wrapped around her was the size of a bed sheet. Harvey said her name was Mama Seraphina. She spat a great deal as she talked. She took Ivy's hands. She was crying and saying she was so sorry. Ivy was wondering if she meant she was sorry that her parents had died. But then she said that Maurice was now in heaven with the Lord. He had been helping with the wash and he had slipped, hit his head, and passed out with his face in a full wash basin. He had drowned.

Ivy slapped Mama Seraphina. Then she punched her. She heard Harvey yell but she was healthy now and quick. She was out the door and running to the gate before he could get around his desk to catch her.

All she knew just then was that she wanted to run. But halfway down the driveway, she saw the Maasai guards moving to close the gate. She realized she could not escape. Although she was a fighter, she was no match for the Maasai with their spears and swords. She did not care. She decided she would fight them. They killed lions when they were still children. She would make them kill her.

It was an old Maasai with gray hair that tried to stop her. She kicked and punched him but now she was crying uncontrollably. He did not fight back even though she wished he would. He held her still and spoke to her gently. A younger, fat Maasai grabbed her hands. She screamed at them to just kill her. She begged them to. The young one looked to the old one. The old man laughed a bit. She had never been so close to a Maasai before. This close she could tell they smelled of smoke and ash and meat. The old man wrapped his arms around her to hold her, and she felt the fight leaving her, felt herself folding into him, surrendering.

"Pole," the old man said. *"Pole sana."*

Harmony finally got her mother back to their alley where they slept between the green grocer and the mechanic's shop. She was very worried about her because she was still talking nonsense. But Loraine was there and she immediately began taking care of Harmony's mom.

Harmony was hungry, so she told Loraine she would take Michael and beg for food. This was how it continued for days: Harmony begging and her mother laying down and resting. Harmony even tried selling some of their sweets, which she learned she was good at if she found people in nice suits or even *wazungu*. They would give her extra money for a sweet every time. Sometimes she would return to find her mother sitting up, but not often. She knew her mother could walk, but not far, because Harmony could tell she had been urinating just a few steps away from their blankets. The cuts on her mother's head were red, yellow, and wet. The bandages turned brown and gray. One time her mother came back from pooping and had some on her hand but did not notice. Harmony cleaned her off.

Her mother ate though, which Harmony knew was good. She sometimes would eat Harmony's portions of food as well, but Harmony said nothing. One day when Harmony was too tired and weak to get up from her own blankets, her mother was particularly restless. She got up and wandered out of the alley. Harmony was too tired and hungry to follow her. She simply hoped that her mother would bring back food or maybe go back to the church and get more sweets and cigarettes to sell.

A few minute's passed. Harmony started to hear a commotion in the street. Usually she would go see, but she was still too tired. But then a child of one of the hawkers ran into the alley and said,

"Harmony, your mother is dead."

Harmony ran out. The sunlight dazzled her eyes and her head felt light. She saw people gathered around a green and yellow *matatu*. Its windscreen was broken and it was turned a bit sideways. On the street in front of it was her mother. Her head was split open. Her eyes were open and she looked alive but there was blood on the ground under her. Harmony screamed and cried until she felt snot running from her nose into her mouth. People were clicking their tongues. Others touched her and told her they were sorry but she told them to get away.

Then a blue police car stopped and two men got out. They were different men than the ones that had beaten her mother but Harmony was terrified nonetheless.

She got up and ran.

Chapter 21

More Shenanigans, Chess, and Pictures I Should Have Taken

The Kenyan school system does not have summer break (Kenya doesn't even have the corresponding seasons). In place of a three-month break, the kids have April, August, and December off. As volunteer coordinator, these months, thirty solid days crying out for structure, become my busy seasons. I bring in more volunteers from Kenya and all over the world. We have eighteen-hour days and if done well, volunteers, staff, and children are happy and I'm sleep deprived.

These months are when the kids go to the movies and play games (hopscotch, soccer, tag, hide-and-seek) for hours. I introduce projects, inter-cottage competitions and cultural enrichment trips to see traditional African dancing or visit museums. The water park is one of my favorites, partly because it wears the children down, but also for the rickety zip line that runs the length of the property. At its highest, it's six feet off the ground, but my favorite part is the way it brings the participants' ride to an end: a wall. No foam or hay pit, no staff member to catch the kids, just a solid wood wall with a rubber mat added as if an afterthought. It's a death trap that would never be allowed in the litigious US, but in Kenya it's a total go. The kids swing off the platform, kicking and screaming their way down until they collide like crash test dummies with the wall at the end. I offer to catch the kids but they insist I don't. It seems slamming into the wall and getting stunned by the abrupt stop is part of the draw. Even when some of the big kids build up serious momentum and peel off the wall like dead flies, it's only moments before they collect themselves and are off running back to the pool, the slides, or for another go on the zip line of death.

There are casualties from the shenanigans. Namely Lassie, one of the orphanage's guard dogs. She is a border collie, but the resemblance is enough for the children to name her after the iconic dog of American television—after all, I am Peter Parker. But Lassie, the product of centuries of careful breeding and genetic selection, is driven bat-shit crazy trying to herd uncooperative children. The children remain engaged in whatever game they are playing at the time, ignoring the barks and nips from the border collie that is forced by her DNA to fruitlessly attempt to corral the children. They are always too many and they are too fast for her. On a Saturday morning it is not unusual to see her literally spinning in a circle, wide-eyed, tongue flailing, her brain short-circuited by a creature her breeding never prepared her for.

There are things that the kids say as well. A cat lives on the premises that the children call "Pussy." The alpha guard dog is a beautiful Rhodesian ridgeback named Tommy. When he sees Pussy he launches into full hunter mode, chasing her down and snapping at her tail. He never catches her but the one time he gets a piece of her tail in his mouth, the kids come running to me. "Ted, Tommy ate Pussy!"

Tommy and I have a relationship of mutual respect. Unlike the Kenyans who see him as a working dog more than a pet, I play with him. As a result he likes me and one day even shows up at the door of my office. He was trained never to enter any of the buildings but his urge to spread out on the cool cement floor in my company is strong. He turns and backs into my room a step at a time, leading tail first. I imagine in his doggy mind he is hoping that by coming in backwards he will perhaps fool me into thinking he is actually on his way out. I watch him as he moves across the room to the far side where he bumps his backside up against the wall and then lies down on the floor, watching me tentatively. For all his canine cognition, I decide I have to let him stay.

After Randolph dies his skin is so tight over his emaciated body that his teeth—once the heart of his becoming smile—now stick out grotesquely as he lies in his casket. It is a funeral that the staff have a difficult time accepting. Randolph was healthy. He had made it to the age of fourteen. He had all the medications he needed to keep his body sound, his virus in check. Yet all are struggling with the notion that he seemed to give up in his final weeks, he stopped fighting, whereas so many other children fight until the end. Bonava, the chief manager in title but really the father figure to every child at the orphanage, is morose like I have never seen him. The house moms and uncles are quiet and withdrawn, especially David, the soft-spoken house uncle who had cared for Randolph in Cottage Red.

But Monica takes it the worst. I sit with her on the balcony of the volunteer house after the funeral saying little, the two of us staring out at the eucalyptus trees and ponds the next lot over, tropical birds flashing overhead like escaped pieces of a stain-glass window.

"He made a choice," I say. "You were the only one who respected it. That's why he chose you to be with him until the end."

"Doesn't mean I have to like it," she says.

The home was founded as a hospice. In a hospice for children the goal is to keep them happy and comfortable. But now with ARVs the children are living. Those kids that grew up without consequences, with only a "keep them happy for today" mentality, are growing up into spoiled teenagers. I network with other orphanages and bring in counselors that have expertise with teenagers. Teenagers bring a whole host of problems, but as Bonava says, they would rather have teenagers and all their problems, than be losing all the children.

I agree.

The teenage girls are a particular problem. I organize a retreat for them with a few female Kenyan volunteers in their twenties that are good role models. We do community building exercises and all the kum-ba-ya stuff I hated on my own church retreats. The girls regularly point out to me that I don't go to church. A few times I have gone at Miriam's request, only to have her make fun of the way I make a half-hearted sign of the cross in mass.

On the second evening of the retreat, among other exercises, I have the girls take paint and write things they would like to change about themselves on some rocks. This is the second half of an exercise. The first half included painting things they liked about themselves on a clay tile, which will be glazed and put on display at the home. The rocks we will toss off the edge of the Ngong Hills, which the girls do not know we are climbing in the morning.

I walk around inspecting; making sure not too much paint is spilled. Ivy writes on her rock that she hits others. Sofie has written that she is lazy in school. Joyce has written that she is lazy and that sometimes she fibs.

I come down to the end of the line where Miriam is still staring at a blank rock. I had a feeling that she would have difficulty with the exercise, in all seriousness, she is a perfect child. I have never known her to get in trouble or to be anything besides helpful. I sit down next to her. She tells me that she can't think of anything.

"That is ok, because you are a very good young lady. But is there anything about yourself you want to get rid of, improve, or change?"

"I have something," she says coarsely and reaches for the paint. I leave her to work. I check on the other girls. Alexis has written in big red letters that she wants to get rid of her temper.

Elizabeth wants to get rid of her laziness in school. Eventually all the girls are finished and I send them inside to wash their hands.

Miriam is still sitting on the ground finishing the final letter on her rock. I come over and sit next to her. There in yellow capital letters, made wobbly by the surface of the rock, is the one thing Miriam no longer wants herself to be: LONELY.

She looks up at me.

"I did it wrong."

"No, if that is something you want to change," I say, feeling overwhelmed. "That is what you can put. You don't have the same problems as the other girls."

"It is still wrong," she insists as she puts down the paint brush. "The things the other girls wrote. Those are things they can change."

Now she does not look at me. She gets up and says she is going inside to wash her hands.

The first time I meet Oliver he is lying on a bed in the sickroom receiving a transfusion of blood. He has a red knit cap on, threadbare in places, a few of its threads beginning to fray, and a few places where different colored yarn has been used to repair tears in it. The nurse explains to me that Oliver is chronically anemic and the doctors cannot figure out why. As a result he has to be transfused every few months.

The first Harry Potter book is sitting on the chair beside his table. I assume that it belongs to one of the volunteer nurses, but when I pick it up Oliver asks me to read it to him.

"It is yours?" I ask.

"Yes."

"Can you understand it?"

He nods. I begin to read aloud to him. The nurse tells me that the transfusion will take five hours. I agree to stay with Oliver and keep him company. We finish the book about the same time the blood bag has emptied out. I call the nurse over. As she unwraps the tape, the gauze, and finally removes the needle from Oliver's arm, he cries out in pain, slapping his hand to his face and pinching his cheek. But there is discipline in Oliver: the transfused arm remains completely still, almost as if he were paralyzed. It was only when the nurse gives him permission that he pulls the arm up to his chest protectively.

I walk Oliver back to his cottage, Cottage Yellow, where Miriam lives. I suddenly realize that I have noticed him before, but only as the quiet child who is always sick and always wears that red knit cap, even on warm days. I just have never paid him much attention.

Oliver walks back to the cottage slowly, holding tightly onto my hand. I ask him which part of the Harry Potter book was his favorite. He says it is the end where they play chess on a life-size board. I ask him if he knows what chess is. He says yes. Can he play? Yes. I ask him how he learned and he says that his grandfather taught him.

When we reach the cottage Miriam opens the door. She knows what Oliver has been through and tells him *"pole,"* sorry. Then she takes him in her arms and carries him to his bed.

Later that night I ask Mum Amelia about Oliver. She says that he is the smartest child in the cottage, perhaps in the whole home. He can read better than the teenagers, and she feels it is a shame that he is always too sick to go to school. She tells me that he came from a well off family. When he arrived he was notably more polite than the other children. He always said please and thank you. He asked to be excused from the table when he was finished eating. He also had been used to eating with a knife and fork and had to learn how to eat with his fingers.

I ask about his grandfather. He is dead, Amelia says. He brought Oliver to the home because he knew he did not have much time left. It was not long after Oliver arrived that he passed away. But no one has ever told Oliver this. They are afraid it might worsen his condition. But occasionally he still asks why his grandfather never visits him.

I get a chess set for Oliver and play him in a game. After only a few moves I realize that there will be no need to restrain myself—Oliver is as good as any adult I have played. In the end he makes a mistake. I take advantage of it and checkmate him, but I do so telling him how good he is and that I hope he will learn from his mistake.

He does. The next time he plays he beats me. He is a complete gentleman in victory. He does not celebrate, but rather asks me if I would like to play again.

There are days when I cringe when Judith, Sofie's mother calls me. I feel helpless listening to her desperate pleading voice on my phone telling me that the doctor has prescribed an antifungal cream for the infection on her scalp—a cream that we just can't afford. I am reminded of my powerlessness when she calls telling me that she has lived too long with her friend without paying rent and she must find a place of her own. I'm slowly realizing the burden of keeping someone alive who is, in so many ways, living just on the brink.

I was the one who took Judith to a lab to get blood work done. We found out that her CD4 count was sixty-eight—that low, anything could kill her. So I took her to an MSF clinic that provided free antiretrovirals. But first she had to prove that she could keep her appointments for three months. Three long months. During that time she received Bactrim in order to fight off any pneumocystis pneumonia. She kept every single appointment. I never doubted she would.

In the 1990s the then head of USAID infamously said that Africans would never be able to benefit from antiretrovirals since they did not own watches and therefore could not keep track of time. Since then, dozens of studies have shown that in many cases Africans have better rates of adherence to their ARV regimens than their counterparts in the west. One of the most common explanations for this phenomenon is the simple fact that Africans are much more likely to have witnessed the effects of untreated AIDS first hand. They are scared into taking their meds.

In Judith's case she has actually experienced the untreated effects for herself. She does not want to again.

Judith finally starts the ARVs. They give her splitting headaches. She also has to eat with them otherwise the pills make her sick and she vomits them back up. But she cannot always afford food. That means more money from me.

"What do you do with yourself Judith, during the day?" I ask.

"Nothing," she tells me. "I was once a seamstress but I sold my machine for food."

So we go to town and I buy her a sewing machine. I am out of money myself—although I know Judith's perception of me as a *mzungu* is that I am infinitely more wealthy than she. But I am spending my last cents on emails and phone calls home to ask for loans or to call in favors from friends, even with Eve giving me discounts at the internet cafe.

The sewing machine works. Judith begins to bring in some income on her own, even though she still needs infusions of cash from me for clothes and rent. Still I hate the fact that it is not easier to help her, that I don't feel better about things, that I will never be able to say "happily ever after" or let go of Judith completely. I am bound by my promise and although I don't regret it, I marvel at how I could never make it again, could never with my means take on anyone more than Judith.

Over time things do improve. Judith gets a contract with a nearby girls school to make uniforms. She also works there some days as a cleaner and once in a while even plays goalie when the primary classes play soccer.

But how long, I wonder, will this last? I watch Judith and Sofie sit together at the orphanage. Judith still keeps her head covered out of embarrassment for her rashes there—a stubborn reminder to me that she will never be quite healthy. I know that the rashes on her head most likely have spread to the rest of her body, producing scale-like scabs, usually concentrated in the places where skin folds, the armpits, the waist, the crotch. Sofie is on ARVs now as well, since her own CD4 count has plummeted and her viral load spiked. Sofie gets skin infections along her ears, not unlike her mother, and it is these similarities that haunt me and remind me that both Judith and Sofie will die of AIDS. We'll all die though, I've told myself. That is not something exclusive to the mother and daughter sitting before me. So I realize I have bought them not life, but time, nothing else.

When it comes down to it, that is all they really want. It is all any of us deserve.

In Kiswahili there is no gender. So the children are constantly mixing up the gender of their English personal pronouns. It reveals Miriam's progressive stance on gender identity when I am looking for Bonava one afternoon.

"Bonava, she went to the store," she tells me.

"Miriam, Bonava is a man. It's 'He went to the store'."

"*He* can be anything *she* wants to be," she says.

The doctor who visits the orphanage a few times a week to check on the children decides to do a spinal tap on Anika, her almond-shaped eyes close tightly, tears at their corners as they force the needle between her vertebrae and into her spinal column. When the fluid comes out and is dark, one of the nurses tells me, "It's too late."

They treat Anika for meningitis but she does not improve. The biting irony was that just a month ago she was responding so well to antiretroviral treatment that her viral load was nearly undetectable. The Canadian volunteers are gone and I'm left to sit with her during the night. When she is awake because of the pain, time is elastic, stretching out, without end. Analgesics have run low and all we have to make her more comfortable are paracetamol suppositories. They are inadequate and I feel the same: inadequate, unworthy, unqualified, to administer them to Anika. I yearn for the volunteers I know she likes more, but they are already back in Canada. I believe she is in renal failure because what little urine she can pass is dark and tea-colored and after some time, while she makes many efforts to use the bedpan, it remains dry the rest of the night.

The next evening she asks to return to her cottage. Mum Christine wraps her in blankets and carries her to the building that for all intents and purposes is her home. The children sing for her and pray before she leaves. When Mum Christine is done carrying Anika back to the sickroom, I see that she is wiping tears from her eyes. I ask her what is the matter and she says, "When the children ask to go back to the cottage, the end is always near. Anika wants to die there, not the nursing room."

Later that night Anika loses the ability to speak. When I'm not sure whether or not she is coherent I ask her,

"Anika, it's me Ted. Ted D. Bear. *Umshumari*. Do you remember me?"

She nods.

"Am I still stupid?"

161

She nods again, the faintest of grins turning the corner of her mouth upwards.

We make it through the night but in the morning when I've gone back to my room to catch some sleep there is a knock at my door.

"We've lost her," Ruth, the nurse from the sickroom tells me.

I initially feel numb upon hearing it. But then I feel the need to dress in one of my best shirts and go down to say good-bye. The sign on the sickroom door reads "No Admittance," but it swings open without my knocking, Bahati, the orphanage receptionist, is waiting for me on the other side.

What claim do I have on Anika? Really? I lift the sheet that they have covered her with and there is nothing ghastly there, just the same face I had been looking into these past few days and the longest eight hours of my life the night before. It strikes me that with her face so emaciated, her features, the taught skin, the prominent cheek bones, the hollows under the eyes, the lips pulled back over her teeth, she now resembled Randolph.

I feel teary then, but I first ask what happened. Ruth tells me that Anika's breathing became labored. They tried putting her on oxygen but while they were holding the mask to her face she, in Ruth's words, "Left us."

She is in a green dress now with cotton in her nose, ears, and mouth. I think of the pain she had been in and to be back in this body would only bring her more suffering. I am also angry. Angry that now in death there is no one to truly mourn her. The nurses are busy preparing the children's medications. Bahati returns to the front desk. The people closest to Anika in life, the staff, all are paid to take care of her. Granted, I know they love the children, nearly as much as their own, and I know my thoughts are uncharitable, but the loneliness of her orphanhood bears down on me and I'm just spiteful. I write a good-bye letter to her in my room. Apologizing for not being as good a nurse or sweet a person as Monica, the German volunteer, or as cool as the Canadian ones; for erasing her picture on the digital camera, for the time I ripped a Band-Aid off her skin too hard, but also thanking her for making me smile and making a "stupid" guy feel useful. Then I fold it up and seal it to place it in her coffin.

Chapter 22

The Things We Carry

I'm not sure when the turning point came in my recovery. Just like I could not pinpoint where my tip downwards into depression began. I remembered the first impulse I had to kill myself, nearly a year before I was hospitalized. It terrified me, but I learned to live with it, for it only reoccurred in infrequent intervals, even if the intervals became shorter and shorter.

I remember in the hospital the intervals had shortened to nothing so that a broken record of a voice kept replaying in my head, "Justkillyourselfjustkillyourselfjustkillyourself." Again, it was the drugs that blunted this impulse, I'm sure of it. I remember after going twelve hours without the impulse, my psychiatrist said I could be released from Cottage Green to the halfway house. I deferred, waiting until I had not heard the voice for 24 hours before I agreed to leave.

I improved. It was not without setbacks, but in general, the trajectory was upwards. I graduated to being an outpatient at the hospital and then to the point where I only needed to see my psychiatrist once a week.

He was a balding Indian man with rimless glasses like my own. I had disclosed to him, in the worst of my sessions while still in Cottage Green, the crushing guilt, shame, and remorse I had experienced for leaving the children behind. I blamed myself for abandoning them, for not doing more.

"I never even wrote the book I went there to write," I said.

"Why don't you now? You have the time."

He was right, for although I was out of the hospital and working in my old research assistantship, I was still waiting for the next semester to begin in order to resume my classes. I shared with him my concerns and challenges of the past, my litany of stumbling blocks, not the least of which was my own character in my writing.

"I would like to make it more about the children," I told him.

"Why not both? You've certainly done some healthy self-examination in your work with your friends in A.A."

"Even if I wanted to write more about the children, I never had time to chase down all their stories. After a while, I was just too busy working. Writing seemed like a self-indulgent luxury in light of so many urgent needs. Plus, how could I share their stories while respecting their privacy?"

"Improvise."

"I don't want to be Greg Mortenson."

"Don't be. Call it fiction, or metafiction, whatever the New Yorker literary critics are calling it these days. Be Tim O'Brien. Haven't you read *The Things They Carried*?"

I hadn't, but I ordered it on Amazon that afternoon.

He stayed on me about the writing, bringing it up in every session. I shared with him every fear as it came up.

"I don't want to be Jason Russell."

"Jason and Invisible Children have done a lot of good."

"But maybe he is a narcissist."

"You are not a narcissist. That is a professional opinion by the way."

But I had more worries.

"I did not ask the kids for permission. Even if I use their stories in a novel, isn't that a form of exploitation, another white westerner, taking advantage of a vulnerable African kid's story to sell copy?"

He tapped his notebook with his pen. "Why don't you ask them?"

Chapter 23

Kiserian

The next morning, they led Miriam to her new home: Cottage Yellow. It was nicer and larger than her old home, but she had to share it with fourteen other children. She was introduced to her new mother, Mum Amelia, who seemed nice but strict. Miriam was afraid of her and wanted to be good so that Mum Amelia would like her.

Miriam's bed was on the other side of the cottage, where the older girls slept—the younger children, the babies, and toddlers slept on the side with the kitchen, where Mum Amelia's bedroom was. The bunk underneath Miriam's belonged to a girl named Frieda. Frieda was very thin, like Miriam, and had very light skin. She was pretty and told Miriam that they could be friends, which made Miriam very happy. From that day onward, where Frieda went, Miriam followed.

The other children in the home had lost their parents as well. Many of the children were sick. Frieda said they all had *ukimwi,* which was also called *hacheyevee.* Because of *hacheyevee* the older children had to go to a private school, no one wanted them in the public schools. The younger children went to the school at the orphanage. Miriam asked if she would be allowed to go to school. Frieda told her that as long as you were not sick you were supposed to. And if you were not sick you could also play on the playground. It was a huge playground full of sand and swings and plastic toys.

If you were sick, you had to stay in the cottage and if you did not get better you went to the death room. The death room was the one Miriam had gone to when she first arrived, it was where the nurses were. Frieda said they all had to go there if they got a cut or

166

needed special medicine—besides the medicines they took each day in the cottages—but if they were so sick that they were spending nights there, then they would not be coming back.

"Where do the children go?" Miriam asked.

Frieda showed her. She led her to the back of the orphanage where there were a number of graves with flowers growing on them and large white crosses.

"They go to be with Jesus," Frieda said. For a moment Miriam pictured Jesus as a man who lived underground—unearth each grave and at the bottom would be a door leading to his subterranean world.

At night some of the sick children would call out for their mothers. They did not mean Mum Amelia, Mum Christine, Mum Grace, Mum Teresia or any other of the moms of the home. They meant their real mothers. Miriam learned from the other children that if you remembered your real mother too much, you would get sick and die. The children who cried a lot and missed their old homes and were sad were always the ones who went to the death room the soonest and never came back.

On the days that the doctor came to see the children, Miriam would have to pass through the death room to see her. There were often *wazungu* there. They were actually all over the home. They did not dress like the *wazungu* Miriam had seen in Mombasa; they covered up their skin. Frieda called them volunteers. They were actually very nice to Miriam, although they spoke *Kizungu* funny and Kiswahili very badly.

But for the first time in a very long time Miriam felt that she was happy. She tried not to think too much of her mother or father, since that might make her sick, but she and Frieda would draw pictures of their families. Frieda had had two younger sisters, but they were dead. Sometimes when they were drawing pictures of their families, they would shuffle the members so that Miriam and Frieda had the same families and they were sisters.

The best part of the home, however, was the schoolhouse. When Miriam had become well enough, she was allowed to go to school. There were many children there younger than her who could read, but the teacher, Teacher Margaret, told Miriam that she could learn at her own pace. Because Miriam was older, Margaret asked her to do a lot of things to help and to sometimes discipline the other children, which meant picking the children up and taking them to their cottages to get spanked if they were bad. In exchange, Margaret would let Miriam take books back to the cottage with her. Miriam had to make sure that they were books with pictures in case she could not read the words.

Every Sunday the schoolhouse became a church. Bonava would teach them in Sunday school, then a priest, an old fat *mzungu* that had founded the home, would come and say mass. The priest was also Father Christmas, so he loved children, and that was why he had started the home.

It seemed that every other week another child went to the death room and another died. Miriam wondered if it was the *wazungu* ladies killing them, but then why would they cry at the funerals, which were in the schoolhouse?

There were lots of clothes at the home. Miriam had clean clothes every day. The drawers with the clothes in them had many names that had been written on them, then scratched off because those children had died.

It did not take long for Miriam to meet Catherine. Catherine was the big sister to everyone. She had bumps all over her face, like Miriam and many other children. But it did not seem to bother Catherine. She read in church and all the adults loved her. She was always eager to answer Bonava's questions in Sunday school. And if there was an argument on the playground, the children would find Catherine. She would listen then resolve the difference. The only exception was if one child had hit another, which was when Catherine would simply send them to their house mothers, with a reminder:

"Would Jesus want you to hit one another? No, God wants us to love each other."

Miriam and Frieda stuck together. If Frieda felt sick one day, Miriam would say she had a stomachache so they could stay in the cottage together. But one morning Miriam woke up and Frieda's bed was empty. At breakfast she asked where Frieda had gone. Mum Amelia said that during the night she had become ill and they had taken her to the nursing room.

Miriam did not want to eat after that. She did not eat lunch either, but Mum Amelia made her eat dinner. Then Mum Amelia let her sleep in a bed on the little children's side of the cottage, close to her room in case Miriam had nightmares. The next morning Miriam went back to her side of the cottage. Frieda's bed was still empty. She asked Mum Amelia if she could visit Frieda in the sickroom. She said they would go later.

When they finally went they found Frieda in a bed with a needle in her arm connected to a bag of water. There was also a baby that was crying a lot. Miriam greeted Frieda and Frieda made a small smile. She was not in her usual clothes but in a long shirt that opened in the back. She was naked beneath it. Miriam wished she had brought her a picture. Mum Amelia told Frieda to be strong, to take her medicine, and come back to the cottage soon. She nodded.

Miriam did not want to go back to the cottage. She wandered to the front of the home where there were no children and sat down under a tree. After a while, Bonava come out of his office and walked over to her. He asked her if she was sad and if that was why she was sitting alone. She surprised herself by saying,

"I don't want Frieda to die."

"We can't be selfish," Bonava said to her. "If she dies she will be with Jesus in heaven, where she will never be sick again and where she will be happy forever."

It did not seem like the children went to be with Jesus, Miriam said. It seemed like they all got buried behind the schoolhouse. Bonava explained that it was their spirit that went to heaven. Their body was just an imperfect shell.

Miriam felt angry that Frieda could be happy without her, but she did not want to be selfish as Bonava had said. Miriam tried wiping the tears off her face, but they kept falling. Bonava told her she should go make a picture for Frieda, a picture that would show Frieda how much Miriam loved her.

Harmony forgot how long she ran. She simply kept going until she could not take another step. But where she stopped it smelled like a toilet. There were street boys around, so she could not stay. She went a little further. She was on Aga Khan Way. She had been begging here before. She went around the corner and saw the old Kenya buses lumbering away from their stages. She walked to the stage and waited until one bus was pulling away. Then she did what she had seen street boys do—she ran after the bus and leapt on through the back door.

She was afraid that people would tell her to get off, but even though some looked at her, they said nothing. With her back against the stairwell, she buried her face in her arms and cried. She did not know where the bus was going, but soon the tall buildings disappeared and things began turning green all around her. She wondered if she stayed on the bus long enough, would she would reach Kericho?

Soon the road became very bumpy because it was made of dirt. Most of the seats on the bus were now empty. Harmony did not take one because she did not want the tout to see her. He did anyway and asked her where she was going.

She said she was going to Kericho. He laughed at her and told her she was on the wrong bus because this one was going to Kiserian.

That was what she meant, Harmony said.

He left her alone and did not ask her for money. He seemed to feel sorry for her because she had been crying. When they finally reached a town where there were cars and people, he told her she was in Kiserian, so she decided to get off.

Kiserian was a small town. It was dirty as well, with lots of trash in the gutters and lots of dirt swirling about because there was no pavement. There were not very many hawkers but there were large mountains behind the buildings. She was terribly hungry but there was such a lump of sadness in her chest she knew she would not be able to sing for spare change. Instead, when she walked by a hawker's stall with a crate of papayas in it, Harmony took one.

The lady that owned the stall was not far away though, and she screamed "thief." Harmony started to run but a man coming out of shop grabbed her. Harmony remembered what she saw the mob do to the street boy and she began to cry for mercy. She said she was sorry and asked that they please not beat her.

The man that had caught her laughed. The woman who had called her a thief asked her where she was from. Harmony told her she was from Nairobi. She asked where her mother was. Harmony told her she was dead. Her story tumbled out, in gasps, in cries of rage, and ended with her crying so much she was unsure if she could ever stop.

The woman told Harmony she could keep the papaya, then she led her down the street to a hotel. Inside the woman spoke to the chef, who was a woman that was younger than she was, but older than Harmony's mother. They spoke in low voices until the older woman came over to Harmony with a bowl of beans and said,

"My friend Maureen will take care of you. In the meantime, eat."

Chapter 24

Displacement

It's Saturday and we're doing activities with the kids in the schoolhouse. I have the children between the ages of seven and twelve. One of them, Tristan, begins to misbehave, jumping in and out of his seat, distracting the other children, and generally being disruptive enough that I decide to remove him from class. With my preschoolers I often pick them up from their seat and carry them to their cottage where their house moms will put them to bed or sometimes spank them.

I fall into the same routine with Tristan, picking him up and carrying him out. But he is not four years old and before I reach the door, I realized I've bitten off more than I can chew. Tristan fights me every inch of the way, grabbing door frames, poles, flower pots, even the edge of the sidewalk. At nine years old, he is no match for me, but I still have to use more force than is appropriate, as I have put myself in a situation where as the adult, I "have" to prevail. I can't lose, but by using force in the first place, I've lost the moral high ground.

Finally at the front stairs of Cottage Purple, Tristan makes his last stand, locking his fingers down on the pole supporting the portico. Pulling him off is nearly impossible, his body is stretched out, taught and sinewy, his fingers turning white where he has them wrapped around the metal support. I peel them free and wrestle him towards the door. I'm reaching the limit of my patience and I notice the door is ajar. I lift him up and push him against the door to open it. But I've miscalculated. The door only appeared open. It is actually warped and the bowing of the wood gives the illusion that the door is not latched in the frame. My attempt to push the door

open, leaning in with Tristan's body, turns into slamming hii
locked door. He is stunned and I see the fight go out of his ey
While he is recovering from the shock, I realize the cruelty of what
I've done and move to comfort him, but at this point his house mom,
Ivy, opens the door. She is not surprised to see him back.

"Tristan, were you misbehaving?" she asks.

"Yes," he mumbles. I try to tell her that he's already learned
his lesson but she calls him inside and orders him to bed—the
equivalent of time out. My own words catch in my throat. I feel like
I've betrayed him and all the children. While there are rules and
guidelines for disciplining a child for the house moms and uncles,
there are none for the volunteers, since it is assumed we would never
be put into that role. I sit outside thinking about which point I went
too far, what I could have done differently.

I never apologized to Tristan. That is a regret I will hold until
the day I die.

After Anika dies I can't concentrate. I'm angry, depressed,
and snap at the staff, volunteers, and the kids. Small setbacks make
me lose my composure completely. It all builds on me until I realize
that I can go home and get away from it all. I change the return date
on my ticket, tell Bonava I'm leaving "for a few weeks," and after a
day and a half on planes and in the Amsterdam airport, I'm home,
my mother waiting for me at the international gate. I explain to her
why I'm home, but as a seasoned nurse she already understands and
gives me the phone number of a doctor she knows at the hospital
where she teaches.

"You should call and talk with him."

His name is Edmund Pelligrino. He is in his eighties and has
memories from attending to patients in iron lungs while he was a
medical student in the 1940s. He has also written extensively on

medical ethics and end of life care. Between his teaching rounds at Georgetown Hospital, he sits down with me to talk. He's not a large man and reminds me vaguely of Frank Purdue in his old Purdue Chicken Farm commercials, but seated behind his desk he has a gravitas that Mr. Purdue never had. I tell him of my sense of hopelessness, impotence, even rage at the death of the children. "I'm just sick and tired of burying kids," I finally say.

He is quiet for a time, his fingers forming a steeple on his desk. His silence prods me on. "There are so many kids growing sick and then dying. I don't know how to put up with it. I feel so crushed inside when I'm standing next to one of those graves shoveling in dirt on an undersized coffin."

He listens. I notice his fingers are gnarled but strong as he flexes them and lays his hands on his desk. In the gentlest voice possible he says, "I don't mean any offense by this, but your pity is misplaced."

I'm a little stunned. How could that be? I'm working in an orphanage, in Kenya, for children with HIV. I've done more with my pity and compassion for others than most do in a lifetime.

✓ "Yes, but you keep talking about yourself and how you feel sorry, for yourself. You are not the one dying."

I sit back in my chair and stare out through the window. I'm back in the North American cycle of seasons. It's spring and the maple tree outside is covered with red buds of new growth. "I guess you are right," I say.

Dr. Pelligrino, among other things, is a classicist, and he asks me if I remember my Latin from high school. I tell him I do. I also remember it from Georgetown where I took four additional semesters.

"Good," he says. "Think of the roots of the word compassion. *Cum patior*, literally, to suffer with. That is the role of the doctor or nurse attending to the sick and dying, to suffer with them. I tell my med students that they are not truly doctors until they have their first incurable case. It is only then that they learn the difference between healing and curing."

I tell him I'm not sure of the distinction myself.

"Anyone can cure," he says with a wave at his bookcase full of books and teaching awards. "Anyone can throw pills at an infection and cure it. But to heal, that takes a relationship between one human being and another. To heal, to exhibit compassion, to suffer *with* a patient, that is the true role of service whether you are a doctor, a nurse, or nurse's aide as you are serving. You can't cure every infection, but you can heal even up to the point of death, even with a terminal patient."

He smiles and for a moment I'm envious of students who get to study under him. "Stop feeling sorry for yourself. Call your airline. It's time to go back."

A boy has jumped the fence of the orphanage, not out but in. He made a slow but intelligent breach, taking his time to study his target before making an entry. I notice him in the late morning. The lot next to the orphanage belongs to a successful tourism operator who is building a home and office for his business. The work is slow because he is not taking out any loans to finance it, but is instead paying cash as he can. As a result the pond, trees, reeds, and rushes remain in view from the volunteer house while the cinderblock structure slowly takes form alongside.

I notice the boy sitting on a eucalyptus stump, singing and talking to himself, kicking his legs and snapping his fingers, all the while facing the fence marking the property line between the orphanage and the adjacent lot. I don't think much of him—seeing an unaccompanied child in Kenya is not an unusual thing. I simply go on my way.

Later in the afternoon, however, a ladder from the construction site is leaning up against the fence. I notice graffiti on the walls as I walk up the stairs of the volunteer house. Someone has written, "Thank you for not smoking." When I climb to the top of the flight I see the boy sitting on the balcony, alone again, singing. One hand he uses to keep the beat, with the other he twirls a stick of charcoal. His feet are ashen with dust, his shirt and shorts faded and tattered at the edges. His hair is also longer and thicker than most of the children at the orphanage, but it is not a complete unruly mess; he has received haircuts, if infrequently.

He won't look me in the eye and does not seem to know English when I try to speak with him. I ask in Kiswahili where he is from and he points to the lot next door. I introduce myself and ask him his name.

"Patrick," he whispers.

I get Kevin, one of our Kenyan volunteers, who speaks with him in Kiswahili that is more fluent than mine. When Kevin asks him where he is from and he points at the adjacent lot, Kevin does not understand. I do and nod at the ladder leaning against the fence.

I ask him if he is hungry. He nods yes. We take him down to the kitchen. By now its dinner time and we are able to get him a bowl of rice and green grams. It's a huge helping. I look away and back and it seems as if he has finished the entire serving in seconds, cleaning out the bowl completely. I get him water next, again he drains his cup with the efficiency of the parched. At this point one of the nuns comes by and recognizes him.

"Patrick, what are you doing here?" she asks him.

His story slowly comes out. We learn that he is a child in the orphanage's outreach program—so he is HIV+. He lives with relatives but as sometimes happens with orphans inherited by extended family, he does not receive the love, attention, or food that the biological children receive. Our clinic in Kibera, where he goes to receive his antiretrovirals, is one of the few places he feels loved and receives any sort of affection. The sisters are a bright spot of consistency in his life. Somehow he memorized the address of the orphanage from reading paperwork or perhaps glancing at the side of one of our vehicles and made the journey from Kibera to here on foot.

The tone shifts. Sister Tiny—who is called such because she is, well, tiny—scolds Patrick for leaving home and jumping the fence. When Sister Tiny is finished, Kevin takes his time to explain all of his transgressions to him and all the rules Patrick has broken. Patrick sits with his hands in his lap, his head down, saying nothing.

I can't help feeling torn as I stare at the cleaned out bowl on the bench next to him. Could you blame him for coming? Doesn't life with the kind nuns, loving house mums, and the other clean, well-dressed children who have their own playground and school seem preferable to the unsanitary mazes of Kibera, clogged with people, sewage, and ashes from burning trash? To me it feels so arbitrary that our kids have food, shelter, even toys and Patrick does not, because he has "extended family" that he should be with.

On the one hand, the episode illustrates a criticism of orphanages: the "if you build it, they will come" problem. Aside from being expensive, orphanages act as magnets for unwanted children who get dropped off or wander in, their families often concluding that it is better to grow up in institutions with Gameboys and razor scooters than with connections to community and family (also called the lucky-orphan perception). In some cases this might be true, but most critics point out that it is difficult to meet the psycho-social needs of children in an institution, and ours, with its celebrity visitors and donors, is not representative of most orphanages—Malaika with its overcrowded rooms, poor sanitation, and inadequate staff is a better example. Gameboys and razor scooters can't replace the love of a family, yet shiny toys draw more and more unwanted children into what many consider is an unhealthy, unsustainable form of childcare.

But all the debates aside, I feel for Patrick. He spends the night in Cottage Red with the other boys, then is returned to Kibera in the morning.

A colleague at Feed the Children found a baby tossed in a trash pit in Dagoretti. The baby was a boy. His face had been mauled by dogs, the torn flesh covered in an oozing miasma of maggots. The staffers at Feed the Children named the baby Lazarus, in a reference to Lazarus from the Bible who Jesus raised from the dead. They felt that this Lazarus survived his own experience of death. When I meet him in the infirmary of the Abandoned Baby Center, he reaches up to be held by me. I do not pick him up.

Staring at Lazarus and the missing side of his head, my mind struggles to make sense of what appears to be an illusion, like the digital effects in a movie. The dogs tore away his ear, part of his jaw, his cheekbone, just up to the eye socket, sparing the eye but placing it just on the edge of what remains of his face. I stand before Lazarus with the feeling that all rules have been waived.

There is a part of me that searches inside myself for outrage, but I find none. I know the place where Lazarus was found: Dagoretti. To me it is one of the worst slums in Kenya. Kibera is the slum most people think of when they think of slums in Nairobi. Kibera has standing. It is the second or third largest slum in Africa (depending on whom you ask). Aid agencies fall over each other trying to get a foothold there. There were 133 different charities doing work there at last count. As an aid worker you have arrived, passed your trial of fire, whatever—when you have worked in Kibera.

For that reason I avoid it for almost two years.

Then there are other slums, smaller ones, that are forgotten, and because of that, worse off. Dagoretti is one of those. With a slaughterhouse perched on a hill overlooking the slum, Dagoretti has the semblance of a thriving economy. Street boys come there from the city to work and earn five shillings a day to spend on glue, on a movie, or to have taken from them by older street boys. Dagoretti has a particular smell. It comes from the blood that runs down gutters into streams where it mixes with raw sewage. These are the same streams which street boys use to drink and bathe.

It comes to me that I know Lazarus' mother, or at least have known so many like her that by now I can picture her well. She's young and unmarried. In Dagoretti her chances of being HIV+ are about 50/50. She's unemployed, she may be homeless, she likely is addicted to local brew—a mixture of alcohol and just about any other chemicals—paint thinner, insecticides, cleaning chemicals—purveyors decide to toss in. I know despite all these things, all mothers love their children and would not leave a baby in a trash pit unless scared, threatened, high, deranged, or all these things. No one in their right mind would do such a thing, and in Dagoretti, who can be in her right mind? Sure Lazarus' mother failed him, but Dagoretti failed her. I look into Lazarus' face and I can muster no anger, only resignation.

It is night. The children have just finished watching a movie in the schoolhouse and they have scattered back to their cottages. Lights in the bedrooms have gone on as they change into their sleeping clothes and get into bed. Miriam is locking up the schoolhouse. When she finishes she runs up behind me and leaps onto me for a piggyback.

"Yah, mule," she says and makes the unique cackling noise that is her laugh.

I take her around the school once and by the basketball court I look up at the stars and ask her if she knows that she is supposed to make a wish on one each night. She says no. I stop and tell her to pick one.

I wait as she leans back and studies the sky. Her weight shifts as she leans left to right to consider her selection from horizon to horizon.

"Have you picked one yet?"

"Nope."

"Now?"

"Nope."

"How about now?"

"Ok, you can go."

I start walking towards Cottage Yellow. I start to wonder what an HIV+ orphan would wish for, given anything, so I ask.

"Money," she said over my shoulder.

"Money?" I say as I put her down in front of Cottage Yellow. "Why money? Didn't Jesus say it is harder for a rich man—"

"Blah blah blah," she cuts me off with a wave of her hand, then becomes very stern, shaking her finger. "You know what is wrong with all the children in the home."

"I do, but do you?"

"We all have HIV."

"Yes."

"It does not go away."

"No."

"And people, they hate us for it."

"I don't. All the people here don't."

"But many people out there do," she says, waving her hand towards the gate. "I want money so I can take care of the children here. So we can take care of ourselves."

"I guess that is as good a sentiment as any," I say.

Then she comes up to me and slaps my face, somewhere between affectionately and painfully. I'm a little stunned.

"That is so you won't forget," she says.

It is a little before noon. The sun is shining bright on the bougainvillea and the flame tree blossoms. My preschool class is running all about me, but Edison has held back a bit today. For what reason, I don't know, but he wants to hold my hand this morning. I oblige and move at his slow pace down the drive, both of us in the warm embrace of the sun.

I don't have a paying job, I own only four shirts, three pairs of trousers, two pairs of shoes, seven pairs of underwear, a couple of books, and a mobile phone. All of it could fit into a duffle bag with room left over and yet, I am happier than I have ever been in my life.

I get to know more of Eve's family. All of them but her oldest sister, who works for UNICEF, live at home. This includes her three other sisters, May, Chiru, and Chloe, as well as her brother Anthony and even her cousin Maurito, who is practically a brother. It is a two-story brick house. The family has one car which they rarely use. By Kenyan standards they are right in the middle of middle-class.

They are also Kikuyu. Stereotypes can be foolish, but they exist in every culture and every society. The Kikuyu, the dominant tribe in Kenya, are known for being industrious and incredibly stingy with their money. One evening when Chloe arrives home with milk, she announces that she bought it from a Maasai and not a Kikuyu.

"Why would you do that?" I ask, thinking that as a Kikuyu she would want to buy from her fellow tribesmen.

She laughs.

"I don't buy from a Kikuyu if I can help it. I am Kikuyu, I know that we will try to cheat you every time. The Kikuyu sellers water down their milk! The Maasai are honest."

Eve's mother, Nelly, is a police officer. The police are
known for being the most corrupt institution in Kenya, regularly
taking more bribes than any other public officials. It is a topic I
would love to explore with her mother, but not knowing her well I
am uncomfortable bringing it up. That changes quickly though when
Nelly learns that I have been to visit Malaika. She tells me how she
once was called to pick up a dead body, only to find a child hanging
in a tree from her wrists, just clinging to life. She asks me how
Agnes is doing.

The first thing that strikes you about Kibera—as long as you
look beyond the raw sewage—is the vitality of the place. To a great
degree, this is due simply to the density of people within the slum:
there are 1.2 million people in a six-square-kilometer area. That is
more than half the population of Botswana. All those people within
Kibera normally do not sit around idle. They inevitably do
something—they have to, to stay alive.

And with children running and laughing, occasional cars
tumbling along the rutted roads, men chopping wood, pounding
metal, teenage girls fetching water, women selling tomatoes,
avocadoes, tubs of charcoal, electric cords, soap, and shoe polish, the
pervasive feeling is that the place is alive.

People move to Kibera from the countryside because of the
promises of work and opportunity that the city holds. And although
the opportunities are often not as numerous as the inhabitants had
hoped, the people still must get on with the business of living.

After you notice that, you would then definitely notice the
sewage. Once again one might imagine taking half the sewage from
the country of Botswana and depositing it, daily, in a six-square-
kilometer area, then building a development of sticks and mud on
top of it. Water and sanitation is the first and foremost problem in

Kibera. Many teenage girls don't go to school. They spend the day crossing the slum with seventy-pound buckets of water on their backs. Along every road there are ditches of green-gray sewage. Even in narrow walkways where there are only inches between dwellings, one has to share the foot space with such streams of effluence. There are places where the streams have swollen to large puddles or even ponds where houses are simply constructed on stilts and built over top.

These streams must be constantly dredged, otherwise they fill with newspapers, plastic bags, corn cobs, avocado pits, wine bottles, and beer cans. The litter is raked out then left in a pile. Once the ooze covering it has dried, the trash is set alight. Hundreds of these piles of trash are burned each day so that there is often a pungent scent of melting plastic hanging in the air, not to mention ash. Gray ash, the same color as the sewage, covers everything. The roads are almost sandy with it.

Then amid all of this you might find a flowering eucalyptus or flame tree growing up between rusted corrugated tin roofs. Why such trees are not chopped down for firewood, when so many other trees have been, I cannot guess.

In aerial photos of Kibera those tin roofs look like a log jam, no space between and no order whatsoever. From above one can't help noticing the housing subdivision that has sprung up beside the log jam. These homes, in great contrast, are white and as neatly spaced as vertebrae on a spine. The contrast is striking, but the subdivision homes seem boring and dull in comparison.

Underneath the corrugated tin roofs, it is interesting to see how similar houses in Kibera are to homes in the countryside. Here they are still made of mud and sticks—those that have traveled from rural regions often only know one way to build a house. The difference is simply the closeness between them. It can be pitch black in many homes since the next house is so close that any sunlight is blocked from the windows.

183

But unlike the rural regions, in Kibera there are movies. Small shacks and huts have chalkboards beside their doors reading: *"Shaq in Steel,* 8:30; *Jackie Chan: Boat to Shanghai,* 10:30; *A Night to Remember,* 4:30;"* (the last of these being pornography). The sound on the movies is turned up in order to advertise to passersby. That noise mixes with the noise of radios playing Celine Dion or Phil Collins. All this powered by electricity that is stolen by jerry-rigged wires from the power lines above.

The power lines are one of the few signs of municipal services. The waterlines are the other. There is a network of fourteen or so quarter-inch pipes that run alongside one another through the slum. All are empty though. The girls that step over them with their buckets collect water from one of the few pumps that pump it from underground.

Then there are the train tracks. As many as five trains a day pass through Kibera, on the same line, the lunatic line, that was built by the British in an effort to make central Africa and Lake Victoria more accessible to trade. The line was supposed to go all the way to Uganda but was cut short at the shore of Lake Victoria as a result of unforeseen expenses and difficulties (including the man-eating lions of Tsavo).

The residents give the tracks only what space is necessary for the running of the trains (sometimes not even that much) and build their houses right up to the edge. Most of the time, the residents ignore the tracks, only paying them heed when a train is grinding past, at which time huge crowds of people build up on either side of the countless walkways that crisscross the rails. In places the steel ties are stolen and used as bridges over refuse streams. Near the western edge of Kibera, a train will pass a clearing where tarps lay covered with drying millet—a key ingredient of local brew, the cheapest and quickest way to get drunk in the slum.

Amid all this are flies. They are pervasive, flying from the shit underfoot directly to the food being sold in kiosks. They land on crippled children and old men and women that cannot move to swat them. There are rats and there are also cats; both drink from the contaminated streams. And there are children. Children dressed in crisp-looking school uniforms, children in tattered clothes, and children in nothing. The youngest ones become covered in the gray ash if they are not supervised, which they often are not. The children can navigate the passageways and alleys of Kibera better than any adult. The paths between houses are packed down into hard earth by the passing of their feet.

This is Kibera. This is where Tabitha is from.

Chapter 25

Something

I wrote to the kids. After ten years they were hardly kids anymore. Over the years they had friended me on Facebook, but I had been leery of being too close to them, as if I were afraid of the loss it might lead to, or afraid that I would simply miss them.

I shared my thoughts of writing a book. Emphatically each one told me I should write it, but not for the reasons I imagined. Not for them, not even for other kids in similar circumstances, but, "for the people who live there in America who can't afford to come to Kenya, so they can know what our lives are like."

They felt that we in the rich, privileged west needed to be more educated—enlightened.

I still debated. I wavered. I was scared. Scared it could all go wrong, scared of the memories and nihilism that had overtaken me, scared of falling into some trap of self-aggrandizement. At the same time I was afraid it would seem like just another self-indulgent solipsistic examination of white guilt—a rambling documentation of what was ultimately just a case of white fragility. I said as much to my psychiatrist again but he just shrugged, impatient with me now. "Anyone ever tell you before that you over-intellectualize things?"

"Maybe."

He let out a sigh, frowned and nodded at the same time as if I had exposed myself in some indisputable way. "You know my opinion: write it," he said. "It will be good for you. It can help you get over the trauma of watching children die. You lost meaning and purpose after witnessing what you did at the orphanage. Maybe, this is a way of getting it back." He waved his pen at me. "And now you have the kids telling you to write it. They trust you. That means something."

Chapter 26

Pigs and People

Maureen's house was nice even though it was a long *matatu* ride away and up a steep hill. The best part was that it had a view of Kiseran below which Harmony thought was very beautiful. Maureen said that on clear days you could see Nairobi. Inside Maureen's yard she had lots of chickens and even a dog. The dog came over to Harmony, barked at her and sniffed her. Harmony was very afraid but Maureen said that as long as he was wagging his tail she should not be worried.

The inside of the house was large and had four rooms, five if Harmony counted the pantry, six if she counted the shower and toilet, but they were partially outside so it was hard to include them. Maureen showed Harmony where her room was and then where Harmony would sleep. The bed in Harmony's room was smaller and there was also a crib beside it. Harmony asked Maureen if she had her own children. She said she once had a son but he had died. Now she felt that God had called her to take care of orphaned children. Harmony asked where the other ones were. Maureen said that she did not have enough money to take care of them forever, but kept them a little while until she could find them more permanent homes.

Harmony told her she wanted to stay with her because she was nice and her house was large.

Maureen next took Harmony to the shower where she made her wash with soap and water. Afterwards she found some clothes for her and threw away her old clothes. Harmony liked her new clothes; they were bright, they were not torn, and they smelled clean.

Harmony liked staying with Maureen. She made food often for Harmony and she even took her to school one day. Harmony was not able to read very much, but the headmaster said she could start next term. Some Sundays they even got dressed up and went to church together, which Harmony enjoyed because she loved to sing and the women all told her she had a beautiful voice.

Maureen often asked about Harmony's mother. Harmony told her everything. Maureen's friend was a social worker and she came and listened to Harmony as well. She asked a lot of hard questions like, what was Harmony's mother's name—Charity. What was her mother's surname? Harmony did not know. What was Harmony's birthday? She did not know. Where was her mother from? Kericho. Did she still have family there? Yes, but Harmony did not remember the name of her grandmother and she certainly did not tell them about her father. She said she simply had never known him or where he was from.

Harmony would play with the children that lived nearby. Most of the children Harmony's age were in school during the day, so she played with little boys and girls. She would pretend to be their mother and they would make *chipatis* and *oogali* out of mud.

Harmony also liked Maureen's friends. She had many but the ones that come over the most were John and Steven. They would come over at night and drink beer with Maureen and sometimes her friend Evette. This drinking was fun because Maureen and her friends would listen to music and dance with Harmony. Harmony would sing for them and they would cheer and clap. Often they would stay all night, which meant that Harmony would have to sleep in bed with Maureen and Evette while John and Steven slept in her bed—which she did not like because the next day it would stink like them.

One night when it was just Maureen, John, and Steven, Maureen drank so much she could not talk straight. She kept telling Harmony how sad she was that she lost her son, but that she loved Harmony and would take care of her. She even offered her some beer, which Harmony did not like the taste of, but then Maureen said she should never drink it anyway. Maureen got very tired then and carried Harmony into her bedroom to go to sleep.

Later Harmony woke. She was in her room and John and Steven were over her. They were pulling her trousers off so that she was naked. She twisted to cover herself but they suddenly became forceful. John held down her arms and Steven pressed her to the bed with one hand on her belly. With his other hand he unzipped his trousers.

Then Harmony saw his penis. It was not like the little finger she had seen on the naked boys running around the village. It was upside down and stiff like a corn cob. So stiff it was like a club and Steven took it and tried to stab it between Harmony's legs. She cried out that he was killing her but John covered her mouth. She bit him and felt flesh tear away like she was ripping undercooked chicken meat off the bone. Then something struck her face. She saw a bright light but did not remember much after that.

Miriam did not know what to draw for Frieda. She thought of making a picture of their families, but she knew that it was not good to think too much about their families at a time like this. She decided to make a picture of Jesus instead, that way Miriam could also show Jesus that if Frieda died, she would not be jealous that Frieda was with Jesus and not her.

When she finished, she took the picture to the death room, but when she entered she saw that Frieda was pooping in a white pot. Miriam went back to the cottage. It was dinnertime, which meant there would not be another opportunity to visit Frieda that day.

She went the first thing the next morning, even before breakfast. She showed Frieda the picture, but she did not seem very happy. The nurse told Miriam she should go to school. After school that day Mum Amelia told Miriam that the two of them were going to visit Frieda in order to say good-bye.

Miriam knew by now what this meant. She began to cry but Mum Amelia told her she will not be allowed to see Frieda if she cried, so she did her best to stop. When they went to the death room, they found Catherine beside Frieda's bed. Frieda was not moving but she was breathing quickly then slowly, then quickly again, like Miriam's father did. Catherine was praying. Miriam hoped that her picture of Jesus was helping Frieda. No one said anything. Finally when they turned to go, Mum Amelia told Frieda that she was a good girl and that they all loved her very much.

Frieda died that night.

Tabitha lived in a world of magic. Other children went to school. Tabitha did not. She would explore Kibera's back alleys with other children. Sometimes her mother would send Tabitha away to go play with her friend Flo. This happened most often when men came to visit her mother. If Flo was not around, Tabitha would go to Dorris' house. Dorris lived down in the same alleyway as the boy with the crippled legs. This boy moved about on his hands and knees. His skin was gray because he did not bathe. His family fed him out of a dish on the ground like a dog and they did not allow him beyond the doorway of their house because he was cursed.

As a rule, when she was alone, Tabitha did not venture too far down back alleyways. But the one day she did she rounded a corner and came upon the crippled boy pulling himself along the ground. Tabitha screamed; so did the boy. Then Tabitha ran in the opposite direction. She was afraid his curse would spread to her and her legs would become twisted as well.

Living in the slum could be dangerous. Tabitha knew she had to be inside by dark every evening because there were men on the streets that drank, as well as ghosts. The ghosts were often the ghosts of people who died in their houses or of people killed on the train tracks.

Tabitha remembered the last man that had been run over by the train. The train whistle had been blown particularly long that morning. But apparently the man still had not heard the train coming—he may have been sleeping deeply because he had been drinking local brew.

It was Flo that had come to get Tabitha and they ran up to the tracks together where there were dozens of people gathered. The man's body parts were scattered over several feet, so the crowd of people was long and spread down along the train tracks. His chest and head were still in the place he had been laying, but his arms and his legs were farther down. His hand had gone the farthest. Flo counted thirteen ties between his body and his hand. It was good Flo counted because Tabitha did not know her numbers.

At one point a street boy reached between the legs of the people gathered and stole the dead man's hand. Tabitha and Flo knew why he had done this—street boys would do anything for money, even work for witch doctors. If a witch doctor was given this hand, he could bury it and then the ghost of the man would come back to find it. Then the witch doctor could enslave the ghost and make him kill the people he did not like. As long as the ghost never found his hand, he would be bound in servitude; however, if he did find his hand he would surely kill the witch doctor.

Harmony could not walk for a long time after that night. It also hurt to go to the toilet. A few days later Maureen took Harmony to a clinic to see the doctor. Harmony did not want to show him where it hurt but Maureen made her. After that she had to stay in the clinic overnight for a long time.

Maureen told her that she should never tell anyone about what happened or else Harmony could get hurt very badly. Harmony promised she would keep it a secret.

Maureen was funny after that. She still cooked for Harmony but she was not as nice as she used to be. Before she would talk to Harmony while she cooked, but now she was silent. When Evette came over, Maureen would send Harmony to her room or tell her to go outside and play.

She did not see John or Steven.

Then one morning Maureen woke Harmony up very early. It was a Sunday and Harmony thought that maybe they were going to church, but they did not put on their church clothes.

Maureen was walking very fast. Harmony followed her down the hill until they came to the matatu stage. There was a crowd gathered there around something in the road. Maureen turned to Harmony and told her that she wanted her to look very closely at the man on the ground.

Harmony said she would. She followed Maureen around to the far side of the crowd. There were many people and many children too. There was even a camera crew there from Kenya Television Network (KTN). They had their camera pointed at the man who was on the ground.

Harmony knew he was dead. There was lots of blood all over him and his jacket. It was because his neck had been chopped open with a *panga*. Maureen pushed Harmony closer and told her to look at his face. She went around and did.

It was Steven. Harmony felt sick and scared at the same time. She went back to Maureen.

"He is dead?"

"Yes," Maureen said.

Harmony looked back at him. She recognized his green jacket now, but had not before because it was covered in so much blood. Because she knew he was dead she was not as afraid so she moved closer. He was on his belly, so she could not see his penis again. She looked at his neck. It was red and white on the inside. She realized it looked much like the insides of pigs and goats when they were slaughtered and hung in the windows of the butcher shops.

Maureen was calling her, so Harmony took one last look and followed. Her mind was suddenly spinning now that she knew that, on the inside, people and animals looked the same.

Chapter 27

Cottage Blue

Maina was one of the Maasai guards at the home. Unlike many of the other guards, who are middle-aged with wives and children, Maina is young and still single, so there is a certain affinity we share for one another, which manifests as the occasional cup of tea we share together wherein I fumble over my Kiswahili and he politely tells me I'm improving.

One Saturday he watched two cars pull up to the gate. One of them parked just outside while the other continued down the drive. Two men got out of the car that had stopped outside the gate and walked up to Maina. They made an effort to be very friendly, greeting Maina enthusiastically and then striking up a conversation by asking abundant questions about the Maasai.

The Maasai were one of the few tribes in East Africa to still cling tightly to their traditional ways. One could see them walking the city streets of Nairobi, the men in their red robes, the women in colorful blue, orange, pink, or any other bright color they might choose. But most Maasai still lived a semi-nomadic existence in the farther reaches of the country. As a Maasai living in Nairobi, Maina was used to the feeling of being a foreigner in his own country. He was patient about answering questions regarding his tribe's customs. When the men asked about the holes in his ears, he explained to them that he was actually Samburu, a tribe closely related to the Maasai, but with a slightly different dialect and unique customs. Maina explained that the Maasai actually made the holes in their earlobes much larger, as opposed to the Samburu who kept them smaller.

The men appeared very interested and had already maintained their interest for longer than most usually did. Maina was already wondering if they were going to ask him for a favor of some sort when the phone in the guardhouse rang. He turned his back on the men and picked up the receiver. An urgent voice told him to close the gate, that a car was leaving and the people inside had kidnapped Hezekiah, a four-year-old from Cottage Yellow.

Maina turned but one of the men was waiting for him with a pistol pointed at his chest. He told Maina that if he interfered, he would kill him.

Hezekiah had been at the home for a few months. He was in a unique position. Both his parents had died within a short time span. His father was Muslim, his mother Christian. Hezekiah was their only child and after their deaths inherited a substantial amount of land, animals, and money. But neither parent had left a will. The paternal side and maternal side had been fighting over him since. The dispute was further complicated by the fact that the paternal side belonged to a sect of Islam that did not believe in any medical treatment. Hezekiah was kept alive by his medical treatment since he was on antiretroviral therapy, which the maternal side would continue if they had custody. The paternal side would not, a certain death sentence.

While they battled things out in court, Hezekiah had been sent to the home, temporarily, until the dispute was settled.

But now, believing that possession was nine tenths of the law, Maina realized that one of the sides was kidnapping Hezekiah. His heart sank as he watched the car come down the drive. There were three passengers in it, a driver and two women in back. They were driving very fast. The man without a gun opened the gate for them to pass through. Watching the car pull through the gate was torture. Maina knew he was Hezekiah's last chance and if the car reached the road they would never see him again.

The man that had opened the gate ran to his car and started it. There was a good deal of traffic on the road and both cars had to wait for it to clear. The man holding the gun looked over his shoulder to see if the car with Hezekiah had pulled onto the road yet. Maina seized his chance.

He swung his arm and struck the gun as hard as he could. It went flying out of the man's hand. Instead of running after it, since Maina did not even know how to use it, he reached for his bow and quiver of arrows—each one had a poison tip. The man abandoned his gun, leapt in the waiting car and screamed at his companion to drive. They pulled out into traffic suddenly, cutting off the car with Hezekiah.

Maina ran to the driver's side of the car with Hezekiah. The window was down and he aimed the arrow at the driver's neck. The women began screaming. Maina asked where the child was, but they said they did not know what he was talking about. Maina wanted to kill the driver, but he knew he could not. If he did, their families would be drawn into a blood feud. Instead, Maina leaned closer, then reached inside, pulled the keys from the ignition and threw them away as far as he could.

The women got out, incensed. They said many derogatory things about him being a backwards Maasai. They opened the trunk and showed him that it was empty. All this time Maina noticed the driver did not move. Maina told him to get out of the car. He refused and said he did not need to take orders from a goat herder. Just then Maina heard Hezekiah call for help.

Something inside Maina broke just then. He rushed to the car door and pulled it open. Maina was short and stout for a Maasai. Most were tall and lean. Maina was barely five feet. The man in the car was over six feet but he had long locks. Maina took the man's hair in his fists and yanked him from the car. He came out screaming. Maina made sure to pull the hair down low so the man fell to the ground.

He looked into the car. Pressed into the seat where the man had been sitting was Hezekiah.

Maina grabbed him in his arms, ran to the far side of the car, putting it between him and the driver. Then he drew his sword. It held the women at bay while he inched towards the gate. By that time Bonava, the moms, and the rest of the staff (including me) were running down the drive. Once he was beyond the gate, Maina began running towards them. He did not stop when he reached them however, he just kept running, past the offices, the nursing room, the cottages, and the schoolhouse, all the way to the farthest corner of the home, the cemetery where the children were buried. There he waited, with his sword drawn, and Hezekiah in his arms, until Bonava came and told him it was safe.

I meet Nea (Kiswahili for radiant, shimmering) while on a visit to a school on top of the Ngong Hills. It has a spectacular view of the lush green countryside that surrounds Nairobi to the east and the parched rift valley to the west. The spot on the hills is called Corner Baridi (Cold Corner) for the cold wind that is always whipping the ridge here. On rainy days with low clouds the place feels more like the Scottish Highlands than Kenya.

The school is a boarding school and a sort of home for children with nowhere else to go. It is one of the few places deaf children can attend and learn sign language. Most of the children who board there go home on breaks but a few remain who are orphans that have been abandoned. One of these is an eleven-year-old Maasai girl fleeing marriage to an older man. Another is Nea. She is not deaf but she is HIV+ and when I meet her she is sick and withdrawn, walking from the cottage where she shares a bed with other children to the schoolhouse with all the lethargy of a child with fever. She is tiny for her age, nine, but has a long face and wide cheekbones and light eyes—it's easy to see how she earned the name "Radiant." I learn that both her parents died of HIV and she was living with her grandmother until she passed away. On this first meeting she is bundled in a winter jacket, scarf, and hat, standing in unpolished shoes on the front steps of her cottage, trying to negotiate the wide mud puddle that encircles it.

The school proprietor's name is Josiah. He is a gracious bear of a man with a wide smile and an easy way with children. He studied sign language on scholarship in the US before returning to establish this school. He is nearly always dressed in a suit and tie and lives on the campus in a furnished home. His college-aged children are also well-educated and attending local universities. They can sometimes be seen walking about the campus with their MP3 players and mobile phones.

Josiah and his family's comfort makes some visitors, including myself, uncomfortable. This is due to the great contrast between Josiah and his family's quarters and the spartan, crowded, unsanitary conditions of the children. At Malaika, Mama Seraphina lives in the same conditions as all her children. Josiah does not. While the children sleep three to a bunk bed with tattered blankets and dirty floors, Josiah's living room is well-lit, furnished with comfortable couches, and even doilies on the end tables. The pig sty, with all its accompanying stench and filth, is adjacent to the children's sleeping quarters and the smell pervades the bedroom. There is no place to study in the children's cottage; it is filled floor to ceiling with bunk beds, the space between them barely wide enough to fit an adult. The school itself is typical for a Kenyan school—bare rooms made of cinderblock, corrugated tin roof, old desks that seat two to three children at a time. Chalkboards sit on the floor and lean against the wall.

So as I sit with Josiah and sip tea, I am of two minds. By Kenyan standards, his school and living quarters for the children are adequate, even luxurious compared to facilities in rural areas. They hardly meet the standards of Rainbow, which is an unfair comparison since Rainbow is a very different institution. Yet the contrast between Josiah's comfortable home and the school and sleeping cottages is stark and sears itself in one's mind.

We sit on Josiah's couches and discuss Nea.

"She is an orphan," he says. "And HIV positive, her health is not good."

Of course not, I think, she is sleeping in a freezing cold shed that smells of urine and pig shit on a mountaintop where the wind never stops blowing.

"She has had a cough for so very long," Josiah adds.

I have the distinct impression that Josiah wants me to take Nea off his hands. She is too much for him to handle, a burden, and there is no one to pay for her. Unfortunately Rainbow is full at the moment. Instead I enroll Nea in our outreach program so she can receive drugs and check-ups. I give Josiah some money for gas.

"Please bring her by our nursing room this weekend. We'll get her checked out."

Josiah promises he will.

Oliver is in the nursing room for days on end now. I make sure he has enough books to read. He has finished the first four *Harry Potters*. When incoming foreign volunteers ask what they might bring to the orphanage, I add to their list of medical supplies the fifth *Harry Potter* book. In the meantime, Oliver burns through *The Chronicles of Narnia*.

I ask Amelia if she is worried that Oliver is in the nursing room so often now. She says that he has been sicker in the past and that he tends to bounce back. His CD4 count (white blood cells) is five (healthy is 1300 to 1400). The clinical definition of AIDS includes a count lower than 300). Oliver's count has been five or lower for a long time, she says, and still he persists. She is right. In a few days he returns to the cottage.

I realize I am completely besotted with Eve: her poise, her equanimity, her sense of humor, her statuesque figure. I take her on dates with the kids, Miriam, Josephine, Tabitha. We go to movies and to Nando's, like a family assembled from spare parts. Once while Eve waits in line, leaning up against the window of a store, I see the entire street as a backdrop to her beauty, as if she is a Goddess and the entire world her dream. One night when it's just the two of us, after I make her dinner, we kiss. I'm so nervous my hands are shaking.

"It's ok," she says. "Your first black kiss?"

"Yes, but I didn't kiss you because you are black."

"Good, cause I didn't kiss you because you were white."

But it's over before it started. I start trying to imagine a life with her back home and once while on a date in a coffeehouse, I ask her if she would move back to the States with me. She becomes quiet and downcast, looking down into her cup of coffee. "It's not my favorite place, Ted."

"The US? But you've never been. How do you know you wouldn't like it?"

"It's not that I hate your home," she said, reaching across the table to touch my hand. "It's just that I love mine. I want to die in Africa, you see. I love it here."

Sadly I understood. I tried to take it as a compliment, so many beautiful Kenyan women would date average looking guys like myself in hopes of a green card and citizenship, but Eve dated me because she liked me, just not enough to leave her country permanently. It betrays my own arrogance in thinking she would immediately want to live in a place away from her family, away from her business, away from this place where the air smells *just so* after the rain, where she tells me even the sunlight has a smell (like drying wood, she insists), while I had not even considered staying for her sake.

I do my best to take her rejection in stride. It's only back in my room later that I find myself crying.

I console myself with the daily drama of the orphanage. As it turns out, the Maasai guards, although brave as warriors, are not skilled at dispute resolution. I learn that Bonava is often called in to mediate bickering among them ranging from whose turn it is to make tea to who was sleeping on the job. I also learn that the children are convinced there is an invisible killer chicken stalking the back garden although after numerous investigations we are not able to find much evidence except for chicken droppings. After a lengthy debate, only some of which I am able to follow for the children conduct it in rapid Kiswahili, it is decided that an invisible chicken would indeed leave behind only invisible droppings, which means (a) the droppings that had been found must have been from regular (read: not killer) chickens and (b) if there is an invisible killer chicken that is leaving invisible killer chicken feces in its wake, we all could be standing in them and wouldn't even know it. As a result, the search is called off while the boys of Cottages Red vow to "Invisible-Killer-Chicken-Proof" their cottages. This takes the form of some traditional charms—feathers, beads, and tiny bones—set on the windowsills along with a number of action figures including Spiderman and the Hulk.

And then there is the endless quest to find Cottage Blue—the missing cottage, since the other colors of the rainbow are accounted for in Red, Orange, Yellow, Green, and Purple cottages. This mystery is a source of great speculation among the children, even though on this particular day when I join the search I make the mistake of questioning whether or not Cottage Blue is where the invisible killer chicken lives, which leads the children to abandoning the search for at least the rest of the afternoon.

Lialabell, one of the children I sometimes read to in the school, came over during story time and tried to sit on my lap. This was not unusual, but the fact that she tries to do so with her legs spread is strange to me. She is eight. She is the only child that does this and it does not seem right to me. Lialabell also asks a lot of questions about what boys have "down there" and what girls have "down there." The other kids her age do not ask these questions.

I think about what a psychologist friend of mine once said: "Sexuality is a box that is always in us that is not supposed to be opened too quickly or too early. If it is, through abuse, the therapist tries to close it as best as he or she can."

I have a hunch that Lialabell has been abused, but her house mum has no idea. After a process of approval and consulting with Rainbow's social worker, I get permission and go through Lialabell's file. After the admissions form I find the following:

Lialabell Kidenda. From Western Province. Age 3. Admitted after being defiled by father. Mother deceased from AIDS related causes. Three siblings. Father was convicted and sentenced to prison. Child could not walk after defilement. Underwent surgeries to correct tearing and other damage. Lialabell is HIV+.

I stop reading. Wondering about the horror of what I just read. It is hard for me to imagine the mind of a serial child abuser, those men who kidnap, rape, and murder children, even their own. Was that Lialabell's father? Or could this have been an uneducated man, whose wife had died of AIDS, who was becoming ill himself, then someone tells him that he can lose the disease by having sex with a virgin . . . but the only virgin around is his daughter. Does he try to justify it by saying she won't remember or that this is the only way he might live so he can care for her? Judith had been ready to kill her daughter Sofie before letting her live on the streets. Would raping your daughter be a lesser evil for both of you to live? Is there any explanation for such evil? How can we prevent it? Is it wrong to even try to imagine what led him to it, how he rationalized it, even if in effort to see that it never happens again? Yet, trying to take a step into his thought process makes me feel cold all over.

I'll never know what motivated Lialabell's father. He died of AIDS in prison.

The dispute between Hezekiah's families does not resolve. We learn that it was the paternal side that tried to kidnap him. To all of our frustration, they still insist on visiting rights. When we object they threaten to sue the home.

After each visit from some of the same people that tried to kidnap him, Hezekiah has nightmares and wets the bed. Mum Amelia is usually so angry she remains in her room, afraid that if she came out she would say something that would get somebody hurt.

The family sits in front of the cottage with Hezekiah. I usually make no secret of the fact that I am watching them. They speak to Hezekiah in Kikuyu, which only a few of the children understand. Mum Amelia is Luhya and does not. Oliver and Miriam do however, so I strategically place the two of them nearby with books that they pretend to read. I have to give Oliver children's books because no one who did not know him would ever believe that he was reading *The Lord of the Rings*. Miriam can recall the gist of any conversation and can alert me if anything is amiss. Oliver can repeat word for word, so between the two of them I have an effective monitoring system.

A few months later, however, Hezekiah begins to suffer from incapacitating headaches. They take him to the nursing room. He is diagnosed with encephalitis. He is treated aggressively, but nonetheless, passes away three days later. When the vehicle leaves, bearing his body away to the morgue, Maina is the last one standing at the gate. He stares down the empty road long after the car has gone.

The families even argue over who will bury Hezekiah. His body languishes in the morgue for months until it finally, simply, disappears.

I am at the market in Karen, buying tomatoes with a volunteer nurse, John, when someone forcefully shoves me aside. As I bend down to retrieve the tomatoes I dropped, I see a street boy running away. He is dressed in ragged clothes and carrying a bunch of bananas in the crook of his arm. Immediately voices are raised all around me.

"*Mwizi! Mwizi!*"

Thief.

Two security guards quickly follow, knocking me and John out of the way. Once he is clear of the market stalls, one guard stops, raises his rifle, and fires two shots.

I watch as the street boy collapses in the middle of the road. People stop on the roadside, startled. John and I are of the first to reach him. He is face down, his eyes wide open. He is panting hard. There is a scattering of pink brain matter on the road before him. The bullet struck him high on his head. His brain stem is still intact, so his body is still struggling to survive even while bright red arterial blood is spreading out all around him—already it has reached the bananas that have fallen alongside.

John moves to take his backpack off and administer first aid, but the officers have come up now. They motion with their rifles for us to clear away. I don't understand. I try to explain that we are trying to help him, that he is not dead.

The officers say nothing. Their eyes are invisible to me behind their sunglasses. If they were not armed I would rip the glasses from their faces. Finally, probably sensing that I am endangering myself, a soft-spoken Kenyan man wearing a Roman collar pulls me aside. He speaks in measured, almost apologetic tones. "They are waiting for him to die," he says to me. "If he lives they must take him to the hospital and that will require them to do a great deal a paperwork. If he dies it will be less work for them."

I take another look at the boy. The "who" of him is already gone, spread out in the brain matter at my feet. The "what" of him is all that remains, and not even that for much longer, I realize, as the people that have gathered take steps back to avoid the growing puddle of red, broken only by the island of yellow that is the bunch of bananas.

Oliver is sitting in the sun wearing his cap. It has faded to a lighter, less bold shade of red. He feels too ill to go to church in the schoolhouse. Everyone is there but us. It is Easter. Last night a record amount of rain fell, flooding streets, fields, houses, and slums. Rumor around the home is that people have drowned in Kibera. I picture women and men trapped in their shanty houses, pounding at the metal roofs that won't give while brown water, carrying all the trash and excrement of the slum, floods in around them. I'm sure they cried for help while they still had air. Or maybe no shanties have been washed away at all. Perhaps the people who have drowned were drunks, who passed out from local brew too close to the stream running through the slum or perhaps they were street boys or small children.

I find it difficult to reconcile those images with the image I have before me of the Rainbow children in their finest clothes dancing and singing to Jesus. It seems such a violation that two such disparate tableaux could exist on the same day, in the same country, in the same hour, or in the same world at all.

But I suppose it happens every day, not just on Easter.

One of the older children is reading the gospel. Mary Magdalene has just heard from the angel that Jesus is not in the tomb. I turn to Oliver and ask him if he is afraid of dying.

"No," he says. I ask him why.

"I know my mother will be waiting for me."

Josiah makes good on his promise and brings Nea to our nursing room for check-ups and refills of her medications on a regular basis. Our doctor, an unassuming Ugandan woman with a gentle demeanor that puts the children at ease, tells me that Nea is sick but stable. "The environment where she stays does not seem good," she tells me. I can only nod my head.

Nea herself hugs me when she sees me. Somehow she has connected me with the improvement in her circumstances—as marginal as they may be. I make sure she has time to play on the swings on the playground, even enduring a long and boring conversation with Josiah in order to delay him from leaving and giving her more time to play. It's warmer and sunnier here in Karen than up at Corner Biradi, and seeing Nea smile and play with other children strengthens my resolve to find a more suitable home for her.

After I see the street boy shot to death in Karen, I go through bouts of irritability and frustration. What good is anything we do, when people can turn on one another so easily? When the answer, to those with so little, to those suffering from injustice, deprivation, oppression, is not to help one another but to hurt?

Then again, was I so naïve as to think otherwise? To think of the world in such simple binaries of good-bad, victim-victimizer, oppressed-oppressor? Had I not already learned that nothing was as simple as I wanted? And if the problems were complex, so too would be the answers.

It was just that I didn't want them to be.

Angry and cross, I take a bus into town to run a few errands. While walking down Aga Khan Way a street girl, no more than seven years old, with a toddler on her back, comes up beside me begging for bread. Usually I ignore street children, while keeping a wary eye on them as well as a hand on my wallet. I think of it as benign neglect. I also feel justified since I am in Kenya to help children. I can ignore these children with a clean conscience.

"*Tafadali.* Please bread," the girl says. Then she touches my hand.

Begging I can tolerate, but not touching. I yank my hand away and tell her in Kiswahili to get away or I will beat her. For just a moment, I'm completely convicted in my righteousness. This was how you dealt with street children who invaded your space. They should know better.

The look of fear on her face as she looks up at me in horror brings me out of myself and I wonder what I have done. But she is already running away, casting scared looks over her shoulder as I try to follow.

I try not to run too quickly as to scare her or make her drop the boy off her back, who is now crying. I call after her in broken Kiswahili and tell her I am very sorry. Nothing stops her. She is a child that thinks only of survival. Realizing this, I say to her I will give her bread.

Now she stops. She is breathing hard. She is still scared but I can sense that she is weighing the risks of trusting me. Food is a powerful temptation for a starving child.

I sit down on the sidewalk as to seem less threatening. I am oblivious to the Kenyans walking by me, surely thinking that I am just another insane foreign do-gooder. I reach out my hand. I say I am sorry again. The girl comes up. I tell her my name is Teddy. She says she is Rebecca. She is fascinated now, to the point that she is ignoring the boy on her back. I ask her what his name is, bringing her attention back to him. His name is Paul. He is her brother. She pulls him off her back and makes him shake hands with me as well. He looks uncomfortable touching a *mzungu*. His hands are gray with dirt and grime.

I ask Rebecca where her father is. *Kufa,* she says, dead. Mother? *Kufa.* Grandmother? *Kufa.* Grandfather? *Kufa.* I asked her who took care of her. She did not seem to understand the question. I know that means no one. She is the provider for her brother and herself.

I tell Rebecca to come with me. We go to the nearest supermarket, which on the inside does not look too terribly different than a supermarket back in the States. With the equivalent of five dollars I buy her enough food to last her a week. I constantly watch tourists give money to street children with scorn, writing them off as suckers for sentiment. If they really wanted to do good they would give the money to an institution or a charity, I think.

But I am not so sure anymore. Rebecca and her brother need food *now*. Of course they will need it tomorrow and the next day and the next week and my handing over food and money now is not "sustainable" as we like to say in aid circles.

But that does not change the need she is experiencing at this moment.

While she follows me in bare feet through the store, a clerk tries to throw her out. I explain to him she is with me. He hesitates at first then leaves us alone. We exit the store and now I follow her to the Kenya Bus stage where there are two other girls her age with younger children on their backs begging. Rebecca calls them over to her to share her bounty.

Realizing I was buying for six and not two, I return to the supermarket, buy the same things, bananas, bread, nuts, milk, and orange juice, then return. Rebecca and the others are still there in the middle of the sidewalk. If one ignored the passing legs of commuters on their way home and the gray sidewalk beneath them, one would think these children were in a field or at a playground having a picnic.

In a way they are. The world does not make room for these children, so their playground, their picnic site must overlap with our sidewalks and our bus stages.

I tell them to be careful and save some food for later, then leave.

Chapter 28

Kursk

I wrote. The writing was hard. Messy. At first it was easy, I just based it on my experience and the experience of children I knew. No need to invent a plot, no challenge in recalling, but then it became more difficult—how much of me should I share? And it was me in those pages, even if I call it fiction—those are my memories, my feelings of unrest, doubt, and sadness flowing out, like black miasma from my chest. I continue to write in hopes that there will be some clarity at the end of the draining. But I don't know. I am reminded of a Russian submariner, who trapped in the darkness of the *Kursk* wrote a letter to his wife, beginning it with the phrase, "I am writing blindly."

Chapter 29

Ukimwi

While Tabitha lived in a world of magic, exploring the maze of roadways, walkways, and alleyways of Kibera slum and all the wonders and terrors offered there, her mother spent more of her time at home. She remained in bed until late almost every morning. It was up to Tabitha, most days, to mix *ugali* or make tea. Some of her mother's men friends still came by and when they came, Tabitha would go and play. Tabitha noticed that while there seemed to be many men that came to their house, few women ever did except for Tabitha's auntie. Besides her, when women came by they sometimes would scowl and some even spit at their door.

Eventually Tabitha and her mother moved to live with Tabitha's auntie. Her mother said this would be easier since she was often tired and Auntie could cook their food. Tabitha liked her auntie, she was a big woman with breasts that were bigger than mangoes that hung down to her waist. But Tabitha was afraid that she would send her and her mother away after the first night they slept in her house because her mother coughed until early morning.

Auntie proved to be very kind, however, and took care of Tabitha's mom. Auntie owned a hotel where they made *mandazis*, and *chipatis* and hard boiled eggs. When Tabitha visited her shop, Auntie would always give her a little something to eat, which made her happy.

Now that they lived with Auntie it was a longer walk to Flo's house and Dorris' house. As a result Tabitha only saw them on Sundays, after church—Auntie made her go to church every Sunday. Her mother would come if she was feeling well enough.

It was after they had begun living with Auntie that Tabitha's skin began to turn white. It started on her head and spread to her hand. Auntie did not know what it was and neither did mother. It did not hurt so mother told her not to worry. Tabitha was afraid, though. She feared that her skin would turn gray and that the crippled boy's curse was spreading to her.

In time some of her mother's friends began visiting again, even at Auntie's home. But there were also new men that came to visit. One of them, Herbert, would bring a radio with him and sometimes he would play it loudly so Tabitha could dance.

But the women in Auntie's neighborhood hated Tabitha's mother even more than at their old house. They would walk by her and call her *"malaya,"* a word Tabitha did not know, but it sounded like *"mbaya"* which meant bad, so she knew *malaya* could not be much better.

Tabitha asked one of the older boys that lived nearby her what *malaya* meant. He told her it meant to "make family," which Tabitha did not understand because the house was small, only one room, and their family had not grown at all. She remembered her mother had had a baby a few years before, but he had died and they no longer talked about him at all.

The boy and his friends offered to show Tabitha what it meant, but she could tell by their giggling that it would be a joke at her expense.

After Frieda died Miriam felt like something had been taken out of her and something sick had been put back in its place. Miriam began coughing more after Frieda died and some mornings she was too weak to get out of bed. Mum Amelia moved her so that she could sleep on her side of the cottage at night. That way when Miriam woke up coughing, Mum Amelia would wake up too, come out of her room and rub Miriam's back. She would also then catch the blood Miriam spat up in a tissue.

Miriam watched the other children go to school, come back for tea, go back to school, come back for lunch, then go play on the playground. The nurses came to see her and she sensed that there was some disagreement between Mum Amelia and the nurses. They did not speak to each other, which was unusual because Nurse Ruth almost always spoke to every one with a big smile. The next day Ruth and Amelia actually exchanged angry words, but they were in *Kiluhya,* their mother tongue, so Miriam could not understand. Finally Bonava came. He spoke to Mum Amelia in *Kizungu.* He did not think Miriam understood, but by now she did.

Bonava and Ruth thought it was time Miriam went to the nursing room, the death room. But Mum Amelia did not want her to go. Mum Amelia was tired of losing children. Even Mum Amelia wanted to cry. Miriam realized that Mum Amelia was like Miriam had been when Frieda was sick—she did not want Miriam to go away and be with Jesus. Miriam did not want to go either. She was afraid.

But Miriam did not want to anger Bonava, who was her father now, so when he asked Miriam if she wanted to go to the nursing room, she said yes. Mum Amelia went into her bedroom and closed the door.

One afternoon Tabitha came home to find Auntie in the house. It seemed like she had arrived in a hurry because she was still wearing the apron and hair net that she wore when she was frying *mandazis.* She was very angry and was screaming at Tabitha's mother in Kiswahili, using the word *malaya* herself, but when she saw Tabitha she became sad and switched to *Kizungu.*

After that no more men came to the house. Tabitha's mother spent more time sitting outside in the sun with Auntie's Bible on her lap. The next Sunday she came to church with Auntie and Tabitha, although she was very weak and coughed throughout the service. She did not come the next week, however. Tabitha would find her on her knees more often, praying to God. Sometimes she would make Tabitha pray with her, even though Tabitha did not particularly like praying for as long as her mother did.

There was not as much food now and the whiteness on Tabitha's head and arm had spread to both arms. Now the first arm had gotten fat and hurt. Tabitha's mother not only was coughing now but she had to go to the toilet very often. Sometimes they would run out of newspaper for the toilet because her mother was using so much. Auntie became worried. One morning she took a few crumpled bills from her change purse and told Tabitha's mother to take herself and Tabitha to see the doctor.

Maureen finally brought Harmony to a home for children called Malaika, run by a big fat lady named Mama Seraphina. At first Harmony liked Malaika. She had a bed to sleep in with two other girls and she had food to eat. She helped in the kitchen regularly so that she got to eat extra, but when Mama Seraphina found out she was stealing, she spanked her and sent her to her room.

Harmony started going to school. They had one at Malaika but Harmony was in a class with lots of little children and the older children made fun of the way she read. Her bed was not very nice after a while either because one of the girls was always wetting it. She would try to sleep out on the couch in the main room, but Mama yelled at her for that as well.

The gate of the home was always open though, so one day Harmony decided she would wander out. Not very far down the street there was a Coke kiosk with some boys standing around it. Harmony smiled at them and asked them for a Coke. They bought her one.

Harmony began sneaking out of Malaika whenever she could to meet the boys. They didn't buy her drinks every time but sometimes they would let her sip theirs. One time they asked her to lift up her skirt and show them herself for a soda. Harmony did. The doctor had looked at her there so she was not as embarrassed this time.

One of the boys had an uncle named Thomas and he was sitting down near the kiosk. When he saw what Harmony was doing, he became very angry. He told the boys to go home and told Harmony he would tell Mama Seraphina what she was doing if she did not go straight back.

On a later occasion, Harmony snuck out and she ran into Thomas again. This time he was on his way home. He was alone and did not tell Harmony she had to go home. He invited her to his house and told her he would give her some sweets.

When they arrived the house was empty. Thomas sat down on a chair and asked Harmony to sit on his lap. He asked her if she would take her trousers off again for him. She said no. He asked if she would take his off. She was not sure, but he promised her fifty shillings.

His penis was like Steven's and Harmony wondered if this was simply what they got like when boys grew up. He asked Harmony to rub it, which she did until he urinated on her, although the urine was white and sticky. Then he gave her fifty shillings and sent her home.

Whenever Harmony could get away she would go to Thomas's house. She made lots of money from him by rubbing his penis. One time he asked if he could rub her in the same place. He promised two hundred shillings. Harmony agreed. Then he wanted

216

to put his penis in her. She said no because it had been done to her before and it hurt very badly. He said it would not hurt this time.

It did, very much. But he gave her four hundred shillings in all and told her to tell no one. If she bled on her underpants, he said she should just throw them away.

Harmony did what Thomas said and went back to visit him regularly. She liked it when he held her up close to him, even if he had a strong smell of sweat and maize. She came to like the smell, it meant someone cared for her and the hole she had felt in her chest since her mother had died felt smaller. Thomas still gave her money but it was never as much again, never more than twenty shillings. Harmony stored all the money in a sock in her shoe, but one of the girls that shared her bed could hear all the coins jingling around. She told Mama Seraphina that Harmony had money.

Harmony was called in to see Mama. She asked Harmony how she was getting the money. Harmony said the boys had given it to her. Mama asked how the boys would have so much? Harmony said she did not know. Mama told her to tell her the truth or she would throw her out. So Harmony did.

Mama sent her to her room. A few days later Mama called her back to her office. Harmony was horrified and excited to see Thomas there. He was dressed in a suit and barely looked at Harmony. He told Mama that he knew Harmony and that she was the girl that kept coming to his house. She had told him her story and he had felt sorry for her. So he had given her some coins. But she was quite a nuisance and he thought Mama needed to take better care of her children. He mentioned that she had exposed herself in front of about a dozen people in order to get a soda.

He left after that. Harmony started crying. She told Mama he was a liar. She told Harmony to shut her mouth and sent her away.

The picture Miriam had made of Jesus for Frieda was still hanging above the bed. She was placed in the same bed that Frieda had been. Other children came in to visit Miriam. They brought her pictures that they hung beside the one of Jesus. Miriam had not realized that she had made so many friends. Many of the little boys that she had disciplined in school came with bad drawings with letters on them. When Miriam asked Ruth what the letters said, she laughed.

"They say, 'I love you Miriam!' I did not know you had so many boyfriends."

Mum Amelia came in to visit her each day. Sometimes she was not even in her Mum uniform, which Miriam knew meant that she had come in on her day off. Bonava came in as well and so did Catherine.

Catherine told her she should not be afraid. Miriam thought she should try to follow Catherine's advice since Catherine was the best child—Miriam had heard many adults saying so.

"Jesus will be in heaven and so will your parents," Catherine said. "Do you miss your parents?"

"Yes," Miriam answered.

"Don't worry. God will take care of you."

Miriam felt better after Catherine's visits. After them she always felt like she was ready to see Jesus. But then Mum Amelia would come in and sit by the bed for hours and Miriam would feel sad again. She liked Mum Amelia and she did not want to lose her. Mum Amelia told her to keep being strong and to fight, and that she loved Miriam. She told Miriam not to give up, to pray that she would get better.

Miriam was confused. Why would she pray to Jesus to get better if Jesus only wanted her to be with him, like Catherine had said? If Miriam prayed to Jesus that she would get better, was that not against his wishes?

Miriam decided not to pray at all. She would just look up at the picture she had made of Jesus. She was afraid of him now. He

218

wanted her to die. Catherine wanted her to die. Miriam wanted to live.

One day the doctor came and she brought many large pills for Miriam. They were white with three letters on them, but Miriam still had trouble reading her letters. The pills were so big they made Miriam gag when she swallowed them. Her throat was always hurting now and they made it worse, as if they were covered in broken glass. When she did swallow them, they made her so sick she wanted to vomit. Many times she did. Blood would come up with her vomit. It also came up with her snot.

Mum Amelia said Miriam had to take the pills though. So did Ruth. So she did. But Miriam only seemed to get sicker. Her skin was now peeling off when her clothes were changed. Some days she could not make it to the toilet so she had to pee and poop in a pot like Frieda had. Some days they even put a diaper on her, which she hated because the wipes they used to clean her were always cold.

One night one of the babies in the room died. After he was dead and they were cleaning him, they pulled a worm out of his nose. No one knew how it had gotten there. It was placed in a pan where it wiggled and squirmed and left wet trails where it moved. Miriam vomited. She was afraid she had worms in her too.

Jesus had come for the baby that night. He might be coming for her soon too.

During the funeral for the baby, while everyone was gathered for the service in the schoolhouse, Mum Amelia came, sat with Miriam, and read to her. Catherine did not come as often now. But Mum Amelia came all the time, whenever she could. Sometimes her hands smelled of cleaning products, sometimes they smelled of *oogali*. Miriam tried not to remember what her own mother's face looked like because she knew what that would cause. She told herself her mother from now on was Mum Amelia.

One night when Mum Amelia came in to say good night to her, Miriam asked her if she would pray with her. Mum Amelia closed her eyes. Miriam did the same and folded her hands together. Then she said.

"Dear God, I love you very much. Thank you for the nice day. Please bless Mum Amelia. Bless the children and Catherine, and Bonava, and Teacher Margaret and Aunt Evelyn, and nurse Ruth, and the volunteers. And Jesus, please give me one last chance."

The money was not very much, so Tabitha and her mother walked as far as they could to the hospital. Only when Tabitha's mother was too tired did they stop, sit down, and decide to catch a *matatu*. Because they had walked part of the way, it would not be as expensive.

When they arrived, Tabitha was very hungry. She told her mother even though she knew they did not have enough money to buy anything from the kiosks that were set up outside the hospital. Her mother began going up to the sellers anyway and in a very soft voice asking if there was anything they could give to her and her daughter. Most of the people said that they were poor themselves and could not be giving away food or else their husbands or wives or their children might not eat. But one man towards the end of the row of kiosks gave them two passion fruits. Tabitha ate hers right away. Her mother placed hers in her pocket. She thanked the man many times and made Tabitha say thank you as well. Her mother told him God would bless him.

The hospital was very crowded. It also smelled funny, like people, but also a smell Tabitha had never experienced before, an astringent smell that burned the inside of her nostrils. Tabitha and her mother sat down at the end of a row of chairs. Every few minutes everyone would get up and move one chair down. The person on the very end of the line would go inside an office where there was a doctor. There were many old people there as well as many children. Some were very sick, some very thin, some with their arms wrapped in bandages, but none had skin that was turning white like Tabitha's.

They had moved only a few times when Tabitha's mother had to go to the toilet. Tabitha hoped it was near because she knew when her mother had to go, there often was not much time to spare. Fortunately the door was just on the other side of the room. Her mother moved toward it as quickly as possible.

She remained in the toilet a long time. When the line moved again Tabitha was unsure if she should move without her mother, but the *cucu* beside her told her it would be all right. Time passed, the line moved again. Now Tabitha was excited because when her mother returned she would surprise her by calling out her name and showing her how far they had moved and how little time they had left.

The line moved two more times. The long waits in between moving seemed to take forever now that Tabitha was paying close attention. But eventually they moved again and again. They rounded the corner of the chairs and were moving in the opposite direction so Tabitha's back was to the toilet door and she had to keep looking over her shoulder.

The line moved two times in succession next. Now the *cucu* bent over and asked Tabitha where her mother was. Tabitha said she had not seen her come out of the toilet yet. This attracted the attention of the old man sitting behind the *cucu*. He said something in *Kizungu*. The *cucu* nodded and said that maybe Tabitha should go check on her mother. She promised to hold the seat for Tabitha.

Tabitha walked over to the door to the toilet and pushed it open. The room on the other side was quiet. The astringent smell was very strong inside but so was the smell of urine and excrement. Tabitha called out for her mother. Her own voice echoed. She called out again but heard nothing in response.

It was a large toilet. Instead of just a hole in the ground, there were walls constructed around what Tabitha thought were many holes. However, when she peered around a swinging door that led to where the hole would be, in place of a hole she saw a shiny white chair. It was a strange seat with no bottom. It had a hole in the middle and water floating inside. It was white and Tabitha thought maybe it was made of polished bone, maybe the bones of the people who had died in the hospital.

She was becoming scared. She called out for her mother again but there was no response. The walls between the seats did not reach the floor and Tabitha looked beneath them. A few feet down she saw her mother's skirt. She made her way down the room and pushed on the appropriate door.

She found her mother on the other side. She was sitting on one of the seats. Her skirt had been bunched about her but it was falling now. The smell of diarrhea was very strong and suddenly Tabitha felt terrible for intruding upon her mother.

Her mother did not seem upset though. She was leaning against the wall, her eyes partially closed. Tabitha moved closer. Her mother was breathing very softly, like she was sleeping. Tabitha called out her name. She whispered something, but her eyes did not move. Tabitha realized she was very tired. Then she noticed that her mother's passion fruit had fallen on the floor. She reached down to pick it up. As she did so, she noticed that diarrhea, blood, and urine were running down the side of the white seat.

She placed the fruit back in her mother's pocket. She told her mother that they were almost to the doctor now. There was a slight change in her breathing, which Tabitha thought meant she had heard her. But still her mother did not move. Tabitha decided to leave her so she could continue to rest.

She went back to her seat in the queue. It had moved one seat over but the *cucu* had kept it for her. She asked Tabitha how her mother was. Tabitha told her that she was resting.

Finally the queue had moved and Tabitha was at the front. She kept looking back over her shoulder. A few women went into the toilet. Each time the door opened, these same women would come out. Tabitha's mother was still resting. Finally the door to the doctor's office opened. A nurse came out and called for the next person. Tabitha did not know what to do. But then the *cucu* spoke, in *Kizungu.* The nurse then asked Tabitha if her mother was sick. Tabitha said yes. Then the nurse called over a second nurse and they went into the toilet together.

Tabitha waited. She did not want to lose her spot in the queue for when her mother came back. She watched as the door opened. But it was only one of the nurses. She ran away and when she returned, she had a man with her and between them they had a bed on wheels. At the sight of this, many people turned their heads. The *cucu* took a hold of Tabitha.

The door opened again. This time one of the nurses was holding it open as the other nurse and the man pushed the cart through with Tabitha's mother on top of it. Then they turned down the hallway and disappeared. The nurse that had held the door came over and told Tabitha to come with her. Tabitha asked if they would lose their place in queue. The nurse said they would be seeing a doctor right now.

She led Tabitha down a hallway. Tabitha kept looking for the bed with her mother on it, but she did not see it. The nurse made her sit down in a chair outside a room. When Tabitha looked inside the room, she could not see much because there was a curtain in the way. She waited there a long time. Finally the nurse came back. She seemed upset. She asked what Tabitha's surname was. Tabitha did not know. She asked what her mother's surname was. Tabitha did not know that either, but she suggested that the nurse ask her mother.

The nurse said that she could not because Tabitha's mother was now with the Lord.

Tabitha knew what this meant. Her brother that they had buried had gone to be with the Lord. It meant that he would not come back and neither would her mother.

A few months later Mama Seraphina took Harmony to a clinic where they stuck her with a needle and made her bleed. She cried. She realized this was her punishment for what she did with Mr. Thomas. She said she was sorry, but Mama did not seem to care. Mama said that they needed to take her blood to see if she was sick. But Harmony knew she was not sick. She felt fine. There were other sick kids at the home. Some children had even died but Harmony was never sick.

But a few days later Mama called Harmony to her office. Mama's Bible was open on her desk and she got up and hugged Harmony against her huge body. She was crying. There was a piece of paper in her hand. She said she had been praying that God would help her tell Harmony the news, but that she was still afraid.

She sat down and held Harmony's hands. Mama told Harmony that she herself had failed Harmony and that God would punish her for it. But God would also punish Mr. Thomas. Harmony asked why. Mama said it was because Harmony had become sick from Mr. Thomas. Harmony said that she felt fine. Mama said it was a sickness, *ukimwi,* that could take a long time to make you sick. But Mama said that all the children that she had ever known that had *ukimwi,* had died of it.

Harmony said she did not want to die. She started to cry as well. Mama said she would do her best not to let it happen, but that it meant she had to send Harmony to a special home for children with *ukimwi.*

Miriam was in the death room so long she lost track of the days. It was certainly months. Although her head hurt and her stomach was always upset, other things got better. Ruth rubbed cream on her skin and it stopped peeling off. She felt like her arms and legs were stronger and she could take herself to the toilet again. When she did go the toilet, she did not have diarrhea any more. Mum Amelia came to visit her and smiled more. So did Bonava, who said he was very delighted she was getting better. She had defied expectations, he said.

Best of all, Miriam could now look at the picture of Jesus and not be afraid. It seemed that for now he had left her alone, left her to live. On Sundays she could hear the children singing in the schoolhouse and she started thinking about the day she would return. She planned to sing very loudly to Jesus because she was grateful to still be alive.

Nurse Ruth often told her how proud she was that Miriam was working so hard at getting better. Oftentimes boys like James, Samson, and Mongai would come and leave pictures for her. Ruth still called them all her boyfriends.

One day the doctor came and finally said Miriam was well enough to go back to her cottage. Miriam felt her heart flutter with the news. Before she went though, the doctor said, they would have to do something about the bumps on her face.

Ruth made Miriam lie down. She put on gloves then began to scrape the bumps away with something plastic. Miriam told her that the bumps would only spread more if she scraped them. That was what Mum Amelia had told her.

"Not anymore," Ruth said. She crossed the room to where a branch of francha-panya was sitting. It was a flower that grew on the grounds and it looked quite out of place there in the clean nurse's station. But Ruth broke it open and dripped the sap on Miriam's face. She said it was a new treatment and that if Miriam was healthy enough it should work.

"Are you sure?" Miriam asked.

"Of course," Ruth laughed.

But there was something else Miriam had noticed. Her voice sounded different as she spoke. She said so to Ruth.

"Yes, you sound old now. It is from the throat infections."

"Will it get better?"

Ruth frowned slightly. "You don't want to sound like a grown-up, Miriam?"

She did not sound like a grown-up, she sounded like a grandmother. But Miriam did not want to be anything like a grown-up. Grown-ups were good at dying. Miriam knew she was good at living. She did not want that to change, but she did not want to offend Ruth either. So she said nothing.

She walked back to the cottage but she did not enter the side where the children were sitting down for dinner. Instead she went to the side where her bed was. This side of the cottage was empty this time of day. She walked into the back, into the bathroom, and stood in front of the mirror.

There was still white cream on her face from the sap and a few Band-Aids where blood had come up under the removed bumps. But her face was not the face she remembered. It was harder now, narrower. It looked the way her voice sounded.

And unmistakably she saw her mother's face.

She turned away. She did not want to look any longer. She went to the other side of the cottage where the other children were, where her new mother waited.

Chapter 30

Ms. Pricilla

I enter Cottage Yellow one morning to find a well-dressed, attractive woman sitting beside Oliver's bed. She has brought him a few brand new books and they are talking quietly. The other children keep a respectable distance. Amelia is cleaning, but doing so with a vigor that tells me she is angry.

The woman's name is Pricilla. She says she was best friends with Oliver's mother. I have never seen Oliver as happy as he is after her visit. Amelia, on the other hand, is not pleased. I ask her why.

"She said she was best friends with his mother, but then why does she never visit him?" she says. "These relatives and friends of the children always come once in a while, but none of them want to take in a child that has HIV. But they will come and criticize us house mothers, saying that we are not doing a good enough job. Maybe we do not have an education and maybe we cannot afford to dress like her, but it does not mean we do not love these children. It does not mean we cannot be good mothers. I don't see her taking care of Oliver."

"But Oliver is happy now. That is all that matters."

She clicks her tongue at me.

"You wait and see if Ms. Pricilla comes back."

Weeks pass and turn into months. Pricilla does not return.

Eveline is a Kenyan woman in her late thirties who teaches in the US. One day while becoming especially passionate with her students about their obligations to be aware of injustice and poverty,

227

especially in the developing world, one boy raises his hand and asks her with a candor only children have, "Why are you telling us all this? Is it because you are not doing anything?"

The question was a bomb dropped on Eveline's life. From that point on she knew she had to go back home to Kenya and do *something*. She decided on helping orphaned children but how she would finance such an operation was lost on her until she was in the ladies' room at a wedding reception. With dark skin, sharp cheekbones, braided hair, and erudite glasses, Eveline is a striking mixture of the intellectual and the exotic. An American woman next to her at the wash basin asked her where she was from. Eveline said Kenya, and after a bit of small talk her whole story came tumbling out. The woman, unbeknownst to Eveline, was a wealthy philanthropist. The woman was won over by Eveline's passion, sincerity, and commitment. A few years later I met her at the opening of Eveline's dream, *Imani* (Faith) Homes. It was a beautiful building on a long and narrow lot she inherited from her family. I had given Eveline advice on the design, and knowing her compassion I mentioned a name to her: Nea.

One afternoon, while sitting in the cottage I see Miriam come around the corner with a child leaning on her arm. For a second I think she is disciplining one of the younger children, but her movements are too slow and gentle for that. I suddenly realize the child is Oliver. She is helping him back from the bathroom. He has grown too weak to walk without help.

I know that Mum Amelia always consoles herself when Oliver is sick with his track record of going and returning from the nursing room, but I sense that perhaps this time will be different. After a brief meeting with Bonava one morning, I close my binder and before I leave his office, I ask him about Oliver. I tell him I know he has surprised people with his ability to recover before, but I am afraid he might not be able to do it again, that this might be his last trip.

"I am afraid it is," Bonava says. He has been at the home for over ten years. He has seen this so many times, with so many children, I trust his assessment. "The best we can do now is to give Oliver the best palliative care possible."

I find myself swallowing hard and excuse myself.

Chapter 31

Superman

When I was little I thought I was Superman. Not pretended—*believed.* I had a cape I would wear and I remember vividly running and jumping through my yard, launching out in the air waiting to take off and fly.

Only to fall flat on my face.

Where others might have concluded—accurately—from each failure that they were not Superman, I concluded the opposite. After all, for a moment—*just a moment*—hadn't I left the ground before I fell? A flight of only seconds seemed about right for my age, my point of development. Give me a couple years, I thought, and I would be able to take to the air for longer flights, eventually soaring to incredible heights and incredible speeds in order to break the sound barrier.

Go deeper. Is it natural childhood development to mix fantasy and reality, or is there more to it?

I'm an only child, so I never had to compete for attention. I was always a little prince. Entitled. Spoiled one might say. Perhaps I never learned that lesson of humility, humbleness, human-ness that siblings provide, that sense of being together, of well-being, even in a crowd. Am I still in adulthood acting out childhood fantasies of saving the world? Am I still playing Superman? To what extent have I internalized and believed in my own unquestioned, unearned privilege?

And deeper. Why would I do such a thing? Well my mother's cancer of course, at least that was what the fellow patients diagnosed with depression, bi-polar disorder, schizophrenia, and other mental illnesses, told me in group therapy sessions. When I was five, she

230

was diagnosed with breast cancer. She survived, but at a cost. She admitted to pulling away from me to focus on her recovery. She stopped hugging me because she felt self-conscious after a mastectomy. For a few years in my most formative stages of development I felt I was left on my own. And so the ego defense rose up. I had to be a good boy—the best possible boy, Superboy—so that my mother would love me again.

So in adulthood, in those group therapy sessions, it's not about privilege, entitlement, youthful ambition, not even hurts suffered in high school. To my fellow patients, I'm still chasing those same fantasies from early childhood.

"You're not that different from those orphans you were trying to 'save,'" Martha, a survivor of two suicide attempts tells me, staring me down across the circle of gathered patients.

So my deepest fear is losing my parents, something I did emotionally at a critical age—a mother no longer available to me. So I revisit my scars by examining the similar wounds of others. I first work with orphaned children with HIV in shelters in DC, which I choose because it seemed difficult but for some reason I feel uniquely qualified for. I can't go the route of other ordinary people. That would not fit with my concept that I am special. Terminally special. Then I keep using my superpowers for recognition—fitting in with the messages fed to me about being talented, elite, powerful, benevolent. So I sought out more extreme cases: Africa, where the scope of loss was that much larger. Where as a westerner of European descent, another preexisting narrative waits for me, ready-made.It is that of the great white heroes, from missionaries to public health officers, Peace Corps volunteers, and well-intentioned teachers from the West, conquering disease, ignorance, and darkness. Africa, place of myths and willing misunderstanding. Not India, not Brazil, but Africa, the *dark* continent. There are African countries, Ghana, Zambia, South Africa, Kenya, where millions of people live and die in ordinary lives, making friends, lovers, mortgage payments. Then there is AFRICA, that projection of western European fantasy. I was going to the latter as much as the former.

What better place to be Superman, a great white knight?

So that is why I—we—do it perhaps. Me, Jason Russell, Greg Mortenson? I heard it said that aid workers, journalists, activists, are always running from something, whether a breakup or a breakdown. Maybe I was running into mine, small difference. That would fit a hackneyed, well-worn narrative.

I see others who come there. I see myself in them, zero to hero. Average folks who would be forgettable back home are suddenly celebrities in a country where most people have considerably less earning power. Men will speak to you with deference, women will chase you. All the while you are drunk with power and the admiration of people back home who think you are living the hero's journey.

What they don't see are the folks who can't go back home. No longer acculturated to home. Too used to being first. Too used to being a big fish in a small pond. And maybe, just maybe too in love with the beauty and brutality of the place. Some of the two-year-wonders can't go home to the comfy suburbs and mini-malls, can't leave the adventures behind. When you have watched the moon rise over the Rift Valley, or a herd of wildebeest marching into a river, or smelled the earth after it rains on the savannah; when you have saved a child from certain death, you feel alive. And so with acknowledgement to Mr. Wainaina, Africa is very intoxicating to us foreigners. Maybe we see this in a way the resident cannot, just as it took a Frenchman, Alexis de Tocqueville, to see the nuances of America that the residents were blind to.

But Wainaina's point is more complex and I see that now. The foreign visitor as writer—as a bridge character—trope exists thanks to the inequalities of privilege that allow one young, white person to visit Africa after another. To "find or lose himself"—as Teju Cole points out in his brilliant essay in the Atlantic: *The White-Savior Industrial Complex*; to publish *another* book (like this one), and debut *another* film about it (like Kony 2012) then return comfortably to his life of privilege. I'm the first to admit we're all too often caught up in the sentimentality of it to wonder why more Africans can't move to the US or Europe and enjoy the same privileges, to be mistaken for saviors, to be viewed as celebrities.

So I went. I did all the things I did and I was happy, falling into the same traps of sentimentality and privilege, and white savior tropes that valid critics deride.

But the idealist in me still thinks of a story Father McLeod once told me. It was about a man walking along the seashore after a storm. The storm had washed hundreds of thousands of starfish up onto the beach where they would be dried, shriveled, and killed by the sun. While the man was walking along the beach he encountered a boy who was picking up the starfish and tossing them back into the water to save them. The man, looking at the innumerable starfish on the sand, said to the boy, "What are you doing? You can't save all of them, what you are trying to do does not matter."

The boy bent down, picked up another starfish, which he threw back into the sea, saying to the man, "It matters to that one."

So I think what I did mattered to Miriam, Josephine, Tabitha, Jamina, Winnie, Ivy, and the girls/gremlins I read to at night. I mattered to Oliver who had a friend to play chess with and bring him books.

Sentimental, yes. But in the moment, I don't know if the children would have asked me *not* to be there.

None of it is something I can easily resolve.

And I still left. Like every other Two-Year-Great-White-Knight-Wonder. Perhaps my depression and anxiety, came about from not being able to reconcile it all and guilt for having fallen into the same old tired roles. Ultimately, my psychic injury derived from this inability to reconcile narratives: I am Superman, but I saved so few. I loved Kenya, but I left. I am a savior but really I am just human. More than that, I'm a participant in a system that contributes to over simplification of complex social issues and the infantilizing

233

of people. Was I "building capacity" or undermining agency? What of faith? I believe in God but he kills children and I hate him. Who are the "good guys" if everyone is guilty?

As Dr. Weena said, the world is not a good or bad place, it's just a place.

And all too complicated for me to figure out with my cultural biases, my privilege-induced blind spots, and my woefully inadequate superpowers of intellect and writing. For each time I try, I only see my own flaws, my own insecurities, my own neediness. I feel utterly incapable of reformulating an identity in all this confusion.

But did that matter to Miriam or Oliver?

And still nothing ever computed because the admiration, the appreciation, never amounted to the things I needed/wanted. So at thirty-five I was still stuck with little savings, no job, and a return to school staring me down. Grandiose choices left me without material comforts. I am a kid still trying to play Superman who has not realized he is Clark Kent, and only Clark Kent.

At other times I try to nurture a less critical reading of myself. Could I see myself as just a well-meaning white kid, lucky, affluent, loved, sensitive, moved by the suffering of others, raised with humanistic values, who wanted to give back, who loves to travel, and the variety and exoticism, the mind broadening experience it brings? Can I credit myself, without being arrogant, as being a young man who tries to see people as people, not as projections or stereotypes, who threw himself into the face of the fire in hopes of finding wisdom or maturity? All at once, I can see that I am and always have been naïve, sentimental, ambitious, grandiose, privileged, over confident, insensitive, and compassionate.

But it inevitably brings me back to the same conclusion: I have struggled to accept the painful lesson that the world is not fair, that in reality bad things happen to those who don't deserve them and there seems to be no adequate explanation for it.

Maybe I'm just struggling to accept the fact that I will never learn to fly, that kids still die, and someday I will too.

Chapter 32

Time

The nurse turned Tabitha over to a very nice lady named Gertrude. She had an office that was on the far side of the hospital that did not smell strongly. It was a relief to Tabitha's nostrils.

She asked where Tabitha lived. Tabitha said Kibera. The woman asked where in Kibera. Tabitha said the name of the *matatu* stage, then she said their house was not far from the video house and was between St. Matthews School and Auntie's *mandazi* shop.

Gertrude nodded. She asked if Tabitha could find her way there from the *matatu* stage. Tabitha told her she could. Gertrude said she would leave work early that day in order to take Tabitha home. In the meantime she asked if Tabitha was hungry. She told her yes. It was nearly lunchtime, so Gertrude left and returned with a plate of rice and green grams. Tabitha finished them quickly. So quickly in fact that Gertrude asked her if she wanted another plate. Tabitha said yes. Gertrude returned with more. While Tabitha ate this plateful, Gertrude asked her why she and her mother had come to the hospital.

Tabitha told her about her mother being sick and about how people had called her a *malaya*. Then she told her about the cursed boy and how his curse had spread to her. Gertrude said that curses were only superstition. Tabitha listened carefully, but was not sure if Gertrude really knew what she was talking about. Tabitha showed Gertrude her fat arm that was turning white. Gertrude said it was not from a curse but from a disease and that she would have a doctor look at it.

Gertrude took her back to the side of the hospital that smelled. She spoke to a doctor in *Kizungu*, then he looked at

Tabitha's arm. While he did so, the nurse that had held the door for the bed with her mother appeared. She said her name was Lucy. She asked Tabitha how she was doing. Tabitha said she was fine but asked if she could see her mother. She remembered when her brother had gone to be with Jesus that his body had to be buried. Before it was buried it had lain in the house for a while on the table. Tabitha wondered if her mother was lying somewhere. But Lucy told her she would not be able to see her. Tabitha assumed this meant her mother was already buried.

When the doctor was finished Lucy spread cream all over Tabitha's arm and even put some in her hair. Then she told Tabitha she would have to take some of her blood. She warned her that it would hurt and she should look away. Tabitha tried looking away but when it started to hurt, she screamed and looked down to see Lucy sticking a long needle into her and blood coming out of the spot. She tried to jump away, but she did not realize that there was another nurse behind her that suddenly held her very still.

That was when Tabitha started to cry. She missed her mother and called out for her. Lucy told her it would be over very soon. She pulled the needle out and put a piece of white cloth over the place where Tabitha was bleeding. Tabitha could not stop crying now. But once Lucy had put the glass with her blood in it away, she came over and put her arm around Tabitha.

She smelled nice although she also had the smell of the hospital on her. But her body was soft in a way her mother's had not been for a very long time. Tabitha suddenly felt tired. Lucy carried her to a bed.

Tabitha woke in the afternoon. Lucy was there as well as Gertrude. They said they both were going to take Tabitha home. Lucy and Gertrude seemed to have lots of money because they boarded the *matatu* right outside the hospital and did not walk at all. They rode along until Tabitha told them their stop was coming up. They alighted at the *matatu* stage that stopped beside the road leading to Tabitha's Auntie's house, then began to walk.

Tabitha felt very important with her two guests and she walked quickly because she was eager to introduce them to Auntie. However, when they reached their house, nobody was home. Tabitha guessed that Auntie was still at work so she led Gertrude and Lucy to the *mandazi* shop.

Her Auntie was there. Gertrude leaned in to the kitchen through the window and asked if Tabitha's Auntie could come out. She did, walking around and sitting down on the benches where people ate, still wearing her apron and hair net. Gertrude told her what had happened and she became very quiet and for a while had to cover her face. She did not cry but she looked at Tabitha many times and shook her head.

Then Gertrude spoke in *Kizungu*. Lucy asked Tabitha to take her outside and show her where she liked to play.

Miriam felt like she had struck a deal with Jesus. She felt that because he had let her live, she had to make her life a deserving one. So she tried to be well-behaved all the time. She helped the other children put on their clothes in the morning. After mealtime she would get up and begin cleaning the dishes. If one of the other children stole something of hers, she would not get mad. She would ask for it back and if the child did not give it back, she would let them keep it. It was not worth arguing over.

She noticed certain things had changed. Children did not call the death room the death room any longer. They called it what the moms and Bonava called it: the nursing room. They said it was no longer the death room because Miriam had come back. Other children went and had died since, but now there was always hope. Miriam had beaten the room, so others might as well.

Miriam knew her health was also dependent upon the medicines the doctor had given to her, so she always took her medicines, even though they sometimes made her sick. Some of the other children would hide the pills under their tongues and throw them in the toilet. When this happened, Miriam would explain to them that if they did not take the medicines they would die.

Catherine took her medicines, but they were not working well. She was losing weight and the bumps on her face had swollen one eye shut. She knew she was going to the nursing room soon, but she still called it the death room. She gave all her toys away to other children. She said she was ready to die.

But when the night came for her to go to the nursing room, Catherine was afraid. Her house mom, Mum Esther, asked Miriam to come over and speak to her.

Catherine was sitting in her bed. Miriam asked her if she wanted to live. Catherine did not answer. She started to cry and the tears did not fall off her face, they got lost in the bumps there. Miriam did not know what to say, but she knew Catherine liked to pray so Miriam knelt down beside the bed and started to pray that Catherine would get better soon. When she finished she was surprised that Bonava had appeared in the doorway.

Miriam was afraid she was in trouble and that perhaps Mum Amelia was looking for her and had sent Bonava. But Bonava simply said that Miriam's prayer had been a very beautiful one. He came over and knelt beside Catherine's bed as well. He asked Miriam to pray for all of them. She closed her eyes and did. When she finished, Bonava said to Catherine,

"Catherine, it is time."

Catherine put her arms around Bonava's neck and started sobbing and crying. She put her face, covered in bumps, against Bonava's cheek and he did not even flinch. For the first time Miriam saw Bonava crying. Even Mum Esther was upset. She touched Miriam on the head and said she should go back to her own cottage.

Miriam obeyed. Her own room was dark and filled with the sound of the children breathing and murmuring in their sleep. She went to the window and through it watched Bonava carry Catherine in through the door to the nursing room.

Miriam knew Catherine was not coming back.

Mama put Harmony in a very nice dress that was still stiff from drying on the clothesline and led her to the car. Harmony waved goodbye to the children but they did not seem to understand she was leaving forever. As they left the gate she wished she could have said goodbye to Agnes, who had just started speaking to people. For the past few months Agnes had been silent, except to speak to Mama Seraphina, whom she slept with at night because of her nightmares.

They rode in the car for a short while but they did not go far. Harmony could still see the Ngong Hills where Mama Seraphina lived, when they made the turn that Mama said led to her new home.

Harmony reflected that she had had many homes and she wondered what this one would be like. As they pulled up to the gate she saw there were Maasai with spears and swords guarding it. This scared her. But as they drove down the driveway, they passed orange, avocado, and flame trees. Mama remarked that it was a very beautiful home. She said that she would pray to God for Harmony to be happy there.

There was never a burial for Tabitha's mother. For the next few weeks Auntie was very nice but also very strict about putting the cream on Tabitha's skin four times a day like Lucy and Gertrude had instructed her to do. Tabitha also ate more food than she ever had in her life. Auntie bought her bananas, avocadoes, and papayas, in addition to *chipatis* and *mandazis* (Tabitha would not touch passion fruit however, she was sure it was wicked and the man that had given the passion fruits outside the hospital had been the devil in disguise). Auntie told Tabitha that it was Gertrude and Lucy that had left them money for her food and that Tabitha should have been very grateful. Auntie made sure that Tabitha thanked God in her prayers each night for Gertrude and Lucy.

During the day Tabitha now spent her time at Auntie's hotel. Auntie insisted upon this. Tabitha was glad because she did not like being alone in their house any longer. When she looked at the empty bed, she would miss her mother very much. Sometimes she even cried.

In time, Gertrude and Lucy returned. Tabitha was very happy to see them both. The day they came Auntie was in her best clothes. Gertrude and Lucy told Tabitha that they were taking her to a new home that would be full of children and where Tabitha would no longer be sick. Tabitha asked Auntie if she would visit her. She promised she would.

Auntie walked them to the *matatu* stage. Before climbing aboard with Gertrude and Lucy, she gave Tabitha a bag with *mandazis* wrapped in newspaper. Then she told Tabitha to be good and to continue with her prayers every night. Tabitha promised she would. Auntie rubbed her eyes and stood in place, staring at the *matatu* as they drove away until they turned the corner and she was gone.

As they rode the *matatu* Tabitha was excited about her new home. She asked Lucy many questions about it. Lucy said that she would have a new mother and brothers and sisters there. She also said there would be toys and water so she could wash every day. Tabitha told Lucy she did not like washing every day because the water was cold. Lucy said they would have hot water at the home.

The home had a gate with Maasai guards and a long driveway. The grounds were not unlike the hospital's with lots of grass and trees. Gertrude and Lucy introduced Tabitha to a man named Bonava. Tabitha could hear other children playing nearby and asked if she could join them. Bonava said of course she could.

Around the corner there was a playground with dozens of children. They were in bright clean clothes and their skin was shiny and black. As some ran by her, Tabitha saw that a few had bumps on their faces and even a few had whitish scalps like hers. Almost all of them had their hair shaved from their heads.

There was a set of swings. Tabitha had seen swings on the grounds of St. Matthew's school in Kibera. When one of the children leapt off a swing, Tabitha sat down upon it and began swinging herself.

She had never been on a swing before and she never wanted to get off. A few children came by, asked her what her name was and where she was from. One told her she would have to get off the swing, but when she told him that Bonava had told her she could swing on it as long as she liked, he went away.

Eventually the children were called inside to their cottages for baths. Tabitha saw older children, with hair, chasing after the younger ones, ordering them into the cottages. Soon Tabitha was the only child left on the playground. No longer feeling possessive of the swings, she explored, climbing up into a wooden hut on stilts and sliding out the other side on a metal slide that was still hot from the day's sun.

One time when she reached the bottom of the slide there was a woman in white waiting for her. She knew Tabitha's name and said her own name was Nurse Ruth. She had a melodious voice that Tabitha liked immediately. She asked Tabitha if she wanted some medicine for her skin. Tabitha said that she did. Nurse Ruth turned and started walking away. She called after Tabitha to come with her. Tabitha scrambled to her feet and followed.

A few months after Catherine died, a volunteer was helping in the schoolhouse and she noticed that Miriam was still reading books for five-year-olds. She asked Miriam how old she was. Miriam said twelve. The volunteer was an old *mzungu* lady with a son named Leo, so they called her Mum Leo. Mum Leo asked Teacher Margaret if she could work alone with Miriam. Margaret said that was fine.

They went and sat outside the cottage and Mum Leo asked Miriam to write a few letters. Miriam did and she asked Miriam if she realized some of the letters she had written were backwards. Miriam had not. Then she asked Miriam to read from her books. Miriam confessed that she could not read but that she usually studied the pictures, hoping that the words would start making sense.

She said that Miriam was had dyslexia, a funny word Miriam had never heard before. She asked if Miriam had always had trouble reading. Miriam said yes and told her how she had been expelled from school because they thought she was lazy. Mum Leo nodded and said they would work together.

They did. Every day. Mum Leo would bring colored plastic strips that you could see through. She would place them over the text of a book and make Miriam read. Miriam found that when the plastic was there the words stayed in place. Mum Leo also brought a tape recorder and when Miriam could read a few lines, Mum Leo would tape her. Then she would play her own voice back as she read the lines again. Somehow this made the words stick in Miriam's brain so that when she saw them again she remembered them.

But it was a strange experience to hear her own voice. It sounded more like an old grandmother on the tape than it did in real life. Mum Leo asked Miriam if she was excited to hear her own voice. Miriam did not want to say no, which was the truth. She did not want to lie and say yes either. So she simply said maybe. Mum Leo laughed. Miriam did not know why. *Wazungu* were nice but crazy.

Chapter 33

Home

Eveline, her social worker, and I visit Nea at Josiah's school. Eveline is also a bit uncomfortable with the contrast between the children's dorms and Josiah's home. Upon meeting Nea, Eveline wants to talk to her away from everyone else. We sit down on the edge of the soccer field, the wind whipping the grass about us while the sun occasionally breaks through the cloud cover racing overhead. Nea is quiet, sitting with her knees up, her head perched upon them. She seems to hide under her heavy jacket and knit cap. Her eyes do not meet ours.

Eveline introduces herself, warm, maternal, full of energy. She asks if Nea is happy.

"Hapana." No.

She asks Nea if she wants to come with her to a different home.

"Ndyio." Yes.

It struck me later how miserable Nea must have been to leave a place that was familiar to her and go with a complete stranger. Then again, the attention of a warm, nurturing, beautiful woman is very appealing to an orphan who lives with such a hole in her heart. Eveline stood up, Nea's eyes following her every move now.

"We're going," Eveline says. "We're getting her out of here."

I had just seen the beginnings of a new family. Nea became one of Eveline's first children at Imani Homes and I was indebted to her for it. My own narcissism wanted to believe that we had saved Nea's life, and perhaps we had. It is Nea I thought of on bad days when I felt discouraged; I could at least point to her life and say, "I made a difference." She thrived at Eveline's home, immediately connecting with Eveline's biological children and the other orphans. Eveline also arranged for Nea to receive regular medical care. That, along with the warmer climate down from the hills, allowed Nea to thrive. She was a bright spot in my career, no doubt, yet a few years later when I visit Eveline, I am served humble pie, for Nea, this child I had "saved," does not even remember me. I'm just another *mzungu* to her.

But she has Eveline. And if she has blocked out all those cold miserable months in the hills, that is fine with me. She has a home now.

Oliver is placed in the nursing room the next morning. When I go in to see him, he is wearing a hospital gown, his hat has been removed, and it is sitting on the table across the room from him. I barely recognize him. He is emaciated. Before AIDS was called *ukimwi,* it was called slim-disease by many Africans. Doctors today still don't know what causes some AIDS patients to waste away and others not to. Whatever the cause, Oliver has been wasting away these past few months, a process that has been hidden from me by the extra layers of clothes he always wears for warmth.

His legs are as thin as his bones, making his knees look enormous. He looks, to me, like a stranger, warped from the child I have grown to know.

His breathing is irregular with short, short, short, and then long pauses between breaths. There is another volunteer on duty. She is a student from the Netherlands that wants to become a doctor someday. I sit myself down on the floor beside her and put my hand on Oliver's head. I tell him hello but that is all. I wonder if he is even cognizant enough to recognize it is me. After a few hours however, I grow tired. I have been having trouble sleeping and the night before

I had finally fallen asleep so late that I heard the first roosters crowing as I drifted off.

I get up to go to bed, but then Oliver takes a deep rasping breath and says, "Ted, please stay."

There is no saying no. I return to cradling his head. He speaks up again to say, "Thank you, very."

When I start to doubt that Oliver will last until the morning, I dial Mum Amelia on my mobile. It is her day off, but I know she will have her phone on. She answers and I tell her she might want to speak to Oliver. I hold the phone to his ear while she tells him she loves him and that he is a good boy. She tells him she will be there in the morning to visit him.

As they had with Anika, the seconds ticked by like hours and I reflect that I never understood this expression until I had worked in a hospice for children. There had been nights when working the night shift was easy and a sick child would sleep soundly though the night. But other nights, he or she would cry and scream most of the night. I had held such children and was always shocked when it seemed like hours of such torment had passed and I would look at the clock to see that it had only been five minutes.

This is turning into one of those nights. Oliver is in great pain. I know his hemoglobin is so low that his blood is barely oxygenated. He has to take five breaths where he once just took one. The effort is making his diaphragm work as quickly as if he was running a marathon—a process we can see though the skin just covering his ribcage. What else might be going wrong with him and why, I don't even know. He has not been able to keep much food down. He says his joints hurt, his stomach hurts, his abdomen hurts, his throat hurts, his head hurts.

Later, the Dutch student is replaced by another volunteer, an American nun in her sixties. When I return after a brief nap, I find her beside Oliver kissing his hands repeatedly. She has recently retired and come to Kenya to administer to the sick in her retirement. Each time she kisses Oliver she closes her eyes in a swoon of religious ecstasy. It irritates me to say the least. I know that each times she closes her eyes she sees her Lord Jesus and when she opens them and looks at Oliver she sees him in just another form: Oliver, the living embodiment of her Christ, the ultimate love of her life.

She is my friend, but at that moment I hate her. She is making Oliver into some fetish of religious worship that he is not. In my eyes he is not Jesus. He is a kid who loves pasta marinara, *Harry Potter*, *The Chronicles of Narnia*, and *Lord of the Rings*. He is a child that loves learning, who can beat me half the time at chess. He is a child who used to play beneath a tree covered in passion fruit vines in his grandfather's yard. He is a child that is not afraid of death because his mother is waiting for him. He is a child we have all deceived by not telling him that his grandfather would be waiting there as well—if one believed in such things.

But I say nothing to the nun. Maybe she is just trying to comfort him through touch and I just can't accept the idea there might be anyone better suited to care for Oliver than myself.

Oliver becomes increasingly restless, writhing and crying out in pain every few minutes. At one point Oliver turns to us. His face is twisted in pain. He looks terrifying and grotesque. In an angry, accusatory voice he says, "Please help me!"

I look at the clock. It is just after midnight and Oliver is due for another dose of codeine in ten minutes. His last dose is wearing off and I imagine that is why he is in increasing discomfort.

I cross the room and find the bottle. I use a cereal bowl and spoon as a pestle and mortar and crush a pill into a fine powder. The only drinkable liquid available is orange Fanta. It would not be my first choice and I can only imagine what the carbonation might do to Oliver's stomach, but it is all we have available. I pour some into the bowl, swirl it around then bring it over to Oliver.

I lift him up and lift the Fanta with flecks of codeine in it to his mouth. He can't move his lips well on his own. I have to pour it

247

into his mouth myself. It sits there about his tongue for a long time. He finally swallows.

Then he screams. I can see his esophagus well at this point and the passage of just this tiniest bit of liquid has been excruciating for him. I lay him back down on the bed where he breathes even harder as he makes up for the breaths he missed while swallowing. I look in the bowl at what I realize now is an enormous amount of soda for him to swallow. I curse myself and realize I have gone about this all wrong.

I search through the medicine cabinets, full of self-loathing and a familiar sense of inadequacy. I miss Weena who has returned to California. I yearn to talk to my mother. She has worked as a hospice nurse and I feel like there are so many little details, little comforts, that I should know right now that I simply don't, and as a result Oliver is the one who suffers.

The nun is beside Oliver's bed, kissing his hands again, humming a church hymn.

There are no codeine suppositories. In the past they have been an alternative to having the children swallow pain killers. I am forced to go back to the bottle of pills. This time, however, I crush the pill in the spoon itself then add just enough soda to fill the spoon up. I return to Oliver. The nun holds him up. I tell him I have his medicine.

"I already took the medicine," he says.

"You have to take it again."

"It hurts."

The nun's face is softening. I can sense that she wants to relent. But the anger of Oliver's own words is still with me. His accusatory face is still fresh in my mind. I become firm with him, answering his conviction with my own.

"Oliver, if you want me to help you, if you want the pain to stop, you have to take this."

He nods. I don't think the nun approves of me speaking to a dying child in such a tone but she moves to hold Oliver up anyway. I

248

bring the spoon to his lips. Moving has disrupted his breathing and we wait for it to become regular once more. Then I pour the concoction into his mouth.

It remains there a long time, soda orange and chalk-white froth. He is taking hissing breaths in through his nostrils. I think of the stories he has told me over the months about his family. I recall how he always cooperates in the laboratory, even when they have to perform painful, invasive tests. I remember how staff members, volunteers, and children have all told me that Oliver is such a brave boy.

I'm hoping he can summon that courage now. I begin to think he has given up. The liquid is just sitting there in his mouth.

Please Oliver.

He closes his lips and swallows.

This time the pain is too great for him even to make a sound. His face simply contorts and he looks up to the ceiling while he utters the smallest of cries. The nun and I hold him and lower him to the pillow. He is exhausted. But the codeine takes effect. He begins to writhe less. Eventually he closes his eyes and drifts into something like sleep.

I'm spent. I have already stayed well beyond my shift. Tired as I am, I know I am of little use, and, if anything, a danger to Oliver. I tell the nun I am going to get some rest and that I will be back in an hour.

Oliver dies while I am sleeping.

When Mum Amelia arrives in the morning, I try to relate to her Oliver's last few hours. What strikes me is that even in his dying moments, he remained the polite, thoughtful boy we had always known him as. He said please and thank you. And in the end, I tell Mum Amelia, his courage did not falter.

I know on some level this must please her, but she shows no emotion. Her face is still and as expressionless as stone. I know her by now though. She will go back to her room in the cottage and weep there in private. As for me, I weep right in front of her.

A few days later we bury Oliver on his grandfather's property up near Meru. The older children from Cottage Yellow, Miriam, Alexis, Tabitha, Jamina, Josephine, and John, attend the service. They even carry his coffin to the grave. It is a light load considering Oliver's weight at the end. The grave is deep, deeper than the other graves we have buried our children in and there is something about that finality I do not like. I take comfort in the fact though that his grave lies between that of Oliver's grandfather and mother.

Back at the house there is rice with beans or meat served by a few of Oliver's distant relatives. Pricilla is there but she pretends not to recognize Mum Amelia or myself.

Always a mixture of bravado and vulnerability, I notice Miriam is especially subdued. While I am eating my own beans and rice in the farthest corner of the yard, I find myself staring at a round shape in the bushes. I realize that it is a passion fruit. I stand up and examine the vine. It winds around a low but wide bush. Beneath its long drooping branches there is room for a child to play and create an entire imaginary house with rooms and halls.

I call Miriam over and show the bush to her. I tell her that this is where Oliver used to play. She stands there, passively staring. I become aware that it is only my own foolish sentimentality that wants her to say something, do something, that will lend this moment some significance.

Instead she simply picks two passion fruits from the vine. She hands one to me and places the other in her pocket, then returns to her bowl of rice and beans.

Alexis has just started school at one of the public schools. These were the schools that rejected the kids from Rainbow because of their HIV status. It took a supreme court case to get them to allow our children in, but discrimination remains.

Alexis is fourteen. She is pugnacious and forthright. The boys of the orphanage will testify to her being a tomboy and very competitive in soccer. Bottom line: Alexis is tough. She is from Cottage Yellow and many volunteers assume she is the one who taught Miriam her strictness (I'm not so sure, I think Miriam is a tough disciplinarian at heart, but I digress). Alexis is one of the big-girls of the house and she is often put in charge of the younger children, however, at times her tough mask slips. On a retreat with the teenage girls, I remember my sense of shock when she came up to me at the breakfast table holding her antiretrovirals in one hand, a glass of water in the other, her brow furrowed, her eyes wide with worry.

"I can't take them with water so early," she said.

"Why not?"

She twisted her mouth into a frown, darted her eyes side to side and said in a soft voice, "I'll throw up."

It's a rare show of vulnerability from her and I can read in her reluctance that the admission is against her nature. But stuck with me for the duration of the retreat, her hand is forced.

"No problem," I say, making as little show of it as possible. I was eager to be her co-conspirator, preserving the tough exterior she prided herself on. I realized it protected her from the world, a world that—she later tells me—she felt rejected her from birth and really never stopped.

Alexis is a total orphan. No one knows where she came from or who her extended family might be. As the orphanage begins to focus more on re-integration, sending the children to stay with family on the holidays, Alexis and a handful of others have nowhere to go and often go home with staff members.

251

It's Alexis who at her new school feels the full brunt of discrimination. When she goes to join the boys in a soccer game at lunch, they stop the game and pull the ball away from her. They tell Alexis that girls can't play. As if she were at the orphanage, she argues with these boys, insisting that she can and that she is likely better than their best player. Then the real reason comes out.

"We don't want to play with someone who has AIDS," one boy says, his words hitting her like a fist. The taunting snowballs from there, the most painful of many phrases hurled at her: "You won't even be alive. You won't even be here in a few weeks."

That's the barb that cuts the deepest and stings the most. Alexis, so fierce in other circumstances, is defeated.

She is quiet around the cottage for days after that. Stubborn and independent, she does not disclose what happened or how she feels about it to anyone, although from the way she is short with the younger kids, hitting and punching them when she loses her temper, it's clear she is not herself.

She does not seek out any grownups for guidance and instead counsels herself. Days, weeks pass. She prays, at first for the boys to be punished, then for strength. Time does not make the hurt less but time provides another revelation that she would share with me later.

"I realized I was still here. I wasn't dead. I was taking my medicine and I was fine."

The revelation reignites the fight in her. She seeks out the same cadre of boys at school, stands among them in the middle of their soccer game and says, "By the way, I am still here." It becomes her mantra. Getting off the school bus each morning she bounds over to the boys to greet them with the same phrase.

"I am still here." Whether she sees them passing on the stairs, "I am still here," the hallway, "I am still here," the classroom, "I am still here," the library, "I am still here," the head mistress' office, the school clinic, the bathrooms, she repeats, "I am still here."

Over time Alexis is herself again. I find it a shame that sometimes the children have to take it upon themselves to change

252

hearts and minds, to counter discrimination and stigma, but unfortunately it's the unfair burden of an unjust disease.

But in the end Alexis wins. (She always does.) She is one of the few girls that now plays soccer with the boys.

And she *is* better than most.

The night of Oliver's burial, we have a dinner of pasta marinara in Cottage Yellow to celebrate his life. The children decorate the walls with posters asking Oliver to pray for them. They draw pictures of Oliver alongside angels. When the meal is finished and I am doing dishes, Miriam begins clapping her hands, bringing the children into a uniform rhythm. They begin to sing.

Mama Wambui
Kenya Mama we,
Alinitu tuskamarinda
Akaniambia wambui ako wapi
Siku mbali mpenzi wangu
Alikufa na Malaika
Nikaenda hotelini
Nikakuta sister Esther
Akinipa chips kidogo
Ongeza Ongeza
Ongeza Ongeza
Chips!

Mama Wambui
You are Kenya's Mother
They were making fun of my dress
I asked where Mama Wambui was
Many years ago

My lover died
He died in sadness
I went to the hotel
I met sister Esther
She gave me a few chips
Add More! Add More!
Add More! Add More
CHIPS!

The dancing, clapping, and the happy voices feel incongruous to the sadness I have been experiencing the past few days since Oliver's passing. But then I admit that my sadness is not misplaced: all these children may face similar ends as Oliver. There is no cure for AIDS, nor are there easy answers to poverty, inequality, and injustice. The tragedy of Oliver will be repeated, I know, over and over again, millions of times.

And yet, strangely enough, there will still be these children, dancing, singing, and laughing despite it all. It dawns on me tonight that although there is tragedy and loss in this world, it coexists with moments of mirth and beauty and children are stewards of that joy. It's one of the world's miracles that in war zones, slums, refugee camps, orphanages, and even AIDS hospices, children will still play, sing, and laugh.

Years later as I write this, I still think that is something worth fighting for. Most importantly for me, it's worth living for.

Afterword

I hope this story does not read as one of unmitigated tragedy. I hope it is a story of resilience and a testament to what some determined people—however flawed—and some brave children have accomplished in the face of striking odds and even more striking indifference. Many of these children are young adults now, going to school and/or working jobs. Some have become social workers in hopes of helping other children. Some are even parents themselves now—with improvements to prevention of mother-to-child-transmission (PMTCT), HIV-positive women can give birth without infecting their children. So today, those children I knew are generally doing the same mundane things all of us do—they just have to take a few more pills in the mornings than the average Joe and are hypervigilant about safe sex.

But I should also warn the reader to beware of narrative. In 2006, I wrote the following conclusion to the stories in this book:

Tabitha still struggles in school. Having experienced malnutrition, illness, trauma and growing up in an environment as deprived as Kibera, she simply missed critical milestones in her psychosocial and cognitive development. At approximately twelve (we can only guess her exact age) she still reads like a six-year-old. Her grasp of English has been slow and frustrating. Even the other children find her somewhat backwards. As I have picked up Kiswahili, I've realized that Tabitha is the butt of many jokes.

Ivy's performance in school has been consistently average. She has been attending classes regularly and is only two years behind most children her age. She can be disruptive in class and there have been numerous instances of her bullying other children. Learning to resolve her differences without resorting to violence is something she still struggles with. Although she has turned eighteen, she still insists, again to the point of physical violence, that she is only fourteen—the age she was at when her brother died.

Lialabell shows every sign of growing up a completely well-adjusted and affable child. There have been no further instances of sexualized behavior and she shows no signs of remembering what her father did to her.

I was present the night Jamina asked Miriam what made the children at the home different from other children. Miriam looked to me to explain, but I deferred back to her. Miriam proceeded to tell Jamina in plain terms that there was a disease in their blood that made the children at the home sick very often. This was the reason they all had to take medicine. Jamina asked if the adults like Mum Amelia, Bonava, Teacher Margaret, even myself had the disease. Miriam said no. Jamina's next concern was for me and whether I would get it from sitting close to her. Miriam again said no.

I was prepared next for a deluge of tears from Jamina, however, she simply returned to reading Green Eggs and Ham. I realized that for these children, finding out that they had HIV was not an event, but a process. They grow up hearing the acronym but it is only over time that they come to be aware of the implications.

It turns out that Harmony has the gift of near-perfect pitch and a dazzling voice. One afternoon while she was sitting in front of her cottage singing, a visitor to the home overheard her. The visitor happened to be a woman who makes children's music. A few weeks later she took Harmony to a recording studio and let her sing backup and even solo on a few songs. Since then, Harmony and a group of children from the home have sung backup for a famous Kenyan pop musician. That particular song made with the children remained number one in Kenya for over a month.

Harmony someday hopes to meet her favorite singer, Shania Twain.

Rebecca I lost touch with. Weeks would often pass when I would not see her, only to have her surface to my great relief. My hope is that she, her brother, and her friends are in a home somewhere. The alternatives keep me awake at night.

The best plastic surgeons collaborated to repair Lazarus' face. His head is still misshapen and always will be, but the wounds healed and there is hope that as he grows older, further surgeries might be able to help him look more normal.

Judith continues to support herself working as a seamstress and as a part-time cleaner at a girls' school down the road from Rainbow Children's Home where Sofie still lives. There are even days when Judith feels well enough to play goalie in a soccer game with the students. Sofie seems taller each day. She shows all the indications of growing up to be tall like her mother. Judith is eager to teach Sofie how to sew. "It is important to pass on knowledge," she tells me while she gestures to Sofie. "After all, people are growing up."

Miriam. Do wishes come true? In 2000 a young businessman in London received an email from a college friend working in Nairobi. The email was a list of children at a home for orphans with HIV/AIDS that needed antiretroviral therapy. He saw that one child had a more expensive regimen than any other. He signed up to sponsor her.

It was Miriam. The drug azidothymidine, otherwise known as AZT, had been one of the first to give patients with HIV hope in the eighties.

Since choosing to sponsor Miriam, his business has become highly successful, making him a millionaire before he was even forty. He visits Miriam regularly. He took her on a trip to Mombasa to revisit the city she was born in as well as a trip to London. He has pictures of the children, especially Miriam, on his walls at home— more than a few people have asked him if Miriam was his daughter.

A few years later, he ran for a seat in the national parliament and won. Now that he is a UK Member of Parliament, I like to think that the children in Africa have a voice that is heard directly by some very influential people.

That voice sounds a lot like a grandmother.

Succinct, pat, a nice bow to tie on the end of all the threads. In 2006 it was all true. But if I ended it there, the reality of the following years would be obscured. With few services available for students with dyslexia, Miriam struggled mightily in high school. As of this writing, in 2018, she is working while also taking college classes. She is still determined to reach a point where she can "give back" and take care of others the way people have supported her, but even now I have an email from her in my inbox indicating she has to visit the doctor because of some a persistent chest infection. It's especially worrisome since two other members of her age cohort at Rainbow have passed away from illnesses this year, illnesses that would normally be treatable in higher resource settings even with compromised immune systems. Most of the grown children have become internet savvy and so I've been witness to their grieving real time in their posts and messages.

But Miriam inspires me daily with her persistence and resilience. She has been through traumas that dwarf my own and yet she still endures. Her dream is to be a counsellor so she may use her own experience to help others. I also know it would be a role well suited for her and her talents, including her incisive ability to read people and her talent for verbal expression. We speak weekly on Skype and I hope that with proceeds from this book we can make her dream a reality.

Singing has also been a gateway for many of the young adults now "graduated" from Rainbow to travel the world, performing for a variety of venues. To say that I am proud of them is an understatement. This very year I met one of the young women who inspired the "Harmony" story in these pages while I was in Washington DC. She has a burgeoning singing career and frequently speaks out for people living with HIV/AIDS. I got to see this dazzling, radiant woman perform her own original songs at a fundraiser full of DCs most influential. For her to be able to sing and even profess her HIV status to a room of strangers was, in her own words, transformational. The next day she traveled to New York City where she met Jay Z, Neo, Nicki Minaj, Alicia Keys, Rihanna, and Beyoncé while also being featured in a series of interviews and articles as a success story. When I contemplate the hills and valleys of her journey, I feel a sense of vertigo on a nearly cosmic scale. Her proximity to fame far exceeds mine at this point, and I wouldn't have it any other way.

Social media allows me to see how the children's lives are unfolding like the lives of many young adults: with a cast of boyfriends, girlfriends, bosses, teachers, rivals—mixed in with a series of concerts, coffee houses, first jobs, first loves, and first days at university. I can self-praise on this one point—I had pointed out to Father McLeod that once Rainbow had ARVs they had to start thinking differently—they were a home with growing children, not a hospice. To his credit, he responded. The orphanage works hard to reintegrate children with relatives and society, as growing up in an orphanage can lead to isolation and stigma. This was the direction the field was going, while I was still working at CARE, with a major shift from residential care to community care. As a colleague once said to me: that kid in the hut might not have a Gameboy like the kid at the fanciest orphanage, but the kid in the hut has something else— love, belonging, roots.

This has led to unexpected costs, as the expenses of raising a child into a teenager and young adult through secondary and tertiary education are considerable, which is why proceeds from this novel will go towards the further education of not only Miriam but other children of Rainbow too.

A further update: Judith eventually became successful enough in her sewing business that she was able to support herself and Sophie, who was able to move back in with her mother. Sophie, tall like Judith now, is now at university studying fashion and design and most recently has been blowing up my phone with her thoughts on the costume design of Black Panther. Her Instagram feed is constantly updating with her burgeoning sense of fashion.

The specter of HIV hovers in their lives. So does rape and sexual assault. Aside from the recent deaths, almost every single young adult has a story of rejection after disclosing their HIV status to someone they were interested in dating. It disgusts me to report this but too many of the young women graduated from Rainbow have experienced sexual assault and date rape, as Kenya still suffers from a rape culture and a toxic sense of masculinity.[3] Professionally the grown children face tough odds as well. Without as many family connections as children raised in intact families, they have struggled to find jobs in a limited market where sexism, tribalism, and discrimination around HIV status are still prevalent and "who you know" still plays an outsized role in securing entry-level positions. Some of them also experience memory problems and cognitive difficulties akin to early onset dementia, which has been documented as a side effect of long term ARV use.

And ultimately, there is the uncertain future they feel looming. When Josephine remembered my birthday recently, she asked me how old I was. I told her thirty-eight. She replied, "I hope I reach thirty-eight someday."

Then she went on to invite me to Snapchat, because . . . well, life goes on.

As I watch their hopes and dreams playing out in their status updates, tweets, and videos, they often express the same determination and optimism I found so inspiring in children like Alexis. Sarah, in her twenties now, who was a teenager when I was at the orphanage, recently posted the following on her Facebook profile: "Nothing is impossible. The word itself says 'I'm possible.'"

So in the final analysis there is no tidy ending. The children who have survived face life, with all its peaks and valleys ahead of

---

[3] This is true of my own country and culture as well, but there is diminishing impunity for offenders in the US, while Kenya still has a long way to come to catch up.

them. They have suffered. Some of them are suffering right now and they will all suffer in the future. But they will experience joy, wonder, and exhilaration as well. That is life, and the fact that we *all* have it ahead of us, feels like a triumph.

~ A Debt of Gratitude ~

A note of gratitude to friends and family who not only supported me through my own journey but also through the crafting of this book. Thank you to early readers, Linda, Ra, JJ, Ed, Kathy, Jack, Ruby, Tara, Dean who helped me to believe that there was merit in sharing these stories.

Special thanks to Helene Gayle, MD MPH, a Global-Health-Gender-Equity-Crusader-SHERO. Her leadership, mentorship, and support over the years has been invaluable. I know if I can accomplish a fraction of the things she has accomplished in her life and career, I will be able to consider my own life well spent.

Thank you to all my friends in the recovery community who continue to support, nurture, teach me, and check me when I most need it.

Thank you to those on the Rainbow Children's Home staff, the donors, and the directors and all supporters like them, who endeavor to do what they can to help those in need.

Thank you, especially, to my editors and friends Bethany Gower and Sara Kenley who insisted on nurturing and polishing this work, free of charge, because they believed in the project and because they are awesome. Also, to Agata Broncel at Bukovero Designs who continues to craft transcendent covers that go so far beyond what I could ever request or even imagine.

And of course, deepest most profound thanks go to my brothers and sisters of Rainbow Children's Home. Thank you for letting me into your lives and your hearts, and for trusting me with your stories. Thank you for your support in how I have represented them here. It's been a joy of my life to come alongside you and watch you all grow. It is a journey I hope we can continue, together, the rest of our days.

~ Thank You for Reading ~

Thanks so much for reading and sharing our journey. There is a companion piece to this book. It is lighter read, a young adult novel called *Jamhuri, Njambi & Fighting Zombies*. It is a piece I wrote for the gremlins whom I read to at bedtime each night at Rainbow Children's Home. The kids wanted a story with characters that looked like them and lived in a place they could recognize. The story is fun and zany, just like the gremlins, and has been the genesis of an ongoing series that I hope to continue.

There are two Kenyan organizations not mentioned in the pages of this book that I have worked with for many years that I wanted to endorse here. I support their visions, their missions, and how they accomplish them.

Little Rock Early Childhood Development Center in Kibera: http://littlerockkenya.org/newsite/ Little Rock was founded in 2003 in order to fill a gap in services for children with special needs in the poorest communities in Kenya. Little Rock provides crucial services through trained staff and volunteers in an inclusive, accessible environment. Their work is nothing short of inspiring. Places like Little Rock are all too rare in Kenya. They are committed to supporting children with developmental, neurological, and physical difficulties. Little Rock is one of the few places where a child with learning difficulties, like Miriam, can find help.

Sauti Kuu Foundation: http://sautikuufoundation.org/en/startseite-en/ Sauti Kuu's goal is to create a platform for disadvantaged children and young people worldwide that allows them to uncover their strengths and realize their full potential to live independent successful lives. Sauti Kuu works with children and youth in rural regions to enable them to develop realistic and sustainable socio-economic structures. They utilize locally available resources that will guarantee financial independence. In the process, the Sauti Kuu team fosters a spirit of empowerment, helping young people to realize that they do not have to be victims of their social backgrounds or their environments.

Finally, your honest reviews wherever books are sold or discussed online **really matter.** They help bring credibility to independently published writers like myself and provide potential readers with information that helps them discover new stories like this one.

If you enjoyed this book and would like to more about Ted Neill, his Belong Blog, and the social justice organizations he supports, visit TENEBRAYPRESS.COM. To contact the author, you can send an email to TENEBRAYPRESS@YAHOO.COM

Made in the USA
San Bernardino, CA
26 October 2018